Networks for Learning and Knowledge Creation in Biotechnology

Scientists in the biotechnology industry are responsible for many inventions that have led to the development of a vast array of products and technologies, in the areas of therapeutics, diagnostics, and agricultural and veterinary products. This has been possible through various intra- and interorganizational collaborations between the academic and private sectors, and through the establishment of networks for learning. In *Networks for Learning and Knowledge Creation in Biotechnology*, Amalya Lumerman Oliver shows how, in many respects, the organizational structure of the industry parallels one of its most important innovations – recombinant DNA (rDNA). She shows how the concept of recombination may be used to explain a number of organizational features, including new biotechnology firms, the formation of university-based spin-offs, scientific entrepreneurship, and trust and contracts in learning collaborations and networks. The result is an integrative account of how multiple theoretical perspectives can be used to understand the structure of the biotechnology industry.

AMALYA LUMERMAN OLIVER is Associate Professor of Organizational Sociology in the Department of Sociology and Anthropology, The Hebrew University of Jerusalem, Israel.

Networks for Learning and Knowledge Creation in Biotechnology

AMALYA LUMERMAN OLIVER

CAMBRIDGE
UNIVERSITY PRESS

CAMBRIDGE UNIVERSITY PRESS
Cambridge, New York, Melbourne, Madrid, Cape Town, Singapore, São Paulo, Delhi

Cambridge University Press
The Edinburgh Building, Cambridge CB2 8RU, UK

Published in the United States of America by Cambridge University Press, New York

www.cambridge.org
Information on this title: www.cambridge.org/9780521872485

First published 2009

Printed in the United Kingdom at the University Press, Cambridge

A catalogue record for this publication is available from the British Library

Library of Congress Cataloguing in Publication data
Oliver, Amalya Lumerman.
  Networks for learning and knowledge-creation in biotechnology /
Amalya Lumerman Oliver.
    p. ;   cm.
  Includes bibliographical references and index.
  ISBN 978-0-521-87248-5 (hardback)
  1. Biotechnology.   2. Biotechnology–Research.   3. Organizational learning.
  I. Title.
  [DNLM: 1. Biotechnology–organization & administration. 2. Biomedical Research.
  3. Diffusion of Innovation. 4. Interinstitutional Relations. 5. Knowledge.
  TP 248.2 O48n 2008]
  TP248.2.O45 2008
  660.6072–dc22   2008028872

ISBN 978-0-521-87248-5 hardback

This book is dedicated to my father, Haim Lumerman, who is my source of inspiration and whose deep love and stamina have always guided me.

If only you stayed with us a bit longer ...

Contents

Figures

Tables

Acknowledgements

This book is an outcome of many years of research in the biotechnology industry, of discussions with colleagues and students, and reading of research materials which were contributed by many important colleagues. Many of my initial ideas about networks in the biotechnology industry were developed while I was a graduate student at the University of California at Los Angeles (UCLA) and I thank my advisors then, Lynne Zucker and Phillip Bonacich, as well as Marilynn Brewer and Peter Kollock. These initial insights and interests were further diffused into additional directions of interest, including "open" and "closed" science and dilemmas associated with these social structures, new organizational forms, and processes associated with them, with university–industry technology-transfer, interorganizational learning, and scientific entrepreneurship. Two very special lifetime colleagues and friends deserve special acknowledgment. Julia Porter Liebeskind has shared with me many hours of intellectual discussions, joint fieldwork, data collection, and critical thinking on many of these topics. As a result of some of these discussions Chapter 5 was written jointly. I thank Julia for sharing with me her wisdom and for her collegial generosity. In a parallel vein, Kathy Montgomery has shown me the great value of collaborating with close friends who can offer many complementary assets. These past collaborations exemplified to me how the notion of exchanging core ideas and building arguments through counter-arguments can bring about incredible complementarities. I am deeply committed to our many years of collaborative work and hope for many more such challenges. Woody Powell was generous with offering comments on several occasions; Michelle Gittelman was willing to share exciting research insights and Joe Lampel was always generous with insightful stories, events, and analytical synthesis.

My colleagues who are my partners as convenors of the EGOS standing working group on interorganizational networks, David Knoke and Marius Meeus, were always ready to help and encourage. In addition, there were many participants in the past few years in the networks track who provided helpful comments and ideas about networks, structure, and processes – especially Anna Grandori, Benson Honig, and Jeorg Sydow.

The research for this study was supported by generous grants from NSF (dissertation improvement grants), Bi-National Science Foundation, Israel–US (with Julia Liebeskind) (1996–1998), and from the Israel Science Foundation (2006–2008). In addition, small but most valuable grants from the Shaine, Eshkol, and Silbert centers at the Hebrew University were very helpful at various stages.

Some of my students were involved in discussions and research on issues related to this book. I thank deeply my bright and enthusiastic students from whom I learned a great deal while acting as their advisor: Shimrit Barda, Iris Biruti, Roni Factor, Einat Achituv-Du-nour, Leonid Beckman, Noa Bar, and Galit Klein.

It is a blessing to have wonderful and supportive colleagues. My colleagues at the Department of Sociology and Anthropology at the Hebrew University, provided much support and gave good advice whenever needed, especially Nachman Ben-Yehuda who offered instrumental and cognitive support for writing this book. I thank my very special colleagues, Vered Vinitzki-Serussi, Eyal Ben-Ari, Boas Shamir, Michale Shalev, Barbara Okun, and Guy Stecklov, for their special collegiality.

I would like to thank Paula Parish, the editor of Cambridge University Press, for her sensitive, efficient, wise, and invaluable professional guidance throughout this process.

My family was always by my side. My beloved mother, Tova, and my brother, Shmulik, and his family, were a source of care and special warmth. Finally, my life-partner and husband, Nir, and our very special sons, Avital and Yaniv, are the light of my life. I thank them deeply for their unique qualities and for providing unconditional support and understanding.

A few of the chapters or sections of chapters in this book were published previously as parts of journal articles:

Liebeskind, J. P. and Oliver, A. L. (1998) From Handshake to Contract: Trust, Intellectual Property and the Social Structure of Academic Research. In Lane, C. and Bachmann, R. (eds.) *Trust Within and Between Organizations* (118–145). (Parts reprinted with permission from Oxford University Press.)

Oliver A. L. (2001) Strategic alliances and the learning life-cycle of bio-technology firms. *Organization Studies*, 22, pp. 467–489. (Parts reprinted by permission of Sage Publications Ltd, © Sage Publications, 2001.)

Oliver, A. L. (2004) On the duality of competition and collaboration: Network based knowledge relations in the biotechnology industry. *Scandinavian Journal of Management* 20, pp. 151–171. (© 2004, reprinted with permission from Elsevier.)

Oliver, A. L. (2004) Biotechnology entrepreneurial scientists and their collaborations. *Research Policy* 33, 4, pp. 583–597. (© 2004, reprinted with permission from Elsevier.)

Oliver, A. L. and Liebeskind, J. P. (1998) Three levels of networking: implications for the study of interorganizational networks. *International Studies in Management and Organization* 27, pp. 76–103. (Parts reprinted by permission.)

Oliver, L. A. and Montgomery, K. (2000) Creating a hybrid organizational form from parental blueprints: the emergence and evolution of knowledge firms. *Human Relations* 53, pp. 33–57. (Reprinted by permission of Sage Publications Ltd, © Tavistock Institute, London, UK, 2000.)

Introduction

The biotechnology industry has been characterized by a wealth of interorganizational collaborations and networks for learning, a feature that resulted in and contributed to the high level of innovation in the industry. In this industry, scientists in the biological sciences developed drugs, diagnostics, waste management systems, agricultural products, or veterinary procedures through various intra- and inter-organizational collaborations. These dense and crucial collaborations contributed to some unique features of industry structure, of types of organizations operating in the industry, and of the scientists involved in the process of scientific discoveries.

This book offers insights into organizational processes, structures, and outcomes which are associated with these networks of collaborations. The insights are based on integration of several "recombination features" of organizational elements that emerged in the biotechnology industry. In many respects, the emerged organizational structure of the industry is isomorphic with the central initial technology-invented recombinant DNA (rDNA). Thus, the book focusses on the following general question: How does our understanding of institutions, organizations, goals, learning, intellectual property rights, and collaboration forms contribute to our understanding of the emerging networks?

Hence, based on previous and ongoing research, the book highlights the following elements of recombination.

- *Recombinations of institutions themselves*: universities and biotechnology firms; through extensive collaborations of various types and alliances between universities and biotechnology firms, products are developed. These collaborations lead to various recombinant forms of organizations and interorganizational networks.
- *Recombinations of organizational elements within new firms*: biotechnology firms are trying to make money whilst attracting and retaining academically trained scientists who will continue to

undertake academic-style research, leading to new institutional forms that are based on the recombination of university and industry institutional elements.

- *Recombinations of business goals and scientific goals*: universities have now adopted many new business norms that are expressed in various features of recombinant goals. These mixed goals may have an impact on the operation of universities and on scientists' research behavior and choices.
- *Recombinations of collaboration and competition*: the complexities of the research and development processes lead to recombinations of interorganizational collaboration and competition trajectories.

These features are introduced in the nine chapters of this book. Chapter 1 deals with collaborations in the organizational context: issues of micro-, mezzo-, and macro-studies, and introduces the overarching framework of the book. It begins with the concept of "collaboration" and then introduces the levels of analysis that are crucial for understanding the knowledge creation and learning processes within and between organizations. The chapter aims to show how different levels of analyses – such as the industry level, multiple interorganizational level, dyadic level, organizational level, and scientists' network levels – are crucial for understanding knowledge creation and learning in biotechnology. The chapter argues that the use of various methods of interorganizational network analysis may bring to the fore hidden processes if based on a multi-level and multi-unit approach. An example argument illustrates that what may be seen as networks of collaboration, with the aid of additional types of network data, can be seen as intents for competition or appropriation. The aim of Chapter 1 is to establish the analytic elements that will be used further in the book, and to illuminate the complexity involved in a multi-level, multi-unit of analyses framework.

The second chapter provides an overview of the biotechnology industry through the lenses of organizational and networks scholarships. The organizational literature does not only exhibit a steady increase in the number of studies on the biotechnology industry all over the world, but also a widening of the spectrum of related organizational topics related to this industry covered by such studies. Although initial organizational studies of the biotechnology industry focussed mainly on interorganizational networks of collaborations, new research is also focussing on patents, scientific citations, strategy, firm emergence, entrepreneurship, intellectual property rights, trust, learning, and university–industry technology transfer.

The aim of the second chapter is to provide an integrative map of the research conducted so far on organizational aspects of the biotechnology industry. The chapter also reviews the available literature on related "knowledge-intensive" industries (such as information technology (IT) or nanotechnology) in order to search for possible similarities or differences, and to question these patterns.

The emergence of an industry with unique features may lead to the evolution of new organizational forms, which either did not exist previously or had gained only minor representation thus far. The task of Chapter 3 is to discuss issues related to organizational forms for learning and knowledge creation that are dominant in the biotechnology industry. The structure and process associated with the organizational forms of new biotechnology firms (NBFs) are discussed, along with university–industry collaborations, university–industry research and development (R&D) consortia, university spin-offs, and incubators.

Entrepreneurship in science is not a new phenomenon. The history of science provides evidence of many scientists who were also entrepreneurs. However, in the context of the biotechnology industry this phenomenon becomes both more dominant and widespread, as well as wider in terms of the different features of entrepreneurship it represents.

Chapter 4 focusses on the individual-level phenomenon of scientific entrepreneurship. "Scientific entrepreneurship" or "entrepreneurial scientists" are recombinant conceptualizations which have not been commonly used in either scientific or entrepreneurship literature. In this context we witness research on academic scientists who establish knowledge firms, or on university "star" scientists who work collaboratively with firm scientists. Modern processes that aim to capture the value of intellectual property rights entail the process of claiming patents over scientific inventions in order to licence the rights to future use of these inventions by interested parties. Claiming for patents rights over academic research may serve as another feature of entrepreneurial scientists.

This chapter asks the general question: What defines the "entrepreneurial scientist?" Specifically, it focusses on explaining scientific collaborations by scientific capital (various ranges of specializations), intellectual capital (patents), academic tenure, research settings (institutional affiliation), and valorization of human capital (laboratory size).

The issue of science and discoveries in the context of private versus public knowledge creation and learning from an academic perspective is explored in Chapter 5. Knowledge creation and learning in the biotechnology industry cannot be understood without clarifying the institutional arrangements and norms under which such knowledge is created. Universities and industry operate under different institutional arrangements and norms, yet they collaborate constantly in order to create the knowledge needed for innovation in biotechnology. This chapter, written together with Julia Porter Liebeskind, aims to explore the rich details of two breakthrough inventions in order to offer a better understanding of the academic perspective on the normative decision-making process regarding the patenting and protection of intellectual property rights of academic knowledge. The chapter follows the historical debates over the decision to patent or not to patent discoveries that emerged from academic research, and asks whether the decisions that were made had an impact on the diffusion of these discoveries.

The core of Chapter 5 is based on a discussion of intellectual property rights in the general context of open and closed science. To demonstrate these issues, we present two case studies of pioneering inventions in biotechnology that were either not patented (monoclonal antibodies) or not exclusively licensed (rDNA). These two fascinating cases of ground-breaking inventions illustrate how academic science was affected by the norms of industrial science. The debates over questions of whether and how to patent academic research reflect one feature of recombination – of "open science" as unpatented academic research and of "closed science" as patented industrial research. This chapter also discusses issues related to the nature of public research and the current trend of privatization of university intellectual property rights. In addition, it highlights some points of conflict between scientific discoveries directed for the benefit of the public at large (the commons) and capturing knowledge for privatization needs and profit-making.

Biotechnology-related basic research conducted in universities is considered to be a requisite for the development of industry applied research. As a result, the role of university–industry technology transfer offices and patent applications has become increasingly significant in the past two decades. Chapter 6 deals with the search for university–industry technology transfer. The technology transfer process is based on recombination of basic academic knowledge with applied industrial knowledge. This chapter is dedicated to the effort to understand the search process for technology transfer collaborations from the academic point of view. It is based on qualitative in-depth interviews with academic scientists, technology transfer officers, and university R&D vice-presidents, and offers a rich description of contrasting metaphors for the search for technology-transfer collaborations. I name the two types of metaphors: "linear" versus "chaos" metaphors and analyze the central assumption and logical building blocks that lead to two distinct modes of the search process.

Previous research provided some tangible evidence that commercial interests have the potential to, and in fact sometimes do, have an effect on the nature of trust in academic science. By offering a wide range of evidence found in the area of academic biotechnology research we can examine how the success of commercially oriented collaborative research calls for a number of different forms of trustworthy behavior on the part of collaborators. Chapter 7 is dedicated to describing and illustrating the role of trust in scientific collaborations. It argues that that owing to the recombination of commercial interests into academic research, a broader form of trust is required to support the research relationship than is required to support a normal academic relationship.

In Chapter 8, the discussion moves from the micro- to the macro-level of analysis, and shifts the focus to NBFs. The chapter deals with organizational learning and strategic alliances whilst focussing on recombination and duality of competition and collaboration. It is based on a dialectical approach associated with illustrated duality. This dialectic is based on the conjuncture of two sets of elements throughout the organizational learning process – exploration for new, unique, and innovative research and development directions, and exploitation of the chosen dominant design for the R&D focus of NBFs. As indicated in the literature, the learning process in biotechnology is heavily attributed to strategic alliances between biotechnology firms. However, it is argued that it is essential to establish a dialectical view of the learning process associated with product development in the biotechnology industry. Therefore, only by understanding the internal dynamics of exploration and exploitation over the life-cycle that is associated with organizational learning, can we decipher the recombination of collaboration and competition in strategic alliances. In addition, at different levels of analysis, as well as in different institutional environments, we may observe the duality of collaboration and competition. The major contribution of this chapter is an epistemological and methodological one. I propose that the use of an assisting tool, titled the "flexible prism" methodology, is important in order to "break" the single light into the spectrum of colors that frequently coexist within strategic alliances. This will enable us to understand that collaborations and competition are not orthogonal but are interwoven within exchange-based collaborative strategic alliances. In order to further elaborate on the suggested duality, a discussion on the issue of positive externalities of competition and negative externalities of collaboration is added.

Chapter 9 suggests new directions for organizational research in the biotechnology industry. This chapter summarizes the general findings and arguments presented in the book, and offers new directions for research. The new research directions are related to trust in knowledge-based collaboration, levels of analyses in studying learning networks, process issues in interorganizational collaborations, as well as including failure or conflicts within interorganizational collaborations.

1 | *Networks, collaborations, and learning and knowledge creation*

The primary goal of this chapter is to introduce the overarching framework of the book. It will start with the concepts of collaboration and learning. Then, we introduce the issue of levels of analysis, which is crucial for understanding the knowledge creation and learning processes within and between organizations. Specifically, the chapter will show how different levels of analyses – industry level, multiple interorganizational level, dyadic level, organizational level, and scientists' network levels – are crucial for understanding knowledge creation and learning in biotechnology. The aim here is to establish the analytic elements that will be used further in the book, and to illuminate the complexity involved in a framework based on multi-level and multi-unit analyses.

Networks of collaborations and learning

Science organizations are experiencing constant changes – in part due to environmental opportunities and constraints, which lead to adaptive changes, and owing to the changing nature of the scientific process in various scientific areas. For example, if science must advance through the joint research of large groups of scientists, as in the case of physicists working around a supercollider, the structure of the organization of the scientific work is expected to change. The structure of groups may change to incorporate large groups of scientists and multiple projects may emerge to accommodate the needs of experts who will seek other experts for learning collaborations. The flow of knowledge will be shaped and reshaped as the groups of scientists will continue to explore collaborations. Consequently, changes in the organization of science are expected as both the internal procedures and allocation of resources of the hosting organization will change along with the norms of conducting scientific work in this organization.

Thus, changes in the opportunity structure, central actors, technology, resources, and flow of information in a scientific field are expected to lead to further changes in the structure of science, networks, and learning. These processes are nicely reflected in the area of biotechnology research.

The theoretical lenses of the present study are based on the underlying assumption that biotechnology-related scientific work is organized within a complex, ambiguous, and highly competitive environment. For most organizations in this organizational field new knowledge creation is essential for survival, yet knowledge is distributed between various organizations, including biotechnology firms, university, research centers, national agencies, and large firms. Since knowledge is distributed between various organizations and institutions, various forms of interorganizational collaborations and learning are needed.

Learning processes vary in terms of structure and process. Pisano (1996) differentiates between the concept of "learning-by-doing," which has featured prominently in the literature of technological innovation, and the concept of "learning-before-doing," which is associated with problem-solving that occurs long before a new product or process design is introduced. Pisano (1996) explores the impact of different learning strategies on development performance, with detailed data on 23 process development projects from pharmaceuticals and biotechnology, and his findings indicate that "learning-by-doing" is essential for efficient development in an environment such as biotechnology, where underlying theoretical and practical knowledge is relatively thin. In contrast, the need for "learning-by-doing" is far lower in environments such as chemical synthesis, where underlying theoretical and practical knowledge is deep enough to enable the design of laboratory experiments which effectively model future production experience. We learn from Pisano (1996) that in emerging technologies like biotechnology, which are typically characterized by less mature theoretical underpinnings and less accumulated practical knowledge, it is simply impossible for developers to anticipate and respond to manufacturing concerns without actually doing their work in the actual production environment. Thus, the locus of development competencies within organizations may be technology life-cycle-dependent. The high level of uncertainty about theory and accumulated knowledge may also be one of the forces which enhance the need for interorganizational and interinstitutional learning exchanges.

Knowledge-intensive organizations are targeted at enhancing knowledge creation, and appropriating this knowledge by transferring it into resources or forms which may be commercialized (such as patents and licencing, products, consulting specialties, and so on). Maximizing commercializing ability demands that the organization's most valuable resource (knowledge) should be well bounded within the organization.

On the other hand, it is well known that in the biotechnology industry the knowledge needed for the commercialization of related products does not exist under one organizational roof, but, rather, within the boundaries of various organizations (Powell & Brantley 1992; Liebeskind *et al.* 1996; Powell, Koput & Smith-Doerr 1996; Oliver & Liebeskind, 1998; Oliver 2001). Thus, it is argued that in order to commercialize science-based products in the biotechnology industry, interorganizational collaborations of various kinds are of vast importance.

Collaboration is a complex concept and has been interpreted in many ways (Huxham 1996, pp. 7–8). Definitions include, for example, "working in association with others for … mutual benefit," "a distinct mode of organizing … an intense form of mutual attachment," or "a new type of organization … type of transformational organization." Whilst collaborations are valuable, argues Huxham (1996), they are also difficult because of inherent hazards associated with them.

The "networks-for-learning" approach focusses on interorganizational networks as resource-generating entities that have the ability to enhance learning in collaborating firms. Powell, Koput and Smith-Doerr (1996) contend that the locus of innovation will be found in interorganizational networks of learning rather than within individual firms. This work contrasts the strategic approach (Teece 1986; Williamson 1991) that deals with the calculation of risks versus returns in pooling resources with another organization. This latter view contends that effective collaborations are hampered by lack of trust, difficulties in gaining control, and differential ability to learn new skills. As we will see, the literature introduces two main lines of argument: one deals with the risks in interorganizational collaborations and the other highlights the advantages of such collaborations for the benefits of the firm.

The sociological insight offered by Powell, Koput and Smith-Doerr (1996) deals with learning as a social construction process wherein knowledge is created in a social community context. This approach is based on the view of von Hippel (1998) that the trading of know-how requires the establishment of long-term relationships, and on Cohen and Levinthal's (1990) concept of "absorptive capacity." The argument that was raised by Cohen and Levinthal (1990) states that a firm with high absorptive capacity has a greater capacity to learn, and hence is adept at both internal R&D and at conducting R&D collaborations with other organizations. Thus, outside sources of knowledge are often critical to organizational innovation. March and Simon (1958, p. 188) were pioneers in offering the argument that innovations usually result from borrowing rather than invention. They also maintain that the ability to exploit external knowledge is a critical component of the innovative process. Further, the evaluation and utilization of this knowledge is a function of prior related knowledge which includes basic skills such as shared language and knowledge of the technological and scientific developments.

The biotechnology industry is a relatively new phenomenon: it is an industry that has emerged from basic university science, with revolutionary implications for "doing science" and for science-based industries such as pharmaceuticals, food, and energy. One of the most salient characteristics of the industry to date has been the use of collaborative relationships to conduct exchanges between new biotechnology firms (NBFs), established pharmaceutical firms, universities, and other non-profit research organizations. These collaborative relationships exist at both the interorganizational level (Barley, Freeman & Hybels 1992; Kogut, Shan & Walker 1992; Powell & Brantley 1992; Oliver 1993; Powell, Koput & Smith-Doerr 1996) and the individual level (Liebeskind *et al.* 1996; Zucker, Darby & Brewer 1998 to name only a few of the early studies), forming a dense network structure among the actors in the industry. These collaborative relationships, it is argued, have allowed biotechnology firms to access commercially valuable scientific knowledge and complementary commercial assets as the industry has evolved, thereby allowing both NBFs and established pharmaceutical firms to reduce their risks and costs in this arena.

Levels of analyses: issues of micro-, mezzo-, and macro- in the study of networks

It is important to clarify when the subject of research is learning networks that there are at least three generic types of network relations. These three types were specified by Oliver and Liebeskind (1998):

- Intra-organizational network relationships that operate at the individual or interpersonal level.
- Interorganizational network relationships that operate at the individual or interpersonal level.
- Interorganizational network relationships that operate at the organizational level.

In differentiating between these three types of networks, the primary argument suggested was that each of them has different features and serves a different purpose within the overall process of biotechnology research and commercialization.

The three types of networks represent two distinct levels of analyses: individual- and firm-level. To date, we still know very little about the interrelations between these two levels, cases of compatibility of patterns, or lack of them. We also lack understanding about what happens when these networks do not match, or how the use of one network structure or process may enhance and increase the productivity and efficiency of the other network levels. Related questions would open the area of research of learning networks to new theoretical and empirical directions. Examples of such questions are:

- To what degree do past interorganizational collaborations on the organizational level affect new interorganizational collaborations on the individual level?
- How can biotechnology firms best enrich their intra-organizational learning networks by the individual-level interorganizational networks of their scientists?
- What happens to the personal individual networks of scientists when they become employed by biotechnology firms that have their established interorganizational organizational-level learning networks? Do the scientists abandon their individual networks in lieu of the new organizational networks in which they participate, or do firms encourage them to transform their individual-level networks into formal organizational networks?

Another level of analyses, not always acknowledged in interorganizational network research, is the level of the industry as a whole, or the subsectors within the industry (Powell *et al.* 2005). Evolutionary theory of networks argues that we cannot fully capture lower levels of networking activities without understanding the general and specific structure of networks on the industry or subindustry sector. Thus, firms operating in industrial settings, in which R&D interorganizational networks are dominant, will not only have a higher propensity to search for R&D alliance partners, but may also find it easier to find them. When collaborative R&D is dominant within an industry, all the actors in the industry are expected to have a higher inclination and propensity to form such alliances.

By the same token, in an industry in which the rate of entry of new firms is high we may find another pattern of networks associated with the industry level. Since new entrants are less known and established in the industry they may experience network entry barriers, and thus be able to form alliances only with other new entrants. In this context, Powell *et al.* (2005), in a most impressive study of network dynamics and the evolution of the biotechnology field, found a clear picture of a continuing flow of new entrants into the field, yet these new entrants have "high-quality" links to other well-connected organizations. This pulling-in of newcomers reflects the process of "sponsored mobility" as new firms are assisted by existing firms at their initial entry to the industrial network.

Integration of levels of analysis

Once again, the primary argument here is that each of the three suggested networks serves a different purpose within the overall process of biotechnology research and commercialization. Oliver and Liebeskind (1998) argued that exchanges of new scientific knowledge take place primarily through interpersonal network relations, both intra-organizational and interorganizational. Thus, "networks of learning" in biotechnology are embedded within the context of personal relationships, whereas interorganizational ties serve primarily to support the commercialization of knowledge, and encompass transfers of "commoditized knowledge" in the form of intellectual property rights and of assets essential for commercial development.

In addition, Oliver and Liebeskind (1998) observed that individual-level network relationships in biotechnology were becoming increasingly encumbered and influenced by organization-level policies and practices. This change in the level of organizational influence on individuals' actions fosters and promotes the formation of certain types of individual ties, and inhibits the formation of – or even severs – other types of ties. Thus, there is a reciprocal interplay between individual-level network relations and organizational policies.

The dense pattern of interorganizational ties observed between NBFs and other organizations arguably reflects the fact that NBFs, as new firms, lack many of the resources and capabilities required to commercialize their discoveries (Teece 1986; Kogut, Shan & Walker 1992; Oliver 2001). Alliances with incumbent pharmaceutical firms allow an NBF to conduct research while the incumbent firm provides "complementary assets" (Teece 1986), such as marketing and distribution, product-testing capabilities, and development capital. Whilst a number of NBFs have managed to develop these capabilities internally over time, many remain specialized in R&D. Many NBFs therefore occupy an intermediate position in the biotechnology industry: between universities, where basic scientific research is conducted, and large established firms, where biotechnology products are brought to market (Arora & Gambardella 1990; Liebeskind *et al.* 1996). Consequently, the survival and success of NBFs depends on their network ties, since structural positions are an important determinant of competitive success in the biotechnology industry.

Research on networks of collaborations

Much of the research on network relations in biotechnology has focussed on organization-level ties between organizations. Shan (1990), Barley, Freeman and Hybels (1992), Kogut, Sham and Walker (1992), and Powell *et al.* (1996) have all examined the organization-level ties among NBFs, whereas Pisano (1990) as well as Arora and Gambardella (1990, 1994) have examined organization-level ties between NBFs and large pharmaceutical firms. Most recently, scholars of strategic alliances in biotechnology could show a large and detailed picture of the networks within the industry. This was achieved by the use of advanced network graphic methods, large-scale datasets, and advanced statistics by Powell *et al.* (2005). Their study focussed on collaborative ties between all actors over time, offering us an evolutionary approach to the industry based on the alliances that were formed longitudinally.

However, other research suggested that interorganizational ties represent only part of the overall set of network ties in the

Table 1.1 *Number of scientific collaborations resulting in published research classified by exchange governance mechanisms*

	No. of research publications		
	Firm X	Firm Y	Total
No. of publications	503	345	848
No. of publications based on research collaborations with external scientists	257	256	513
Percentage of total	51	74	60
Of which are governed by market (contractual) arrangements that are:			
Interorganizational	0	2	2
Individual-level	0	0	0
Number of publications produced only by scientists-employees	246	89	335
Percentage of total	49	26	40

Sources: Corporate records, North Carolina biotechnology database, Bio Scan. (Cited in Liebeskind *et al.* 1996.)

biotechnology industry. For instance, Liebeskind *et al.* (1996), who studied the organizational mechanisms through which NBFs source scientific knowledge, found that interorganizational agreements were unimportant in these exchanges. Rather, the NBFs these researchers studied sourced scientific knowledge through a dense network of individual-level ties among firm scientists and university scientists, almost none of which were governed by an overarching interorganizational agreement (during the period covered by the study). In that study the economic importance of individual-level collaborations for NBFs was also illustrated, finding that scientists at the two NBFs studied were involved in a very large network of collaborative research projects with scientists at universities and other research organizations (Table 1.1 and Table 1.2 summarize these data).

Another important element of the study of interorganizational ties is the content of the exchanges carried out through network ties. For example, a number of studies classified some organization-level agreements as R&D agreements (Pisano 1990; Powell, Koput & Smith-Doerr 1996), although there are important differences between the two types of ties. For instance, many R&D agreements consist of arrangements whereby the pharmaceutical firm funds a program of

Table 1.2 *Exclusive versus shared patent rights of firms X and Y*

	Firm X	Firm Y
Total number of patents	28	21
No. of exclusive patents	25	19
No. of shared patents	3	2
No. of patents shared by new biology firm (NBF) with institutions or scientists at institutions with which NBF has a formal contractual agreement	3	2
No. of patents shared by NBF with institutions or scientists at institutions with which NBF scientists have collaborated in published research	0	2

Source: Based on corporate records and US Patent Office records. (Cited in Liebeskind *et al.* 1996.)

research at the NBF,[1] and the NBF agrees to license any resulting intellectual property to the pharmaceutical firm, or when a university provides a license to a firm in order to use a patent assigned to the university. In both cases, no direct scientific collaboration is necessarily involved in such an agreement. Hence, it cannot be classified as a "learning" alliance in the pure sense. On the other hand, other R&D agreements may involve active collaboration in research between a university professor and a firm research team, or between two NBFs, which will result in interorganizational learning. These distinctions are not simple to specify and tracing them in large datasets that do not provide sufficient information on the alliances is almost impossible.

Finally, network studies of the biotechnology industry may suffer from problems associated with the study of networks in general – of boundary specification. These arise from the fact that multiple actors are involved in the industry (pharmaceutical companies, NBFs, universities, hospitals, research centers, and others); from the large number of units of each institutional form, and from the high rate of entry and exit over time (Barley, Freeman & Hybels 1992; Powell *et al.* 2005). These complexities reduce researchers' ability to specify stable and compatible boundaries and thus to provide a coherent picture of network relations.

---

[1] New biotechnology firms – for description and clarification of these firms as actors in the biotechnology industry, and as an organizational form, *see* Chapter 2 and Chapter 3.

Levels / Extent	Individual level	Organizational level
Intra-organizational	Intra-organizational individual-level ties	Empty cell
Interorganizational	Interorganizational individual-level ties	Interorganizational organizational-level ties

Figure 1.1 Types of network ties and levels of analyses.
Source: Oliver & Liebeskind 1998

The new dynamic methods for studying networks over time may offer some remedy to this problem, yet a theoretical approach that accounts for the effect of entries and exits is needed.

Based on these limitations, Oliver and Liebeskind (1998) offered a model for studying interorganizational networks in professional and knowledge-intensive industries characterized by multiple institutional arrangements. Our model of network relations in the biotechnology industry integrates partial findings and identifies some directions for future research.

The model

As discussed above, an integrative model must incorporate both organizational-level and individual-level network relations within the biotechnology industry. It must also explain how these two levels of networking interact. Given the two levels of networking that have been observed, three types of network relations may be identified, as illustrated in Figure 1.1. All three types of network relations are important to the commercialization of biotechnology research.

Individual-level

Individual collaborative relationships in biotechnology center on the research process – be it within a single organization or between organizations. Biotechnology research involves collaboration among scientists in many different disciplines, such as molecular and cell biologists, geneticists, and protein chemists, as well as technical specialists (Latour & Woolgar 1979; Rabinow 1996; Robbins-Roth 2000). Collaboration is also necessary because new methods and techniques, which are essential to the generation of new knowledge in this field, require learning-by-doing (Nonaka 1994; Zollo & Winter, 2002). Collaboration thus allows one scientist to access the specialized and most recently developed knowledge of another. In the biotechnology industry, such collaborations between scientists are carried out both between and within organizations. The nature and scope of intra-organizational network relations in the industry are strongly influenced by the nature of interorganizational relations, by the degree to which these are governed by the organizations concerned, and by professional norms within the scientific community.

Interorganizational network relations at the individual level

As observed by Liebeskind *et al.* (1996), one notable feature of NBFs is that they maintain a large number of individual-level research collaborations with scientists at universities and other research institutions. Individual-level collaborations between NBF scientists and university scientists bring together actors who are members of the same profession but who work within very different types of organization. On the one hand, universities are institutions of "open" science (David, Mowery & Steinmueller 1992) where research is advanced through open-ended inquiry into issues that are identified as scientifically interesting (Latour & Woolgar 1986). Research findings are then exchanged through various forms of publication in the interest of advancing science and benefiting society at large (Merton 1973; David, Mowery & Steinmueller 1992).

Collaboration among university scientists is unguided by any managerial hand, and scientists have incentives to discover new findings regardless of their commercial implications. Scientific reputations are established on the basis of priority in discovery, so that publication of results is an integral part of the research process, and "motivates men of science to replace the value set upon secrecy with the value placed upon disclosure of the knowledge they have created … The concern with getting into print is scarcely confined to contemporary science" (Merton 1973, p. 337). University scientists also are free to seek out the best collaborative partnerships they can in order to advance science and their own reputations.

NBFs, on the other hand, operate under a system of conflicting incentives. For one thing, the survival and success of an NBF depends on both attracting and retaining university scientists as employees, and on continuing relations with university scientists who continue to push the frontier of research forward into new areas with commercial potential and who permit the firm to economize on research costs. However, NBFs must also protect valuable research findings from expropriation by competing firms. Thus, NBFs place limits on the individual-level ties of their own scientists, ensuring that sensitive projects are conducted in-house and that valuable products are brought to market in the shortest time possible. Thus, while NBFs are characterized by a high level of interorganizational networking, their ties are subject to the guiding hand of the firm's managers. Yet evidence also indicates that very few individual-level external ties at NBFs are formed under the umbrella of organization-level agreements. One reason for this may be that managers do not know enough about selecting appropriate research partners. Typically, it is NBF scientists who propose collaborative research while managers give (or withhold) permission for collaborations and offer the most attractive incentives to the chosen external scientist. For example, in one of the most successful NBFs we interviewed, scientists selected potential external collaborators whilst their managers established procedures to ensure that these potential collaborators were approached in such a way as to maximize the likelihood that they would be willing to collaborate with the firm.

Although university scientists are not directly subject to the guiding hand of managers, they are nonetheless strongly influenced by the organizational context in which they work. The institutions of public science universities, public research institutes, and public-granting institutions exert a strong influence on the type of research conducted in universities, and on the types of findings scientists must produce to obtain funding (Latour & Woolgar 1986). In particular, these institutions promote the production and publication of new knowledge, and the professional norms that support discovery research (Merton 1973; Latour & Woolgar 1986). Universities also seek to maintain the objectivity of research produced by their faculty through the use of rules and regulations which prohibit faculty members from having a commercial interest in entities which finance their research. Thus, a US faculty member who owns a significant share of stock in an

NBF would not usually be allowed to receive grant funding from that firm (Argyres & Liebeskind 1998).[2]

The differences in institutional influences on NBF scientists and university scientists are bridged to some degree by shared professional norms. Most scientists employed in NBFs have earned doctorates from major research universities where cutting-edge bioscience research is being conducted (Kenney 1986; Rabinow 1996). In addition, many scientists at these firms were once faculty members themselves, and they bring with them many professional and collegial ties that they established during their academic careers. NBFs also seek to cement professional ties with universities by appointing prestigious university scientists to their scientific advisory boards, by holding research colloquia, by having their scientists attend scientific meetings, and by publishing the results of some of their research projects.

Differences in institutional influences on NBF scientists and university scientists are also bridged by contracts that are used to govern their joint research collaborations. Firms seek these agreements in order to secure patents on new discoveries. Universities rely on these agreements to protect their system of open science by ensuring that rights to publish are preserved, and that they do not engender conflicts of interest for faculty. These formal contracts therefore usually provide for: (1) the intellectual-property protection of discoveries made by university scientists through patenting; (2) the allocation of exclusive patent licenses, or the right to negotiate such exclusive licenses, to firms funding university research; and (3) rights for a firm to review manuscripts or other written communications for a limited time before they are made public. Thus, firms are not usually allowed to restrict publication completely, but a university faculty member must accept some restrictions on publication to receive funding from a biotechnology firm.

Collaborative research contracts are typically drawn up under the auspices of university technology-transfer units. These programs' policies and procedures are created to facilitate the commercialization of university research, but they explicitly attempt to reconcile the differences in norms and interests between university scientists and firm scientists by brokering transfer agreements that represent a

---

[2] As intellectual property policies in universities are constantly changing, this policy may have changed since the cited article was published.

livable compromise for both parties. Thus, technology-transfer personnel often provide a bridge between the university's interests and those of commercial firms (Kaghan 1997).[3] This positional bridge may be deeply embedded in personal relationships. At one university, the technology-transfer managers maintained very close relationships with a large NBF in the local area, meeting frequently with the firm's managers and scientists to discuss their research needs. These technology-transfer managers also actively seek out university faculty who are conducting research that may be useful to this firm. Individual-level contracting between firms and university scientists governing the use of research materials, data, and techniques used in collaborations also occurs (Liebeskind & Oliver 1998). Firms' scientists may also initiate frequent meetings with technology-transfer managers to learn about what is new in the academic research pipeline. Such agreements primarily protect the intellectual property interests of firms and were less influenced by the university at an organizational level.[4]

Despite these efforts to bridge differences in interests within individual-level network ties between university scientists and NBF scientists, conflicting interests are ever present. For example, Werth (1995) describes a situation that occurred at one NBF, Vertex, in which an R&D team at the firm was collaborating with a scientist at Harvard, Stuart Schreiber. Schreiber was very self-seeking, talking to many different firms at the same time, and discussing his work openly, even though this undermined his commitments to Vertex and threatened Vertex's priority. Ultimately, Vertex chose to proceed with its research without Schreiber's assistance. According to an Israeli NBF scientist:

> We all end up talking to everyone, even our management-level scientists talk with everyone they wish to share information with, even though they give us clear instructions not to do so. After all, we are all one scientific community which evolved from a few universities. This community has a high need for resources, including materials, substances, and equipment,

---

[3] *See also* Chapter 6 in this book.

[4] Although it must be noted that in the past decade, the literature shows that universities are becoming more entrepreneurial and proactive in terms of seeking collaborations with biotechnology firms. These changes lead to new and different models of technology transfer (*see also* Chapter 6).

which are needed by scientists in other institutions. Hence, if a doctoral student needs to use equipment that we own, we will allow her to use it, because later she will share her research findings with us. If a university professor is doing research using a substance that we have, we give it to him. In return, we can call him when we have a problem. NBFs have gained the reputation that they try to get information out of university researchers, but do not share their own work in return. As a result, at international conferences, university professors avoid talking with us. This is our opportunity to help some university scientists, in exchange for some unspecified returns from them. In the long run the company benefits from such exchanges.

In contrast to universities and NBFs, large pharmaceutical firms are characterized by lower levels of interorganizational networking at the interpersonal level. The main reason for this is that few university-trained scientists are willing to work directly for these firms. A number of considerations underlie this disdain. One is that established firms have traditionally been very secretive, so that a university-trained scientist who chose to work in industry might find herself in a position where she was essentially cut off from reciprocal relationships with university researchers by dint of bureaucratic policy. Lacking any potential for reciprocity, industry scientists have also been traditionally shunned by university scientists, having the reputation of "only wanting to pick our brains, without giving anything in return." Possibly as a result of these bureaucratic rules, working in industry has always been considered inferior to an academic career, to the degree that moving from a university to an established firm has been supposed to signal that a scientist is less talented than others. In addition, large pharmaceutical firms rarely offer scientists the prospect of sharing in the rewards of their discoveries. Typically, patents are wholly assigned to the firm, and scientists receive salaries rather than equity shares, whereas NBFs offer more attractive financial inducements to university scientists, in particular equity ownership.

A number of events have changed this picture. Established firms have altered many of their policies and now allow their scientists to collaborate more openly, and to publish, as do most NBFs (Deutschman 1994). Meanwhile, some NBFs have been bought out by established firms, with the stated intention of providing the established firm with a competency in biotechnology (for instance, Genentech is majority-owned by Hoffmann-La Roche). Thus, while established firms may still have only weak interpersonal ties with the academic biotechnology community, they have moved to forge stronger interpersonal ties with scientists in NBFs.

Intra-organizational networks at the interpersonal level

Although NBF scientists are restricted to some degree from free collaboration with university scientists, their external ties are supplemented and complemented by a dense network of intra-organizational ties. Both our interview data and the existing literature support the contention that NBFs recognize that their scientists are their most valuable asset. Concomitantly, these firms also recognize that their ability to generate scientific discoveries in-house depends on the degree to which they can foster effective collaboration and learning among their scientist-employees. Hence, in addition to seeking to hire the best-trained and most productive scientists, most NBFs are organized in such a way that collaboration and learning are fostered. For instance, most NBFs have adopted an organic organizational structure, intended to support lateral processes and internal learning (Nonaka 1994; Oliver & Montgomery 2000). They also conduct internal colloquia, hold regular research-strategy meetings, and promote firm-level activities designed to foster the personal relationships that provide the seedbed for professional collaborations.

However, intra-organizational networking in NBFs is not all voluntary in nature since they will "force" collaboration where necessary. For instance, Rabinow (1996) described how one of the first NBFs was obligated to actively manage the research process for its invention of polymerase chain reaction (PCR). The scientist who had the idea was a difficult person to deal with and slowed the progress of the project. The R&D manager of the firm had to "force" a scientific team to get the idea developed to a sufficient level in order to obtain a patent.

The open-ended nature of scientific collaboration that characterized many NBFs in their early stages of corporate existence is also being transformed as they mature, changing the way in which interpersonal ties are formed and maintained. In one NBF a dramatic change has occurred over the years. Following an early commercial success the firm recruited hundreds of new scientists and in order to accommodate them new research buildings were constructed. However, because research activities were no longer housed in one building, communication and socialization were interrupted. In addition, security concerns over theft of intellectual property increased so that each research building was locked and closed not only to outsiders but also to other employees of the NBF. Within each building, laboratories were also locked, reducing social communication within each building. Thus, as the NBF grew, social and professional "Balkanization" took place. In another case, the firm's culture changed when the NBF was partially taken over by a large pharmaceutical company. In this case, budget controls were increased, so that the firm's scientists were no longer free to collaborate on spontaneous research projects, again undermining network ties within the NBF: "Once the suits arrived, it was all over."

The growth of the biotechnology industry has also spawned new interpersonal ties within universities. In general, university scientists are free to collaborate with whomsoever they wish, and will tend to collaborate with those individuals who allow them to produce the most significant research findings (Latour & Woolgar 1986). However, the commercial potential of biotechnology has led some university scientists to form exclusive, long-term collaborations with local colleagues because research may be advanced more rapidly when it is being carried out in tandem rather than sequentially, and findings may be protected more effectively when activities are not duplicated and when fewer individuals are involved. Thus, commercial interests serve to foster research ties between faculty members within a given university. Commercial interests may also lead university faculty to sever some of their past collaborative ties in order to maintain clear property rights to their own discoveries. Many faculty members involved in commercially relevant research have also forged new ties with university technology-transfer personnel, as described earlier. Concomitantly, faculty members will seek out technology-transfer personnel to find buyers for their inventions.

In some cases, the personal contacts and capabilities of technology-transfer personnel are critical in faculty hiring and retention. For instance, one university was seeking to hire a highly qualified scientist from the advanced-research institute of an established firm. This was problematic from the university's point of view, however, because the scientist was party to confidential information that could potentially restrict his future research. However, a satisfactory agreement was negotiated between the firm and the university, in large part because the departmental Chair who was seeking to hire the scientist had a close personal relationship with the technology-transfer manager of the university. In other cases, faculty members have left universities which were incompetent in managing technology transfer.

Organizational-level

As pointed out already, most interorganizational network relationships between university scientists and NBF scientists at the individual level are carried out under the auspices of interorganizational network ties at the organizational level.[5] The evidence provided by Liebeskind *et al.* (1996) indicates that many research collaborations take place on a more or less informal level, either governed by limited, individual-level contracts between firms and university scientists, or not governed by formal agreements at all.

However, this picture is changing. There are now many NBFs, and competition for the services of top university scientists is intensifying. At the same time, the number of disputes over intellectual property rights, especially between NBFs, is increasing. As a result, NBFs are increasingly relying on contracts to govern individual-level network ties between scientists. For example, an NBF introduced mandatory formal agreements for all exchanges of research materials, techniques, and data in 1990. Now, every university scientist working with the firm's scientists, or using any materials, data, or technologies belonging to the firm, must sign a formal contract. Before 1990, collaboration was almost entirely informal, and no records were kept even of cell lines, reagents, and other proprietary materials or information that was passed back and forth between collaborators. At the same time, universities are becoming more vigilant about the involvement of their faculty in industry research and about enforcing their policies regarding the ownership of intellectual property. Recently, it has become standard practice for universities to require faculty to sign agreements stating that any intellectual property they generate using

---

[5] This was our observation when we initially studied university–industry collaborations. However, over time, as universities became more sensitive to issues of intellectual property rights and technology-transfer offices were established in every campus, it is estimated that many scientific collaborations between university and firm scientists are governed by specific contractual arrangements which are written to protect university knowledge from appropriation and firms from law suits. In Chapter 7, where the issue of trust is developed, these transitions are described – as originally titled: "From handshake to contract" (Liebeskind and Oliver 1998).

the university's resources or facilities belongs to the university; previously, such contracts were rare (Argyres & Liebeskind 1998). Thus, there are pressures from both sides to increase the formal organization-to-organization governance of individual-to-individual relations. At the same time, universities are increasingly restricting the types of relationships faculty may have with NBFs. Faculty are now generally prohibited from owning equity in firms that finance their research or from taking managerial positions in such firms (Argyres & Liebeskind 1998).

Despite the growing role of formal agreements in the sourcing of knowledge by NBFs, the interorganizational-level network relations of firms remain dominated by contractual and ownership ties with other firms which own assets essential for commercializing biotechnology products (Pisano 1990; Barley, Freeman & Hybels 1992; Kogut, Shan & Walker 1992). These complementary assets (Teece 1986) include capital for product development and for clinical trials, manufacturing capabilities, marketing infrastructure and expertise, and established distribution channels. In these network relations, the nature and direction of the tie are determined by the matching of the firms' needs. Essentially, NBFs which lack these complementary assets obtain access to them by trading away rights to their scientific expertise and their intellectual property to large established firms which lack, but need, biotechnology expertise. Here then individual relationships play little or no role. Organizational concerns are paramount, and the ties between firms are strictly contractual in nature.

Synthesis

This chapter has argued that there are three types of network relationships which are important to the economic processes of commercial biotechnology: (1) interorganizational individual-level network relationships; (2) intra-organizational individual-level network relationships; and (3) interorganizational organization-level network relationships. Each plays a different role in the flow of critical products in the biotechnology industry.

Interorganizational individual-level network relationships between university scientists and NBF scientists play a critical role in allowing NBFs access to university-based researchers in molecular biology and other disciplines. They tend to be initiated and maintained by scientists, and are embedded in their professional and social worlds. Knowledge flows from universities to firms through these ties, allowing NBFs to access the latest developments in research. Hence, whilst economizing on their own R&D costs, the success of NBFs depends critically on the successful pursuit of university science, which is embedded in collaborative research ties among university faculty members.

NBFs are also characterized by important intra-organizational individual-level network relationships. These ties allow NBFs to carry out their own proprietary research programs and so protect their discoveries from appropriation by outsiders. Many of these intra-organizational network relationships are guided by managers who direct scientists to work with one another in order to ensure that discovery and development are taking place as rapidly as feasible, and to ensure that the firm's resources are not wasted in non-essential research efforts. Because university scientists are free to collaborate with whomsoever they wish, universities may or may not be characterized by strong intra-organizational ties. However, commercial research may encourage the development of intra-organizational ties among faculty members as well as between faculty and university technology-transfer personnel, who often play a critical role in fostering individual relationships between faculty and firm scientists. Thus, intra-organizational relationships at the individual level both complement and support individual interorganizational relationships. Both of these types of network relationships play a critical role in allowing NBFs to import and to discover new products and processes. Hence, NBFs' critical inputs are imported through personal ties but not through organizational ties. However, these personal ties are being subjected to increasing levels of organizational intervention from both firms and universities.

Finally, interorganizational ties at the organizational level within the biotechnology industry play a critical role in the actual development and commercialization of products. These ties, which exist primarily between NBFs and large established firms which own complementary assets, take the form of contractual or ownership ties and are formed entirely in response to organizational interests.

The importance of each of these types of network over the biotechnology product life-cycle is illustrated in Figure 1.2. Here, knowledge flows into NBFs or is created within NBFs, almost exclusively through

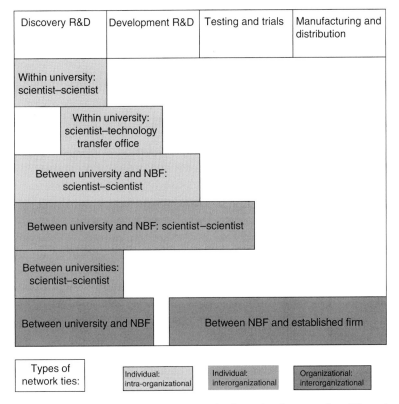

Discovery R&D	Development R&D	Testing and trials	Manufacturing and distribution

Within university: scientist–scientist

Within university: scientist–technology transfer office

Between university and NBF: scientist–scientist

Between university and NBF: scientist–scientist

Between universities: scientist–scientist

Between university and NBF

Between NBF and established firm

Types of network ties:	Individual: intra-organizational	Individual: interorganizational	Organizational: interorganizational

Figure 1.2 Levels of network ties over the biotechnology product life-cycle. *Source:* Oliver & Liebeskind 1998

interpersonal ties. There are few interorganizational ties between NBFs and universities, but their number is growing.

Within NBFs and within universities, organizational rules and managerial influences play an increasing role in determining the shape and direction of interpersonal ties. Finally, products flow out of NBFs to established firms and then on to the marketplace through interorganizational ties, where interpersonal relations have little, if any, role.

These three types of networks, however, are not separate entities but are inextricably intertwined in a number of different ways. First, the individual actions of scientists, technology-transfer personnel, and managers in firms are all influenced to some degree or another by the organizations within which they work, as illustrated in Figure 1.3.

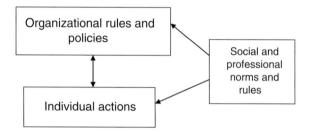

Figure 1.3 Relationships between individual and organizational ties in the biotechnology industry: interests, norms, and constraints.
Source: Oliver & Liebeskind 1998

Organizational rules and policies thus guide the formation and the nature of individual-level network relations. At the same time, organizations' motivations and rules guide the formation of inter-organizational network relations. Lastly, social and professional norms influence both the rules and policies adopted by organizations, and the ways in which individuals acting under organizations' aegis behave. Consequently, although the organizational roles of the different parties to individual ties often diverge, their motivations are harmonized to the degree that they move through different roles and positions in the network. Presently, many individuals occupying key roles in the biotechnology industry are university-trained scientists, working as university faculty, industry scientists, technology-transfer managers, or executives in NBFs or established firms. Sometimes scientists will move from firms back to universities. This rotation allows shared norms to moderate differences in organizational interests among different individual network members. However, as the industry matures, different positions may be filled increasingly by specialists, so that interests may become more difficult to harmonize.

In addition, firms often foster individual ties. For example, an international drug company wanted to develop a line of products based on basic research conducted at a leading Israeli university. To this end, it established a subsidiary company (an NBF) in Israel in the science park adjacent to the university. The chief scientist of the new firm was a professor at the university. Now acting in the firm's interests, he insisted that the NBF be located close to the university in order to produce and sustain ties with university scientists. Formal ties between the NBF and the university have been in existence for many years and are renewed every year. Discoveries made by university scientists, funded by the NBF, continue to be developed by the NBF and are transferred to the international parent company for testing and production.[6]

Another example of the interdependence of individual-level and organization-level ties in biotechnology is offered by the pharmaceutical company Schering-Plough, which acquired DNAX, a one-year-old developing NBF with fewer than ten scientists. The executives of Schering-Plough realized that the DNAX scientists would never have worked in an industrial pharmaceutical company (Kornberg 1995, pp. 121–130). Thus, acquiring DNAX offered Schering-Plough an opportunity to link, via DNAX, to leading university scientists. In order to maintain these network ties, the managers recognized that they needed to attract and retain a world-class scientific staff, as well as to sustain the allegiance of the DNAX founders and scientific advisors. To achieve this, the president and chief executive officer (CEO) of DNAX, appointed by Schering-Plough, nurtured an academic atmosphere which encouraged prompt publication; sharing of reagents, cell lines, and techniques; unstinted physical resources; and generous perks and compensation; minimal security regulations; short-term appointments for visiting scientists; and an ambitious post-doctoral program (Kornberg 1995, p. 130).

This example illustrates again how firms seek to foster individual-level ties between NBF scientists and university scientists. Thus, since the "learning link" is between NBFs and universities, managers in the biotechnology industry understand that learning will not occur in a bureaucratic atmosphere and without a free flow of exchanges within interpersonal scientific networks (inside and outside NBFs). Universities also foster, and sometimes inhibit, the formation of individual ties. A university licensing and relations manager at one of the leading NBFs in the USA explained that university scientists often make contact in order to establish various R&D collaborations. In one case, the university technology-transfer office did not agree to the contract

---

[6] At a later stage, the parent company, which already developed a product based on the knowledge transferred from the university, closed the local R&D facility and moved to another R&D facility.

terms proposed by the NBF for a particular collaboration. A frustrated scientist, who needed this collaboration to further ongoing research, contacted the manager directly and offered to collaborate without a formal agreement. Such informal exchanges were quite common until recently (Liebeskind & Oliver 1998).[7] The NBF manager, however, could not agree to the scientist's request. The university required such agreements and to proceed without one would have damaged the firm's trustworthy reputation and might have led to disputes over intellectual property. In this case, then, an individual-level tie was not formed because a formal interorganizational tie could not be established.

Implications

The model of network relations in the biotechnology industry presented here has a number of implications for research on interorganizational networks.

Implications for theory-building: back to the notion of markets, hierarchies, and networks

The important role played by social networks in the biotechnology industry is supportive of the more generalized argument that social networks may play an important role in fostering organizational flexibility and in promoting efficient organization learning (Powell 1990; Grant 1996; Liebeskind *et al.* 1996; Powell *et al.* 2005). Social network exchanges can contribute to organizational learning by extending the scope of organizational learning and by contributing to the internal absorption and integration of new knowledge because learning involves close collaboration between individuals. In contrast, markets are not a good mechanism for transferring knowledge (Grant 1996).

Using social networks also allows a firm to switch from one source of knowledge to another, increasing strategic flexibility when R&D incurs high sunk-costs (Teece 1988; Liebeskind *et al.* 1996). These arguments have implications for the relationships between bureaucracies

---

[7] Once again, informal university–industry collaborations that were frequently established in the past are very uncommon now, once technology-transfer offices were established in universities.

and social networks, and for the effects of social networks on the founding and growth of new firms.

Given that social network relations are preferable to market relations for sourcing knowledge (Grant 1996), the question arises: How might firms manage social networks? Very little is known about this issue. For instance, in general, do managers direct the formation of social network relations or are they initiated by employees? If these relationships are initiated by employees, how can managers control them so as to ensure that the firms' goals are satisfied? Under what conditions can and may managers govern the nature of these relationships? For example, professionals typically rely on social network relations when they wish to interact without the constraints of formal contracts or other rules and regulations (Kreiner & Schultz 1993; Oliver & Montgomery 2000). Yet, while managers may see the advantages of social networking for the firm, the organizational arrangements which may be necessary to foster the formation of these relationships may conflict with the demands placed on them through the formal organizational bureaucracy, especially the need for accountability. This raises the question of how managers can resolve these two conflicting forces in order to ensure a free and flexible flow of information, on the one hand, while avoiding misappropriation of intellectual property rights and R&D resources, on the other.

Another question that arises is: How can managers control the scope of a firm's social network relations? For instance, to what extent are managers concerned about whether their external network relationships overlap with those of key competitor firms? In their study of two NBFs, Liebeskind *et al.* (1996) provided preliminary evidence that the two firms were involved in a number of overlapping relationships at the individual and the organizational level. However, a satisfactory investigation of this issue would require a full-scale network analysis with availability of data on both levels of analysis. So far as is known, this was not done

An additional question related to the bureaucratic management of social networks concerns hiring. If individuals' ability to establish efficient and effective social network relations is important to firms, do firms hire certain employees because they are active in strategically important networks or are considered central actors in these networks, or both? In the case of the biotechnology industry, there is some evidence that NBFs seek to hire important scientists either as employees or as members of firms' scientific advisory boards. In other industries, firms may seek to hire individuals who occupy central positions in certain business communities or political groups. Similarly, the entrepreneurial success of a firm may be increased if it hires individuals who occupy "structural holes" within an information network (Burt 2005).

Finally, the ability of a bureaucracy to manage its social network relations may depend on its social and institutional context (Granovetter 1985), and the latter's importance to economic performance (Uzzi 1996, 1997). For example, are firms from one country able to penetrate the social networks of another country as efficiently as their own? Or do cultural and other contextual factors inhibit the firm's effectiveness? It is also possible that some types of network relations, such as professional networks, are less susceptible to the effects of local embeddedness.

Social networks and the founding and growth of firms

A second aspect of the relationship between markets, hierarchies, and social networks that merits further investigation is the impact of social networks on the founding and growth of new firms. Because social networks may permit firms to source critical inputs at low cost, it is possible that they can serve as a catalyst or seedbed for new-firm founding. In the light of our model, the founding of new firms in the biotechnology industry may be understood to take place within the context of a dense network of social relationships among university scientists (Zucker *et al.* 1996). Similarly, Saxenian (1994) argued that the founding of numerous software firms in "Silicon Valley" was predicated on the existence of dense social relationships among engineers and other key workers. These insights raise a number of interesting research questions. For example, what types of social networks foster entrepreneurial activity as opposed to inhibiting it? Under what circumstances are fostering networks local or international in scope? When and how do networks of entrepreneurs, knowledge actors, and capital suppliers overlap and supplement each other in supporting new-firm founding?

In this chapter, I have tried to show the complexities of studying organizational networks in general, and, specifically, in the biotechnology industry. Among them I have discussed issues of levels of analysis, process issues related to types of learning in organizational networks, and structural issues related to possible position within networks. The book will further develop these issues offering observations on various segments of this complex and configurative map of analytical questions.

2 | The biotechnology industry through the lenses of organizational and networks scholarship

A review of the organizational literature shows evidence not only of a steady increase in the number of studies on the biotechnology industry all over the world, but also increasing scope of research on many related organizational topics. Although initial organizational studies of the biotechnology industry focussed mainly on interorganizational networks of collaborations, more recent research also focusses on patents, scientific citations, strategy, firm emergence, entrepreneurship, intellectual property rights, trust, learning, and university–industry technology-transfer.

This chapter will attempt to chart much of the research published in recent years on a wide range of organizational issues related to the biotechnology industry. It will also review some literature on related "knowledge-intensive" industries (such as information technology (IT) or nanotechnology), in order to search for possible similarities or differences, and will question these patterns.

The biotechnology industry and central organizational actors

In general, "biotechnology" is not a single technology but a family of technologies that have emerged from basic scientific research in molecular biology, including gene-splicing, cloning, and protein chemistry. The commercial implications of biotechnology are potentially enormous and have been well understood since the 1950s, when genetics research first began to make significant progress. However, it was not until the mid-1970s, that biotechnology became sufficiently advanced to allow commercial development of marketable products. Today there is a large population of firms involved in the commercialization of biotechnological products and processes, and these are commonly defined as the "biotechnology industry."

The industry has two notable characteristics. First, it is populated by a large number of small firms founded for the purpose of commercializing biotechnology research. In the literature these firms are entitled "new biotechnology firms," (NBFs) or "dedicated biotechnology firms," (DBFs). Such firms have been founded since 1976 (Pisano 1991; Barley, Freeman & Hybels 1992; Lee & Burrill 1995; Powell *et al.* 1996) and the founding of Genentech[1] commonly notes the "birth" of the industry. Second, these NBFs are involved in a dense network of interorganizational relationships with other organizations, most particularly large pharmaceutical firms (Barley, Freeman & Hybels 1992; Oliver 2001) and universities (Liebeskind *et al.* 1996; Zucker, Darby & Brewer 1998).

These two characteristics are conjoint phenomena. The founding of a large population of NBFs since 1976 has been attributed to the fact that biotechnology was a "competence-destroying" technology for large pharmaceutical firms. These large firms had historically used a traditional research model, first identifying a new chemical substance and then testing its properties to investigate its commercial potential. Firms' skills and routines therefore revolved around identifying and purifying new substances as well as large-scale clinical testing. In the biotechnology research model, instead, new substances are identified through investigations of the basic functions of cells. This new research model created a new organizational niche (Barley, Freeman & Hybels 1992) leading to the founding of large numbers of NBFs typically by

---

[1] Genentech was founded in 1976, by the late venture capitalist Robert A. Swanson and the biochemist Dr. Herbert W. Boyer. In the early 1970s, Boyer and geneticist Stanley Cohen pioneered a new scientific field called recombinant DNA (rDNA) technology. Upon learning about this development, Swanson placed a call to Boyer and requested a meeting. Boyer agreed to give the young entrepreneur ten minutes of his time. Swanson's enthusiasm for the technology and his faith in its commercial potential were contagious, and the meeting extended from ten minutes to three hours; by its conclusion, Genentech was born. Though Swanson and Boyer faced skepticism from both the academic and business communities, they forged ahead with their idea. The company's goal was to develop a new generation of therapeutics created from genetically engineered copies of naturally occurring molecules important in human health and disease. Within a few short years, Genentech scientists proved it was possible to make medicines by splicing genes into fast-growing bacteria that produced therapeutic proteins. Today Genentech continues to use genetic engineering techniques and advanced technologies to develop medicines that address significant unmet needs and provide clinical benefits to millions of patients worldwide. (Genentech's website: www.gene.com/gene/about/corporate/history/index.jsp)

university scientists in partnership with venture capitalists (Kenney 1986; Zucker *et al.* 1993).

A study of innovation and market structure of the pharmaceutical and the biotechnology industries (Malerba & Orsenigo 2002) found that the pharmaceutical industry is traditionally a highly research and development- (R&D-) intensive sector, which has undergone a series of radical technological and institutional "shocks." However, the core leading innovative firms, and countries, have remained quite small and stable for a very long time, but the degree of concentration has been consistently low, whatever the level of aggregation. The pharmaceutical industry was found to have a stable concentration of firms, and countries, with strong competition between innovators and imitators.

The emergence of biotechnology was a critically important break-through not only in the scientific and technological senses but also in its ability to alter the organizational landscape and composition of actors. It generated a scientific, technological, and business discontinuity for pharmaceutical firms, led a significant number of firms to change their technological identity, and fostered the entry of over a thousand new firms in a 25-year period, alongside a wide variety of new products, processes, and modes of R&D. The breakthrough also led to an increased role for universities and research centers in the commercialization of biotechnology inventions.

Galambos and Sturchio (1998) provide a historical analysis of the development of biotechnology during the years 1970–1996 in which they argue that the transition to biotechnology was a historically unique situation in which there were two very formidable, overlapping transitions taking place in the biomedical sciences and technologies. In the 1970s, small biotechnology firms were the early innovators which led the way and were followed by the large pharmaceutical corporations, which developed alliances of varying sorts with one or more of the biotechnology companies. The large companies exchanged financial support and established organizational capabilities in clinical research, regulatory affairs, manufacturing, and marketing for the smaller firms. Frequently, the biotechnology firms developed "niche technologies" – capabilities using narrowly defined, often proprietary, technological tools. They argued that innovation at large in pharmaceutical companies had always been linked to complex networks of public and non-profit institutions, and the most important relationships were with individual scientists, with public institutions, and with non-profit institutions such as research universities. The new historical development was the growing web of biotechnology contractual arrangements that added a new element to the networks which have traditionally sustained innovation in this industry.

The central question raised by Galambos and Sturchio (1998) is whether the growth of contractual arrangements has been a pheno-menon of the transition of the particular circumstances in the 1970s and 1980s, or whether it has represented a turning point when spe-cialization became more important to the entrepreneurial function than economies of scale and scope or transactions costs. If the second option was true, we should expect the small biotechnology firms to continue to generate most of the initial innovations in the industry, leaving the tasks of clinical and regulatory development, process research and engineering, manufacturing, and distribution to the large pharmaceutical companies.

Evidence shows that most large pharmaceutical firms adopted one of two strategic pathways into biotechnology. The more common strategy was to start by developing highly specific expertise and then attempting to generalize it across a range of different therapeutic categories. One important variation on this strategy was to use the new techniques of recombinant deoxyribonucleic acid (rDNA) as "enabling technologies" which strengthened existing capabilities in drug discovery and development. The second strategic alternative was a generalist approach, skipping the first stage, and attempting to acquire and build upon general capabilities very early in the process of establishing licensing, research, and equity relationships with bio-technology enterprises. Whichever path they selected, by the early 1990s, all of the large corporations had extended their traditional networks by establishing new types of contractual networks with biotechnology firms.

Obviously, the large pharmaceutical firms were slow to respond and thus left a window of opportunity open for small biotechnology startups to emerge and strive (Powell & Brantley 1992). In the 1970s and 1980s they paid a price for leaving open the biotechnology win-dow for as long as they did. If the large pharmaceutical firms had invested in molecular genetics and rDNA technology earlier, they would not have lost about $3–4 billion in total revenue argue Galambos and Sturchio (1998).

Central organizational actors in the industry

Incumbent large pharmaceutical firms

Some might have predicted that the primary organizational actors to emerge in this new industry would have been existing profit-seeking institutions such as large pharmaceutical firms, because of the high level of financing needed to bring such products to the market. The incumbent pharmaceutical companies had well-established research and development (R&D) facilities, had the stability and resources to adapt the new technologies, and were vertically integrated. Thus, given the commercialization needs, a logical collaboration would be between universities or research centers and incumbent pharmaceutical companies. Yet, this model did not become the organizational form that captured the potential in biotechnology products.

Part of the explanation may be found in Hannan and Freeman (1984, p. 157), who emphasize that many larger and older firms suffer from internal inertia that prevents them from being able to reorganize and quickly adapt their strategies and structure to new technological opportunities. This structural inertia provides a window for external entrepreneurs who can more rapidly take advantage of new opportunities.

Further, when a new technology constitutes a dramatic breakthrough it acts both to reduce the value of an existing company's ability to adjust, as well as to create the grounds for generating new kinds of organizations able to exploit the new technology (Abernethy & Clark 1985; Tushman & Anderson 1986). For this reason, Schumpeter (1934/ 1975, p. 83) refers to such "broad and rapid changes to core technologies" as "gusts of creative destruction." As Powell and Brantley (1992, p. 368) note "biotechnology is a dramatic case of competence-destroying innovation because it builds on a scientific basis (immunology and molecular biology) that differs significantly from the knowledge base (organic chemistry and its clinical applications) of the more established pharmaceutical companies." In addition, "biotechnology represents a competence-destroying technology because it required technical skills that were fundamentally different from those with which established pharmaceutical firms were familiar" (Pisano 1990, p. 154). He adds that "for this reason, most of the early commercial biotechnology R&D was conducted by new ventures that formed in the United States between 1976 and 1982 and not by established pharmaceutical firms" (Pisano 1990, p. 155).

An interesting recent study by Kaplan, Murray and Henderson (2003) focused on issues of management cognition in pharmaceutical firms and changes within these firms through a longitudinal study of 15 major pharmaceutical firms in the USA and the UK during the period 1973–1998. Their study aimed at explaining the relationship between management mental models to strategic choice and action in the face of dynamic, discontinuous events. They measured the strategic response of the pharmaceutical firms using four proxies: gene sequence patents (a count of gene sequence patents assigned to the companies); biotechnology patents in general (a count of all biotechnology-related patents); biotechnology publications (a count of biotechnology-oriented scientific publications); biotechnology equity alliances (the number of equity deals between the pharmaceutical companies and biotechnology startups). Their explanatory variable was a measure of recognition by using normalized word count (the total number of biotechnology-associated words) derived from the letters to shareholders from the annual reports of each company.

Additional control variables were uses such as total firm sales and total R&D spending, financial performance (firm operating income as a financial performance), and competitive actions (the sum of patents, publications, or deals for all the other firms in the sample in the previous year). The results show systematic patterns of association between recognition and response to biotechnology. Management recognition, as was reflected in the annual letter to the shareholders, was found to be significantly correlated with the following year's gene sequence and biotechnology patents, and with biotechnology publications, while the relationship between equity alliances and managerial recognition of biotechnology is more complex.

Malerba and Orsenigo (2002), who follow the evolution of the pharmaceutical and the biotechnology industries, confirm the conjectures that lack of cumulativeness in innovative activities, market fragmentation, and the emergence of a new technological paradigm are not unequivocally competence-destroying for the incumbent pharmaceutical firms. They argue that new entrants lack crucial capabilities in product development and marketing, and they do not compete in "protected niches." Rather, they have to face the competition of older firms and products. The NBFs do not compete in the market as a whole, but compete only in submarkets in which they are able to discover and develop their products. Hence, they cannot "win the whole market." Incumbents continue to earn revenues on older products and gradually learn the new technology. Adding that drug discovery and development are costly and take time, NBFs have little hope of displacing the leaders, even in the long term.

The question of whether incumbents are able to adapt to the radical technological changes introduced through the emergence of the biotechnology industry is a central one for understanding the role of incumbent firms. Rothaermel (2001) argues that incumbents may be in a position to adapt to radical technological change via interfirm cooperation with new entrants when the incumbents have complementary assets within their firm boundaries that are critical to commercializing the new technology. In his study of 889 strategic alliances of pharmaceutical companies with NBFs, Rothaermel (2001) found that an incumbent's alliances with providers of the new technology are positively associated with the incumbent's new product development. Further, new product development is positively associated with firm performance. At the industry level of analysis Rothaermel shows that incumbents exhibit a preference toward alliances that leverage complementary assets (exploitation alliances) over alliances that concentrate on building new technological competencies (exploration alliances).

Galambos and Sturchio (1998) suggest that the incumbents were not slow because they were large and bureaucratic. They argue that companies such as Squibb, SmithKline, Glaxo, and Merck had done an excellent job of coping with that earlier transition and once they began to read and respond to the biotechnology developments. Most of the early movers were able to establish appropriate strategies and capabilities in the new science and technology fairly quickly, and all utilized cooperative arrangements with biotechnology firms. Many of the pharmaceutical firms initially stressed a narrow range of therapies and built up specific internal capabilities as they went – the Lilly and Merck strategies. Others quickly built more elaborate networks of contractual relations and sought, through acquisition, the generalized biotechnology capabilities they needed – the Hoffmann-La Roche strategy. Yet both strategies created significant problems for managers and both involved substantial transition costs.

Further, Galambos and Sturchio (1998) indicate that by the early 1990s a few of the early movers had managed their way through the transition and had established the general biotechnology resources and capabilities they needed. At the same time several of the leading biotechnology firms had collapsed or been acquired by other firms, and some of the largest pharmaceutical firms in the industry during the 1960s and 1970s were no longer around to see the pay-off on molecular genetics and biotechnology. But the firms which survived were able to take advantage of the very long cycle of innovation. A new pattern of innovation had emerged in this industry by 1996, one in which biotechnology–pharmaceutical collaborations now played a significant role. With the improved biotechnology capabilities of the largest pharmaceutical manufacturers, Galambos and Sturchio (1998) argue that these will continue to be dominant players in the industry's global markets. Their success with protease inhibitors for HIV/AIDS provides one indicator of this, and evidence that the successful pharmaceutical companies have retained the ability to develop and implement new strategies of innovation suited to a rapidly changing scientific and technological environment.

Another study, by Zucker and Darby (1997), examined the process through which a large and successful incumbent firm transformed its technological identity in drug discovery from a chemical or random screening to a biological or drug-design model. Zucker and Darby (1997) describe how technically sophisticated senior managers championed the transformation that was achieved primarily through hiring many new scientists who embodied biotechnology while existing personnel either acquired the expertise or left. Collaborations with NBFs were used by the firm to substitute for developing internal expertise – judged of marginal value while there were no drug-discovery collaborations with other major incumbents. Zucker and Darby (1997) indicate that the importance of recruiting university "star scientists" led to the development of an overall working conditions and employment package that included stock options, which vest as the drug candidate progresses through clinical trials and Federal Drug Administration (FDA) approval.

NBFs

NBFs (or DBFs) were already classified as the small startups which were established after the founding of Genentech in 1976 for the purpose of exploiting the commercial potential of biotechnologies. In general, NBFs operate within a highly risky environment as they have to deal with both market and private risks (Ramer *et al.* 2001).

The emergence of the biotechnology industry, in the dominant form of entry of newborn firms rather than by incumbent firms, has been raised by a few organizational scholars (Powell *et al.* 1996; Argyres & Liebeskind 2002). On the emergence account, the initial entry of the first NBF was Genentech (1976), which was founded to commercialize products of genetic engineering. By 1982 there were over 200 active NBFs (Orsenigo 1989) and, by 2000, Argyres and Liebeskind (2002) counted that 949 US and large foreign firms existed in the biotechnology industry, whereas 87% of them had fewer than 300 employees. Thus, the number of new small entrants in the USA seems to be increasing constantly.

In the view of this robust entry of new firms, two important research questions are of great importance: "Why were so many of the potential R&D projects in biotechnology undertaken by small, new entrants rather than by large firms with established and related R&D programs in pharmaceuticals, chemicals, and agribusiness, and with the extensive complementary resources and capabilities?" And "Why has this early fragmented industry structure persisted and even become more marked over time?" (Argyres & Liebeskind 2002, p. 202). In their reply to these questions, Argyres and Liebeskind (2002, p. 215) argue, using transaction costs economics (Williamson 1975, 1985), that the economic spread among numerous firms results from the change in the economic activities that did not allow existing firms to govern transactions as efficiently as new firms. This was because existing firms were facing constraints in differentiating their governance arrangements to adjust to requirements of transactions based on new characteristics. Since the early inception of the biotechnology industry was dominated by university basic science (Kenney 1986), it may be argued that firms which wished to attract talented university scientists needed to offer them "university-like" environment and organizational arrangements (Oliver & Montgomery 2000), as opposed to the high level of confidentiality maintained and required in commercial research (Argyres & Liebeskind 2002, pp. 204–205). This argument portrays NBFs as firms which attract the most talented scientific researchers whom otherwise would have considered industrial research to be inferior to academic careers, and evidence shows that NBFs are organized in ways that replicate university-like arrangements

(Liebeskind *et al*. 1996; Liebeskind 2000; Oliver & Montgomery 2000) such as allowing NBF scientists to collaborate extensively with other scientists, to have significant ownership stakes and board representation, and a degree of control over the firm's research agenda.

Not many studies were able to provide such an illuminating understanding of the evolutionary process of the biotechnology industry as a whole, and the positions and roles taken by NBFs, as the seminal work by Powell *et al*. (2005). In this study a nicely developing story on the role of NBFs within the industry is portrayed, starting as early as 1975. It is argued that in the early years of the industry, from 1975 to 1987, most NBFs were very small startups and were deeply reliant on external support out of necessity. At that time, no NBF could establish the necessary skills or resources to bring a new medicine to market. As a result, Powell and Brantley (1992) describe the emerging elaborate lattice-like structure of relationships with universities and large multinational firms. The later work (Powell *et al*. 2005) considered 482 NBFs over a 12-year period between 1988 and 1999. In this study they found that, by 1988, most NBFs supported themselves by selling their lead product to large corporations, which subsequently marketed the medicine in return for a large share of the revenue. NBFs with significant intellectual property and strong research capability were highly sought for collaboration. They also found that a group of first-wave biotechnology firms that were founded in the 1970s and early 1980s (Genentech, Centocor, Amgen, Genzyme, Biogen, and Chiron) became the largest and most visible firms by 1988. In 1989 there is evidence that venture capital was involved in financing NBFs; there were also changes in the capabilities of NBFs. In the first two decades of the industry, the ability to manufacture new biomedical products was a relatively scarce skill, as was the ability to market and distribute a new medicine throughout the world. A relatively small number of large firms had these capabilities, and it took at least a decade before NBFs developed these skills. As a result, the major multinational firms and only a few NBFs were the center of the commercialization ties during the first two decades of the industry.

By 1994, a growing multivocality of the industry is evident. At this stage, well-networked NBFs and pharmaceutical firms developed the capability to finance younger firms, as well as to contribute to basic and clinical science and to commercialize new medicines. The overall picture has become more diverse, with activities with more heterogeneous participants and, by 1997, there is a growing presence of second-generation NBFs that are active in the field; these are also active in pulling new participants to the network through their networks.

In addition to the network structure analyses, Powell *et al.* (2005) found some illuminating statistical findings on the network structures of NBFs. For example, they found that NBFs seek to balance novelty and visibility when they form an alliance with another NBF seeking these two elements in their alliances. In addition, as NBFs age, the importance of partner experience recedes as partners spend more time in the field. In particular older NBFs tend to opt for new partners at the expense of more visible ones.

Being a veteran in the network is an advantage to NBFs and those who are centrally positioned seem to spot up-and-coming newcomers, and escort them into the network. Powell *et al.* (2005) argue that in some cases, these new firms are spin-offs from more established NBFs, and this fact may account for the very strong support for repeat ties with newcomers.

Finally, their results indicate that as NBFs scan for potential collaborators, the diversity of ties is a valuable marker of resources and information. Thus NBFs are constantly exploring new directions through their networks. This may also explain why NBFs favor attachments to partners that are better positioned with more diverse collaborations.

These findings as a whole show how NBFs emerged from a position of a needy organizational form to a position of a fostering form that has the capacity to welcome newcomer NBFs to the network of exchanges. The findings also highlight the ability of NBFs to position themselves in the best network structures that can increase their ability to explore new directions of innovation.

Other studies focussed on the effects of interorganizational ties of NBFs on various performance issues. For example, Gulati and Higgens (2003) found out that various types of interorganizational ties of NBFs have differential effects on initial public offering (IPO) performance and this, in turn, is contingent on the favorability of the equity markets. In the USA, NBFs benefit from having partners with prominent organizations in different ways and at different times: whereas partnerships with prestigious venture capital firms positively affect IPO success when the equity markets are relatively cold for new issues, partnerships with prestigious underwriters positively affect IPO success when the equity markets are relatively hot for new issues. Strategic alliances of NBFs were also found to have a significant effect on IPO success. Finally, Gulati and Higgins (2003) found that network effects are not uniform but rather are contingent upon both the nature of a firm's ties and on the uncertainty associated with the marketplace.

Other studies tried to find out the factors associated with rapid growth of NBFs. Rapid growth of new firms is a highly aimed-for goal in biotechnology. In this context, Niosi (2003) found that most companies that experienced rapid growth in the Canadian biotechnology industry were older (median of 16 years after foundation), were active in the area of human health biotechnology, had obtained patents and then venture capital, established alliances, exported their products, and did not experience any obstacle with consumer acceptance. In sum, age is a main determinant of growth and the sub-area of human health seems to be the sector where rapid growth occurred as it was also the area where firms obtained venture capital more easily. Patents were also related to rapid growth and alliances appeared as the major determinant of growth.

Firm performance of NBFs was also studied by Maurer and Ebers (2006), and their focus was on the role of social capital. Social capital of firms and scientists is considered to be a crucial factor associated with firm success. In longitudinal analyses of six NBFs, they found that firms can realize performance benefits when their members repeatedly adapt the configuration of their social capital to changing resource needs. They show that obligation-based relations based on norms of reciprocity, frequent interactions, and shared identities, lead jointly to relational and cognitive lock-ins and these lead to inertial in social capital. On the other hand, horizontal and vertical differentiation of relationship management and integration of relationship management may enhance the ability of NBFs to overcome relational and cognitive lock-ins.

Universities

Universities are considered the main source of basic scientific research, knowledge, and discoveries for knowledge-intensive industries in general. This is particularly significant for the biotechnology industry in which both the industrial main scientists and innovators as well as breakthrough discoveries emerge from universities (Kenney 1986; Argyres & Liebeskind 2002; Zucker *et al.* 2002). In addition, innovation and patenting in the life sciences are central in universities. Owen-Smith and Powell (2003) contend that by 1998 nearly half (49.5%) of all patents issued to research-intensive US universities were based on life-science innovations.

That universities play such a significant role in biotechnology research is evident; however, there are arguments that the increase in biomedical patenting in campuses and the commercialization of academic life-science research is deeply intertwined with the emergence of the biotechnology industry, which had its origins in university laboratories (Owen-Smith & Powell 2003). As the industry evolved, its ties to academia deepened, with "star" scientists playing central roles in new biotechnology firms (Zucker, Darby & Brewer 1998) and in the transfer of new knowledge from universities to firms (Zucker, Darby & Armstrong 2002).

Since universities are increasingly patenting in the life sciences, it is important to evaluate the importance of their experience and their capabilities for research commercialization. Owen-Smith and Powell (2003) combine a qualitative and quantitative study and present a story of the opportunities and potential pitfalls of university engagement in contractual networks with biotechnology firms. The findings of their study emphasize the central role which firms play as a source of information that facilitates effective evaluation of the potential of often ambiguous faculty innovations. Although establishing connections between academic discoveries with commercial networks is of great value, Owen-Smith and Powell (2003) find that too many linkages may preclude the development of a stable flow of higher-impact patents. In general, they found that the effect of a university's patent portfolio depends on the stock of basic life-science findings in the form of published articles. Significant scientific findings may serve as an entry ticket to commercialization networks which enable universities to develop higher-impact intellectual property.

Finally, Owen-Smith and Powell (2003) argue that the reputations of university scientists also matter indirectly, as researchers who are both highly visible and commercially engaged attract the attention of corporate partners and, in so doing, increase the flow of valuable information into university technology-transfer offices. Although high-impact publications are those that provide an "entry ticket" to information-rich networks in the life-sciences, such access may also contribute to increasing commercial accomplishment. If these two elements occur, scientific reputation might start universities on a path of increasing returns. However, Owen-Smith and Powell (2003) also found that if highly cited intellectual property helps to make universities more attractive to commercial partners, and universities build strong links to a small number of affiliates, then this tight connectivity may reduce overall patent impact. Thus, too much integration across academic and commercial interests may become a danger for universities. These findings fall in well with the belief that university–industry collaborations and exchanges should be perceived as a mixed package with advantages and disadvantages to universities.

Regardless of the complexities mentioned, it is obvious that universities are significant players in the biotechnology industry. Academic technologies are central to the R&D efforts of NBFs, and universities are central players in the inter-organizational networks which constitute the industry's "locus of innovation" (Powell *et al.* 1996; Owen-Smith *et al.* 2002; Owen-Smith & Powell 2003). Significantly, in the early stages of the industry the two most breakthrough and innovative discoveries in biotechnology which led to its birth – recombinant DNA (rDNA) and monoclonal antibodies – were discovered in universities and research centers (for extensive details of these two discoveries *see* Chapter 5).

In an impressive review of the literature of studies on entrepreneurial universities, Rothaermel *et al.* (2007) argue that scholars have recognized that, in addition to internal factors associated with being an entrepreneurial university, the process of university entrepreneurship is influenced by external factors (Etzkowitz 2003), most notably federal laws and policies like the Bayh–Dole Act in the USA (Mowery *et al.* 2001), the surrounding industry (Gulbrandsen & Smeby 2005), and regional conditions (Friedman & Silberman 2003).

In this line of research, a recently developed frame of research refers to the grand role of the "triple helix" of university–industry–government relations as an engine of national-level innovation (Etzkowitz & Leydesdorff 2000). The triple helix thesis states that the university can play an enhanced role in innovation in increasingly knowledge-based societies. The underlying model is analytically different from the national systems of innovation (NSI) approach, which considers the firm as having the leading role in innovation. The focus is on the network overlay of communications and expectations which reshape the institutional arrangements between universities, industries, and governmental agencies.

If universities are becoming central not only in the knowledge creation aspect of biotechnology but also on the commercialization dimension, the resulting question is: "How do universities' inventions get into practice?" Colyvas *et al.* (2002) use a case study methodology to ask this question. Their analysis is based on 11 case studies of inventions created at two universities – Columbia and Stanford. The finding pointed to two major themes: looking at the role of intellectual property rights in facilitating technology-transfer and looking at the role of university technology-transfer offices in bringing inventions to practice. Colyvas *et al.* (2002) found that the two universities took out intellectual property, patent, or copyright on most of their inventions. Such explicit policy has enabled them to reap significant financial returns for some of their inventions.

Although most of the inventions studied were "embryonic" and needed development to be useful, others were useful to industry even without significant further development. In the analysis of intellectual property rights and exclusivity,[2] Colyvas *et al.* (2002) found out that granting exclusivity appeared to be more important for inducing firms to develop "embryonic" inventions, though the dangers of strong exclusivity were also revealed to be greatest for these types of inventions.

As to their findings regarding the role of university technology-transfer offices in bringing inventions to practice, Colyvas *et al.* (2002) found that industry was monitoring university-based inventions well. Strategically located people in industry were well aware of university research projects, even before the universities began to market inventions. Information was elicited through interactions with inventors or their colleagues, or through membership of broader scientific networks. In most cases, the technology-transfer offices were not needed to make contacts with industry, to spread information, or to induce

---

[2] Giving exclusive rights in licensing a patent to a firm prevents other users from using the inventions. This grants the firm a wider protection on the exclusivity of their R&D, yet limits the ability of a university to diffuse this knowledge to the larger community and in this respect is opposed to the idea of "open science" – for further elaboration on this issue, *see* Chapter 5.

industrial interest. Colyvas *et al.* (2002) found that industry actively monitors academic developments and has a range of links with the scientific community, and thus may learn of promising academic inventions via channels other than technology-transfer offices. The role of technology-transfer offices is thus limited to marketing activities for inventions which generate little industrial interest early on, either because of a lack of initial promise or a lack of well-established networks between academia and industry in the relevant technology field. The final and critical conclusion of Colyvas *et al.* (2002) study is that there are reasons to doubt that patents and patent licensing are necessary for effective transfer. This conclusion is highly controversial and debated in the literature, and this topic is elaborated in Chapter 5.

The role of "star scientists" or scientific entrepreneurs in universities has been acknowledged in the literature (Oliver 2004).[3] As indicated above, in the last decade or so many universities have become entrepreneurial, seeking to bring basic academic discoveries to market by use of various technology-transfer methods (Owen-Smith & Powell 2003; Rothaermel *et al.* 2007).[4] This phenomenon is true not only on a university level but also on a scientists' level (Oliver 2004). Whilst focussing on the role of innovative scientists, Zucker and Darby (2001) suggested the concept of "star scientists" to refer to academic scientists characterized by a high rate of innovative discoveries (Zucker, Darby & Brewer 1998).

The argument about the significant role of star scientists was tested in different directions. Studies showed that actual research collaborations between star scientists and firm scientists consistently had a significant positive effect on a wide range of firm performance measures in biotechnology (Zucker, Darby & Armstrong 1998; Zucker & Darby 2001). Collaborations with stars were also found to shorten the time to IPO (firms are younger) and to increase the amount of IPO proceeds (Darby & Zucker 2002). In addition, it was found that, as the quality of an academic star increased and their research became more relevant to commercialization, the probability that the scientist would conduct joint research or move to a firm increased (Zucker & Darby 1996).

---

[3] This topic of entrepreneurial scientists is further elaborated, *see* Chapter 4.
[4] For more details about new organizational forms for conducting research and development research, *see* Chapter 3.

In another study, Zucker, Darby and Armstrong (2002) asked about the value of knowledge (including tacit knowledge) at the time of commercially relevant scientific breakthroughs. They analyzed star scientists who collaborated with biotechnology firms at 112 top US universities, and used as measures items such as joint articles, venture capital funding, patents granted, cumulative patents granted, cumulative citations weighted, total products in development, total human therapies and vaccines in development, total products on the market, total human therapies and vaccines on the market, and total number of employees. Zucker, Darby and Armstrong (2002) found that since tacit scientific knowledge is embodied in individual scientists, working jointly with industry scientists is a crucial transfer mechanism when knowledge has a large tacit dimension, and this is associated with firm success.

The location of top star scientists was also an important factor, as this predicted the location of firm entry into new technologies (both new and existing firms), shown for the USA and Japan in biotechnology (Zucker, Darby & Brewer 1998; Zucker & Darby 2001). This finding was also replicated for the semiconductor industry in the USA (Torero, Darby & Zucker 2001). In this context, Feldman (2003) argues that whilst in its earliest years the biotechnology industry grew up around university star scientists, who licensed innovations to companies, the mode of innovation is now shifting to clusters around universities, and there are many initiatives which attempt to build biotechnology clusters around universities by use of formal technology-transfer mechanisms. However, the presence of universities themselves appear not to be a sufficient condition to promote industrial clusters.

Zucker, Darby and Torero (2002) ask "How do top academic scientists become involved in commercializing their discoveries?" as they aim to explain the mobility processes involved in moving scientists' labor effort to specific firms. Based on the Gen Bank database they found that star scientists move more quickly from academia to commercial involvement if they have higher-quality intellectual human capital (measured in terms of number of citations to genetic-sequence discovery articles) and if that capital is more relevant to firms that are commercializing biotechnology. The opportunities available in the star's own region have a significant effect, and stars have a higher probability of moving to a firm when there are more biotechnology enterprises in their region and a lower probability of moving to a firm when there are more top-quality universities in their region, which suggests a competing influence. In addition, they found that the size of the star's network outside of the university also increased the likelihood of their leaving the university after a shorter period.

The conclusion reached by Zucker, Darby and Torero (2002) is that scientists and the universities, research institutions, and high-technology firms in the USA are faced with knowledge discontinuities that require some kind of technology-transfer mechanism. There are thus incentives for star scientists to construct structures that lower the costs of new knowledge acquisition. These structures include both affiliation and links to firms. They argue that many universities do not place any restriction on a professor's outside employment. To the degree that this is possible, high-technology firms routinely employ the very top scientists across a wide variety of positions, from head of scientific teams to members of scientific advisory boards. Whilst this last comment is true for US universities, it is not so in other countries. In Israeli universities, scientists may work as consultants in firms for up to 20% of their time and part-time appointments in firms are not allowed, whereas holding shares in firms is shared with the university through the technology-transfer arrangements.

Commercialization of academic knowledge requires a process of knowledge transformation, which is considered to be a complex process (Nonaka 1994), and has an impact on the structure of the organizational elements associated with this transformation. In this vein, Zucker, Darby and Armstrong (2002) argue that that knowledge close to breakthrough discoveries needs to be transformed into words, codes, or formulae before it may be easily transferred. These difficulties are inherent to the transfer of tacit knowledge and lead to joint research in which jointly conducted teamwork permits more knowledge-capture of tacit, complex discoveries by firm scientists. A strong indicator of tacit knowledge-capture by the firm is the number of research articles written jointly by scientists working at a firm and the academic star scientists who are working at top universities. Zucker, Darby and Armstrong (2002) state that working jointly at the laboratory bench is a crucial transfer mechanism when knowledge has an important or large tacit component, and suggest that tacit knowledge is embodied in individual, discovering scientists. Thus, star scientists were either fully employed by firms or were governed in their relationships with firms by explicit contracts.

Institutional regimens may generate different structures of relations between universities and industries. One study that aimed at under-standing "how scientific and technological human capital is turned into economic capital" in the French biotechnology industry focussed on the role of university star scientists (Corolleur *et al.* 2004). In a study of 132 founders who created 62 NBFs in France, Corolleur *et al.* (2004) found that, among university-based scientists involved in start-up creation, scientists with a high level of academic production have part-time positions in the firm as scientific advisors. In addition, they found that whilst non-university-based scientists or non-tenured scientists held positions as chief executive officers (CEO) or in top management, the more experienced and productive scientists founded riskier firms.

Regions

Studies of regional development assign an important role for geo-graphical proximity and clusters as possible engines for the development and innovation of biotechnology firms. Such studies of innovation sys-tems are based on two major assumptions: (1) that interactions occur among the chosen population of actors; and (2) that these interactions influence innovations and thereby economic growth. These are strong assumptions about the importance of co-locality within a system to innovation and they should not be taken for granted. Proximity alone cannot explain regional development even if it does clarify the role of firm capabilities, complementarities, networks of collaboration, and exchanges as well as opportunities and constraints.

With regard to theory, regional analysis brings credibility to the competency theory of the region. Knowledge spillover is considered a valuable resource of "added value" in regional knowledge-intensive clusters, as it allows firms to learn through positive externalities from the presence of other knowledge-based firms in the vicinity with reduced direct costs. The spillover of knowledge not only depends on the amount of industrially useful knowledge produced by firms, universities, and government laboratories, but also on the size of the immediate market and other related characteristics of the urban agglomeration.

Within the area of regional development, there are approaches which argue that regional performance should be understood in systemic terms, resulting from interaction between the region and its environment, whereas others have emphasized that regional development is path-dependent, with certain events being more influential on the development trajectory than others (Höyssä, Bruun & Hukkinen 2004). In the context of the biotechnology industry, some studies have looked at universities as sources of regional development and firm density in biotechnology (e.g. Zucker, Darby & Brewer 1998); Feldman 2003; Owen-Smith & Powell 2005) while others focussed on the clustering of firms in regions as a source of innovative activities (e.g. Feldman & Francis 2004).

The next section describes a few studies that focussed on the role of regions and their ability to enhance biotechnology innovation, with the aim of finding some key features that are associated with innovation and success.

In an analysis of the success factors associated with the US Capitol region as a biotechnology cluster, Feldman and Francis (2004) found that three major reinforcing sets of factors accounted for the success. These were preexisting resources, entrepreneurship and the incentives, and infrastructure provided by government. The preexisting resources were mainly in the form of laboratories, bioscience students, and prominent students; the entrepreneurs were an important ingredient to cluster-formation in technology industries, and the incentives and infrastructure provided by the government were in the form of transportation, schools, tax incentives, supporting policies, and public funds for aiding new businesses.

Feldman (2003) argues that while it is known that the existence of knowledge externalities contributes to geographic concentration, the less-answered question is of how regional specialization is determined and how this affects firm survival and growth and subsequently the viability of the regional clusters. Feldman (2003) studied a panel of firms in biotechnology and points to the contribution of the concept of the "anchor firm," which is an agglomerative force that acts as a facilitator to the formation of new dedicated biotechnology firms and has an impact on their growth and the technical specialization of clusters.

Another regional feature that is associated with spillover is network-overlapping. The feature of overlapping networks of collaborations between biotechnology actors constitutes a "nexus of a community of practice" (Porter, Whittington & Powell 2005). In their study of the

Boston region in the USA, the focus was on the intersection of university and commercial science within a geographical region. The leading assumption of the study was that the combination of dense social networks and geographic co-location has been critical to the genesis of the high-technology regions in the Boston area. Thus, in a technology cluster, the network of relationships among participants is the primary source of knowledge. The study is based on four different networks: alliances; founding teams (career history data); science boards (information on scientific advisory boards established by the companies); and inventors (data on co-assigned patents) from the end of the 1970s until the beginning of 2000.

Their study found that the Boston biotechnology community is characterized by diverse and cross-cutting linkages. All the network maps display similar typologies, with a relatively small number of highly connected organizations. Yet, similar to the "anchor firm" concept of Feldman and Francis (2004), Porter, Whittington and Powell (2005) found that all four networks are anchored by public research organizations. Thus, in this context, the research organizations act as an anchor for regional development in biotechnology. The overall centrality of universities and hospitals is impressive yet not surprising based on what we have already learned about the importance of academic and research institutions. Their findings also clarify that the embedding of multiple networks contributed to a dynamic regional economy in biotechnology. These multiple connections provided ample opportunities for the exchanges of ideas and resources. In summary, the Boston biotechnology community is dependent on personal relations between research scientists, on strong, ongoing affiliations among universities, hospitals, and firms, and on reciprocal flows of ideas and personnel.

The study by Porter, Whittington and Powell (2005) also offers us a deeper understanding of regional success in biotechnology. The main key features that may be extracted from this study are organizational heterogeneity and open science.

Organizational heterogeneity promotes opportunities for experimentation and flexibility for firms, and when there is no single dominant actor in the region there is no fixed or constrained mode of operation or direction. Instead there are multiple opportunities for collaborations and exchanges which enhance firms' ability to become competitive. The dense networks that connect these organizations afford multiple independent pathways through which ideas and resources may flow, facilitating research progress.

As to the "open science" feature, the intense scientific competition in Boston created learning cycles which enabled researchers and clinicians to build on the accomplishments of others. This is a significant spillover of the open science community in NBFs. The key feature for success is the predominance of research organizations and universities committed to norms of open science. Thus, the findings on the Boston region show that the intellectual capital of academic and clinical researchers made possible the successful commercial world of biotechnology and the growth of the biotechnology industry in the region. It is important to point out that Porter, Whittington and Powell (2005) found that although the organizational community is simultaneously collaborative and competitive, research spillovers have fueled the overall success of the region.

The role of the social networks and social capital of actors in a biotechnology region was also found by Höyssä, Bruun and Hukkinen (2004), who analyzed a case study of a successful biotechnology region in Finland – BioCity in Turku. These scholars maintained that, initially, the idea of BioCity was conceived through a set of heterogeneous interests but without a clear regional emphasis, whilst only later did the network around the technology center become integrated. Their argument is that technology centers and science parks should not be considered merely in terms of technology-transfer but also in terms of social activity. Collaboration between actors is not just the result of proximity in technological parks or regions, but it may also give birth to such regions. In the Turku case, the construction of the city led to a practice of collaborations and accumulation of social capital that triggered the emerging cluster on a very constructive trajectory of interaction. Thus, Höyssä, Bruun and Hukkinen (2004) highlight the role of informal but organized communication between key individuals from public and private organizations as a key factor contributing to the enhancement of innovation in regions. This enhanced innovation is related not to the short-term innovative activity, but to the long-term development of informal communication between organizational actors in the region.

Another study on regional co-location of biotechnology firms in the Swedish pharmaceutical sector questions the validity of the assumptions about the importance of co-locality for innovation (McKelvey,

Alm & Riccaboni 2003). Sweden, in which there is a strong research policy, has traditionally been a strong player in medical science research. Therefore, it provides an interesting region for studying the relations between proximity of firms and knowledge collaborations. The study is based on data of historical trends for the Swedish bio-technology–pharmaceutical sector between the years 1985 and 2000, and on 215 R&D collaborations made by 67 Swedish firms or Swedish research institutes and 137 foreign partners, out of which 52 were made between two Swedish actors. Their findings show that Swedish biotechnology–pharmaceutical firms engage in knowledge alliances more intensely and frequently than would be expected from only international data. This result indicates that the firms are involved in active, technological collaboration and are not just selling knowledge to leverage economic and complementary assets. As to the geographical co-location, the study found that co-location of partners in the region for formal knowledge collaboration is somewhat less common than might be predicted within the systems of innovation approach.

It may be of surprise that two large multinational companies in Sweden – Pharmacea and AstraZeneca – are not engaged in formal knowledge-collaboration with other Swedish biotechnology firms, and are also reducing their involvement with Swedish universities over time. As to the small and medium-sized Swedish biotechnology firms, the propensity to collaborate with geographically co-located partners differs depending on whether the collaboration is firm–firm, firm–university, or university–university. The overall finding is that geo-graphical co-location is less important for firm–firm collaborations or deals, or for university–university co-authored papers, than for firm–university collaborations. Thus, the co-location knowledge col-laborations differ relative to the type of partner. The interesting finding in this study is that the effect of regional proximity in Sweden is rewarding mainly for firms' collaborations with universities, showing again the importance of research organizations for industrial regional development in biotechnology.

A valuable and most worthy approach for understanding the role of regional clusters in the development of the biotechnology industry is to compare two regional clusters in the same country. This was done by Owen-Smith and Powell (2005), who compared the San Francisco Bay area with the Boston/Cambridge area which are the world's largest and most commercially successful biotechnology regions. In general, their findings show that, despite similarities in scale and outcomes, each region emerged through a distinctive process that continues to influence its outputs. Thus, there is no one single pattern or model of emerging regional development. The variations between the regions suggest that there are multiple pathways to similar outcomes. Their study focusses on the years 1988–1999 and on collaborations between US firms, both public and private, large pharmaceutical companies, investors, government agencies, and public research organizations, as well as on patent and patent citation information for 1976–1999.

Owen-Smith and Powell (2005) found that the Boston and San Francisco Bay area biotechnology communities became more similar during the 12-year period studied. During this period, firms' dependence on public research organizations and venture capital decreased whilst increasing their dependence on the firm–firm component. The differences between the two regions show that the Boston area firms were more dependent on external sources of knowledge and opted to favor more exploratory efforts at discovery. At that time, the San Francisco Bay area biotechnology firms were more self-reliant in terms of knowledge-generation, and were more persistent in their efforts to further development of in-house intellectual property. In addition, the San Francisco Bay area firms were faster in new product development, as well as more likely to pursue novel medicines for larger markets, which are usually more competitive. On the other hand, the Boston firms were more likely to focus on medicine-specific illnesses, slower in new product development, and focussed on less-competitive markets. The differences persisted even when important factors such as market, scientific, and regulatory variables were controlled for.

The Boston firms continued their reliance on public sector research organizations in the region, including the Massachusetts Institute of Technology (MIT), Harvard, Massachusetts General Hospital, the Whitehead Institute, and the Dana Farber Cancer Center. The public research organizations in the Boston area had their effects on the networks owing to their openness to their local networks, using formal contractual arrangements for collaborations with the industry which controlled and directed information transfer. In contrast, Stanford and the University of California at San Francisco (UCSF) are argued to prefer a lack of formal involvement over more informal, non-contractual ties in their regional network, an approach that is closer to the "open science" mission of universities, and which enabled financiers to shape regional innovation.

The paradoxical implications are fascinating. Owen-Smith and Powell (2005) suggest that deliberate efforts by public research organizations to control knowledge flows in networks result in more open and expansive structures, whereas more informal, "hands-off" approaches help to create networks that are more tightly controlled and commercially directed. The co-evolutionary dynamic suggested in the study led to a deeper understanding of sources of regional variation and showed how actions taken by certain actors in the region may have a differential effect on the innovation of the region as a whole.

National-level impact

Nations provide the economic, regulatory, and policy environments in which industries are embedded, and these environments may either enhance or hinder innovation in general and biotechnology in particular. The economic level provides the structure of national opportunities available to the various actors in the biotechnology industry. These include national funding allocated for basic and applied research, the availability of venture capital and of entrepreneurs, national investments in facilitating university–industry collaborations and the like. The policy level focusses on the nature and structure of national policy regarding taxes on entrepreneurial ventures, support for academic entrepreneurs, higher education offering reduced tuition for students in the life-sciences, and on defining intellectual property rights.

In this context, there are studies which provide strong understanding of how nations and their economic and polices differ, and of the differential impact on the various aspects of the biotechnology industry.

National R&D policies are a key factor that may affect the success of the biotechnology industry. In the context of national R&D reforms, Lehrer and Asakawa (2004) argue that the concept of "comparative institutional advantage" suggests that industries in which countries specialize depend not only on the relative costs of classical trade theory but also on the national institutional frameworks that a country's producers are embedded in. However, such institutions are not fixed but evolve over time. To the extent that countries may create or reform national institutions which support targeted industries, they may be able to create sources of comparative advantage that establish specific arrangements but ultimately affect economic factors such as relative costs, the flow of new ideas, and incentives to innovate.

Taking different perspectives on the role of the nation in supporting biotechnology innovation, various studies asked questions about the effect various policies, rules, and procedures have on establishing differences between countries. The next section reviews some of these studies and summarizes their major findings.

National policy may have a major impact on the directions academic research takes. The Bayh–Dole Act, passed in 1980, is considered to have changed significantly the academic arena. The Bayh–Dole Act (Public Law 96–517) gave universities the right to seek patents for scientific discoveries made by their faculty and staff with support from federal funds. The motive of this legislation was to facilitate the commercialization of potentially valuable discoveries. Liebeskind (2001) argues that without clear intellectual property rights firms had few incentives to invest in developing new products. The law shifted patent ownership from government to universities and gave universities the power to seek and own patents as well as license their patents to firms.

As the ownership rights of universities were further expanded under Public Law 98–620, passed in 1984, patents in universities increased sharply, especially in the life sciences. Many perceived these laws as benefiting society, argues Liebeskind (2001), and characterized universities as "engines of economic growth" (Liebeskind 2001, p. 49). Universities now started supplying industry with basic research and potential for new products, and the biotechnology industry has flourished with a range of socially valuable innovations from new drugs for previously untreated diseases to new agriculture products.

Liebeskind (2001) further raises some common concerns about these changes, asking questions such as: Will university ownership of intellectual property rights, which used to create knowledge for the "intellectual commons," eventually shrink now this is common? Or will it undermine its value to society in other ways? These questions and their possible impact were discussed by Liebeskind (2001) in the areas of faculty incentives, the conduct of university research, and faculty–university relations, but will not be further elaborated here.

Yet, the key point here is that national law can have a major impact on the organization of science, and the relations between science and industry in knowledge-intensive industries such as biotechnology.

The social and economic institutional environment in which industries operate may shape the structure and direction of these industries. In a comparative case study between the USA and Germany on the software and biotechnology industries, Casper, Lehrer and Soskice (1999) found that German firms can successfully enter high-technology industries. However, they must do so within constraints created by the broader institutional logic of market regulation in Germany. The social and economic institutional patterns in Germany encourage incremental innovation, long-term relations between firms and their stakeholders, and the accumulation of knowledge and experience. Therefore, technologies characterized by reduced risk and cumulative technologies, such as the platform-technology segment of biotechnology and the services segment of software, fit the inherited institutional framework of Germany better than many other segments of high technology. On the other hand, in segments characterized by more risky and discrete technologies, special effort is required.

As to the biotechnology industry, despite efforts to replicate the American innovation chain, the evidence indicates that the market profile of most German biotechnology firms differs from the activities commonly chosen by American firms and develops a more specialized market.

Another study, by Casper and Kettler (2001), compares the national institutional frameworks of the German and UK biotechnology sectors, aiming at understanding the entrepreneurial models. Through a comparison of four key competencies[5] of small biotechnology firms in the UK and in Germany, these scholars found that the development of entrepreneurial business strategies is strongly influenced by the orientation of key national institutional frameworks affecting technology transfer, finance, labor markets, and company law. Their findings show that the German specialization in platform technologies emphasizes patterns of firm-level competency preservation and a

---

[5] The key competencies include: (1) access to technology; (2) the availability of high-risk finance; (3) the development of human resources within a "competency-destroying" environment; and (4) the development of sufficiently high-powered motivational incentives for personnel in the industry.

lower scientific intensity, which are generally advantaged by German patterns of market regulation. In a similar pattern, the UK has developed a much more market-led structure of specialization in biotechnology that is characterized by a higher degree of scientific intensity and specialization in therapeutic market niches. This structure resembles the US biotechnology industry, yet Casper and Kettler (2001) argue that capitalism research has often emphasized a strong embeddedness of firms within their institutional environments so that it is possible to "read" the organizational characteristics of firms from the architecture of national-level institutions. In this line, they suggest that in Germany there is evidence for a hybridization of business models on the level of business strategy as German technology policies have successfully stretched the established institutional frameworks into new directions. The BioRegio programs in Germany, coupled with financial subsidies and reforms to promote the creation of high-technology corporate governance, led to the creation of extensions of the German model. However, these extensions are dependent on the prevailing forms of organization within the German economy and thus cannot be described as different from the long-established German patterns of company organization. The UK, on the other hand, lacks the type of "non-market" institutions and, as a result, the hybridized business models that seem successful in Germany are not viable within the UK. Rather, the UK liberal market institutional environment seems to strongly encourage biotechnology companies to accommodate themselves to the US model of developing and governing entrepreneurial technology firms.

In an effort to analyze the country effect on the failure of the biotechnology local industry to innovate, Orsenigo (2001) questions why significant innovative activities in biotechnology did not emerge in Italy in what might seem to be a promising area for the growth of this industry. Further, he asks about the nature of the factors that might explain the lagging behind of the Italian and European biotechnology industry vis-à-vis the USA.

Orsenigo's argument specifies the factors associated with the lack of growth, including the weakness of the local scientific base, weak ties and separation between industry and academy, lack of venture capital, and tendency of European companies to collaborate more with US firms than with European ones; the non-existence of intellectual property rights as a result of the lack of patents for published scientific discoveries. In addition, he observed a regulatory climate in Italy that did not restrict genetic experimentation. Thus, he concludes that the lack of preconditions such as the scientific and industrial base, the organizational structures linking science to industry, venture capital, and intellectual property rights hindered the development of the biotechnology industry in Italy (and generally in Europe, apart from the UK).

Another comparative case study on Germany and Japan focusses on issues such as employment rigidities, institutional incentives, intellectual property rights, and historical discontinuity as well as the role of the public-sector of universities and biotechnology policies. Lehrer and Asakawa (2004) argue that the patent statistics give a basic indication that the German and Japanese lagged behind in biotechnology in comparison with the USA in the 1990s. Germany and Japan also lagged far behind the USA in the number of biotechnology firms (there were over 1300 biotechnology companies in the mid-1990s in the USA while Germany and Japan had well under 100 each). The pattern they found was that Germany and Japan were both overly dependent on established firms for conducting R&D in biotechnology, whilst startup companies are usually more important for patenting in biotechnology. Thus, the lack of NBFs in Germany and Japan hindered the development of the biotechnology industry in these countries. By the mid-1990s, the need for startup firms to build an internationally competitive biotechnology base had become manifest. As a result, Germany and Japan established policies to create more biotechnology startups, and highlighted the institutional framework required for biotechnology innovation by reforming the R&D policy toward greater support of public-sector universities. Thus, Lehrer and Asakawa (2004) focus on the important role of NBFs and university-based research on biotechnology innovation.

The role of governments is central in specifying policy and thus shaping the structure of innovation in biotechnology, yet the structure or type of governmental policies is important as well. A distinction between "bottom up" and "top down" strategies is highlighted by Niosi and Bas (2001). They argue that for biotechnology in Canada economic concentrations of firm' competencies are associated with regional concentration. In the Canadian biotechnology industry by 1997 there were 282 domestic biotechnology NBFs, and close to 350 in 2000; 71 of them were public and almost all of the largest firms were active in human health products. Despite the large number of NBFs, 12 firms, half of them in the large cities, held over two-thirds of the Canadian patents in biotechnology. The three main Canadian biotechnology clusters are located in the three largest cities and each one of them had at least one major research university nearby and a large venture capital pool available to them.

Niosi and Bas (2001) argue that government laboratories only marginally countered the market forces that tend to concentrate biotechnology activities in a few large cities with strong university and venture capital environments. This observation is related to the characteristics of government policies. If university-creation represents a "bottom up" strategy and the establishment of government laboratories represents a "top down" one, then the bottom up approach to biotechnology, in which universities are the basis for new firms and industrial dynamics, seems adequate for the advancement of the industry. Their analysis suggests that government policies may facilitate Canadian biotechnology clusters if the laboratories are relocated to the largest metropolitan areas where there is a potential for clustering.

Feldman and Francis (2004) argue that the role of government in industrial development, in general, and biotechnology development, in particular, is not single-dimensional. Their analysis of the US Capitol region in biotechnology led to the observation that various levels of government have unique roles to play. This is particularly true for high-risk and potentially high-return industries such as biotechnology. In the development of the biotechnology industry, the role of the federal government in the USA was different from that of the states and counties. The federal government set a national research agenda that specified funding priorities through grants and laboratory funding as well as through establishing regulations and standards for the industry as a whole. Local government in the USA, such as state and county government, has played and continues to play a different role in the development of the biotechnology industry. Not only is local government involved with more mundane issues, such as issuing building permits for special laboratory facilities, but it is also more focussed on attracting firms to its location. States and counties within states actively compete with each other to gain promising firms by providing tax incentives, dedicated funds, and aid-application preparation for incubators and other business services and educational opportunities.

The institutional environment

In organizational theory, the institutional environment is "characterized by the elaboration of rules and requirements which individual organizations must conform to if they are to receive support and legitimacy from the environment" (Meyer & Scott 1983, p. 140).
It is hard to differentiate the economic and policy effects from the institutional ones as they are co-dependent, but it is nevertheless important to acknowledge the institutional environment effects separately from the effects of formal measures of economy and policy. This distinction is offered by Silverman (1970), who argues that the conceptualization of the environment of organizations also needs to capture the sources of meanings for the members of organizations in addition to just supplies and outputs. Scott (1995, p. 116) argues that researchers in institutional theory have realized that although organizations confront and are shaped by institutions, these systems are not necessarily coherent or unified and the effects may be complex, unstable, or inconsistent.

The institutional environment results in practices and actions taken by firms and individuals, and these may affect various features of the biotechnology industry. For example, the institutional environment regarding intellectual property rights may affect the level of informal scientific exchanges of knowledge, ideas, materials, or technologies. As the intellectual property rights regimen becomes more formalized in assigning and monitoring the rights to privatize knowledge, the structure of exchange networks between scientists may change.

In this respect, an analysis of the networks, learning, and knowledge creation in the biotechnology industry is always limited if the complex institutional environment in which the industry and the networks are embedded is not accounted for. The institutional environment may be accounted for either by direct measurement of actions, expressions, or practices or by attending to the accounts or perceptions of key actors in the industry as they specify the general features of their institutional environment.

The institutional regimen in which firms operate has important ramifications on the constraints and opportunities that firms need to confront while acting. Thus, adhering to the importance of understanding institutional environments and their role in biotechnology may improve our understanding of how learning networks are shaped in the biotechnology industry.

For example, in the context of biotechnology, the issue of intellectual property rights regimens is of great importance. The degree to which the institutional environment provides opportunities to develop intellectual property rights is expected to affect the rate of intellectual innovation and the degree to which scientists and universities will be open for collaborations and exchanges while aiming for profit-making goals. Changes in intellectual property rights regimens may have significant effects on academic science, industry direction, and innovation systems, yet the effects may be complex and incommensurable.

A central element attributed to the institutional environment regards the nature of the interrelations between scientific knowledge and innovation. Gittelman and Kogut (2003) argue that until the sixteenth century, scientific endeavors were secretive in order to withhold knowledge and the powers associated with them. Only then did the process of the institutionalization of science encourage the validation and diffusion of ideas as open to public scrutiny. In order to support these new institutions of openness, norms that standardized the language and presentation of results developed under the auspices of academic journals were established. Within this new institutional environment the careers of scientists were tied to their success in publishing these results in prestigious journals and confronting possible resulting public criticism. The evolvement of science led to fragmentation into distinct communities characterized by separate identities, journals, and models of experimentation and validation. These norms create incentives such as professional ranking as related to effort and scientists' desire to broadly disseminate results to earn respected reputations. Within laboratories, science is "manufactured" through a process in which scientists seek power and alliances to persuade each other that they occupy important positions and thus a published paper is perceived as a legitimate tool of persuasion and a symbol of achievement. The argument that science could drive commercial innovation was a major justification for public support of a nation's scientific infrastructure. Since university-based science is not ready-made for commercialization, a dilemma for universities seeking strategies to increase their revenues, as well as for firms seeking to profit from scientific knowledge, has emerged. Chapter 5 will discuss the dilemma concerning patenting academic research through an in-depth case study of the two central discoveries in biotechnology.

In this context, Coriat and Orsi (2002) describe the new intellectual property rights in the USA that resulted in major changes in the US system of innovation and, specifically, in the increasing privatization of knowledge domains and activities that were previously public. These changes resulted from the combined effects of a response to US perceptions of increased foreign competition, of the emergence of major new technological opportunities in biotechnology and information communication technology (ICT), and of a series of regulatory changes that have paved the way for increased involvement of the financial sector, through direct investments in firms whose main activity comprises R&D.

As mentioned earlier in this chapter, the first major change in intellectual property rights is the 1980 Patent and Trademark Amendments Act, well known as the Bayh–Dole Act. This Act paved the way for strategic changes in R&D policies by creating a series of incentives and legal tools allowing public research institutions such as universities and public laboratories to patent their findings and to exploit the financial results either directly through the startup of new businesses (university spin-offs or joint ventures with industry) or through exclusive licenses to external for-profit institutions. Justification of the Bayh–Dole Act was based on the logic that if firms have exclusive rights to exploit new discoveries which stem from basic research being carried out in state laboratories, the investment returns on public research will be enhanced and corporate competitiveness may be restored.

This law has triggered the privatization of academic research in the area of molecular biology. These changes have been carried out through transferring, exclusively or non-exclusively, many inventions and discoveries in basic molecular biology research programs into the hands of private firms. Following this law, additional new regulations which encouraged the entry of venture capital into the new high-technology firms that were emerging from the research sector were introduced. Coriat and Orsi (2002) mention two of the financial regulatory changes worthy of note: those that allowed pension funds to invest in venture capital firms and to take stakes in "risky" companies listed on the National Association of Securities Dealers Automated Quotations (NASDAQ) system and those that brought about the transformation of the NASDAQ into a stock market that specializes in innovative firms. The changes in this institutional regimen had an impact on the flow of financial resources to biotechnology.

Another aspect of the institutional environment shown to affect biotechnology is the degree to which entrepreneurship is institutionalized along with related technological practices. Casper and Whitley (2004) found that institutional explanations show that the diffusion of entrepreneurial patterns of organizing technology firms differs across European economies. They suggest that the concept of comparative institutional advantage helps to explain patterns by which new technologies are developing in Europe. Their findings show that firms within coordinated market economies such as Germany or Sweden have developed institutions that give advantage to long-term and incremental innovation strategies which are based on competence-enhancing human resources practices. These practices are perceived as inhibiting radical innovation paths. On the other hand, less coordinated entrepreneurial institutions associated with the US and UK innovation systems support business models demanding extreme flexibility, and thus allowing for competence-destruction needed for radical innovation. Thus, the differences between institutional environments were shown to affect the type of innovative systems in different countries.

Comparing biotechnology and other knowledge-intensive industries

The biotechnology industry is only one type of knowledge-intensive industry. Examples of other industries in which knowledge is the central asset are information technology (IT), nanotechnology, and the semiconductor industry. Comparisons between the biotechnology industry and related knowledge-intensive industries may provide us with deeper understanding of both the unique and the general qualities associated with industry structure, innovation, and of learning.

Semiconductor firms are considered to be different from biotechnology firms. Sorensen and Stuart (2000, p. 90) argue that although these firms have also taken on many strategic partners of late, and sometimes outsource chip fabrication, the larger producers have tended to perform many segments of the value-chain in-house, and thus they are different from biotechnology firms.

In a unique comparison between 150 semiconductors firms and 237 randomly selected dedicated biotechnology firms during the period 1987–1994, Sorensen and Stuart (2000) found that, in general, older firms innovate at a higher rate. Yet they argue that aging has two seemingly contradictory consequences for organizational behavior, and specifically for innovation. Initially, older firms' experience with a set of organizational routines leads to gains in efficiency. However, in rapidly changing environments, the fit between organizational capabilities and environmental demands declines with age. Their results show, consistently for both industries, that as organizations age, they generate more innovations and produce new patents, but these gains in competence have a price tag of an increasing divergence between organizational competence and the environmental demands they confront. Most impressively, these results are generally consistent across two very diverse technological contexts, semiconductors and biotechnology, even though this industry is younger than semiconductors. Finally, as firms become older, they tend to work on refinements of older areas of technology, and this is true for both the semiconductor and biotechnology industries.

The first chapter of this book introduced evidence that the biotechnology industry is heavily embedded in various kinds of interorganizational and interinstitutional networks. Thus, comparison with other industries raises the question of whether the dependence on networks of collaborations is a central feature of these industries as well. Very few studies focus on such possible comparisons. One study, by Petersa, Groenewegenb and Fiebelkornb (1998), compared the networks between industry and public-sector research in the areas of materials technology and biotechnology. The major findings reveal that the core actors of the biotechnology field are more active in more projects, than those in the materials field. In addition, Petersa, Groenewegenb and Fiebelkornb (1998) found that biotechnology networks links are denser and more intense than in other fields. Finally, in biotechnology the links between the industry and the public sector are more homogeneous than in the case of materials technology. The higher density of the biotechnology networks results from the fact that the core organizations are nearly all connected with each other and the connection of the core organizations to the rest of the field is higher than in new materials.

In both networks public–private cooperation is taking place. In both fields there are a considerable number of universities, companies, and research organizations working together. However, the balance between participating organizations in the sectors is different. While universities and research organizations dominate the biotechnology field, private companies dominate the new materials field. This difference is most prominent when the core networks are compared. In sum, Petersa, Groenewegenb and Fiebelkornb (1998) conclude that the overtly science-oriented nature of biotechnology versus materials technology is reinforced when the institutional composition of the clusters is compared. In biotechnology, universities and the institutions concentrating on basic research constitute the core cluster, as opposed to materials technology, in which a more mixed picture exists.

The nanotechnology industry is the most newly developing knowledge industry, having developed in the last 60 years. Woolley (2006) describes nanotechnology not as an industry, but as a technology that may be applied to many industries. The technology is a collection of tools and approaches rather than an industry and, in fact, nanotechnology is being used in many different industries.[6] Woolley (2006) argues that nanotechnology falls into the community definition as it crosses many industries, but these are united by the underlying and essential technology.

In the editorial note for a special issue of *Research Policy* on nanotechnology, Bozeman, Laredo and Mangematin (2007) maintain that, despite the initial organizational research on nanotechnology, there are many additional questions that need to be asked. These questions include: "What are the relevant innovation strategies in nanotechnology?" and "What are the respective roles of incumbents and startups in the innovation process?" Many of the questions that have scholarly answers in the area of biotechnology still need further investigation in nanotechnology.

Yet some findings are of interest. For example, Zucker and Darby (2003) summarize the similarities they found in their comparison between biotechnology and nanotechnology. These scholars argue

---

[6] These include pharmaceuticals, optics, ceramics, micro-electro–mechanical systems, energy, scientific instrumentation, textiles, and more. The National Science Foundation defines nanotechnologies as the development and use of products that have a size of <100 nanometers. Nanotechnologists manipulate single molecules, atoms, and structures at the nanoscale. The first firm established for exploiting the potential of nanotechnology was established in 1994 (Woolley 2006).

that, as in biotechnology, firms enter nanotechnology where and when scientists are publishing breakthrough academic articles. Thus, the roles of top scientists and academic breakthrough research are crucial for commercialization. In addition Zucker and Darby (2003) found that the skill-level of scientists (level of education) is important. Similar to biotechnology inventions, the need for top scientists' involvement is important for appropriation of nanotechnology.

In a recent study, Zucker *et al.* (2007) show that the capacity of producing new science and technology in a given space and in a given domain is highly correlated with preexisting codified knowledge (in the form of articles and patents) in this space and domain, thus arguing that science and technology are cumulative in nature. In addition, they found that geographic proximity, high-technology firm creation and circulation of tacit knowledge through human resources in nanotechnology are similar to the recent history of biotechnology.

In a comparison between biotechnology and pharmaceutical incumbents over 20 years, Rothaermel and Thursby (2007) test a model where knowledge performance (as measured by the number of patents granted) depends on the articulation between the internal knowledge base of firms and their absorptive capacity, which is marked by R&D alliances or acquisitions of small R&D firms, or both. The study demonstrates the critical role of alliances at early stages, whilst a shift in favor of internal R&D investments occurs when technologies and instruments become commercially available. For a wider set of incumbent firms which have at least one patent in nanotechnology, their findings show different results where internal R&D investment is the critical factor, and when technological change is associated with a radical innovation that is embodied in physical capital the ability of incumbent firms to exploit the invention depends on the firm's R&D expenditure. Rothaermel and Thursby (2007) cautiously suggest that the difference between biotechnology and nanotechnology may be attributed to the fact that nanotechnology is younger and thus at a different degree of maturity in the technology life-cycle.

3 | New organizational forms for knowledge creation in biotechnology

As suggested in Chapter 2, the most important organizational form that emerged in the biotechnology industry is that of the new biotechnology firms (NBFs) or, alternatively titled, dedicated biotechnology firms (DBFs). The emergence of this form has attracted many scholars, who gave various explanations for it. The present chapter will introduce the concept of new organizational forms, and will illustrate this by use of a few examples of organizational structures that aim at enhancing learning and knowledge creation in the biotechnology industry. The first part of this chapter (based on Oliver & Montgomery (2000)) suggests an account of NBFs as a new organizational form. Further, the chapter introduces additional new forms for conducting biotechnology research, such as consortia, university spin-offs, and incubators, and will highlight their central internal features.

NBFs

The biotechnology industry is characterized by the emergence of a new form of knowledge organization: NBFs. In the early stages of this industry, the new form was developed through a creative collaboration between leading scientists and venture capital entrepreneurs to capture the new opportunity (Kenney 1986; Kornberg 1995). In this way, venture capital provided the mechanism for introducing the new technologies important for future economic growth. This direction of organizational evolution is consistent with the observation of Van de Ven *et al.* (1989) that environmental niches do not preexist but are constructed through a continuous interaction of entrepreneurs and organizations toward the establishment of new organizations which take advantage of underutilized and non-redundant opportunities of a "structural hole" (Burt 2005).

To illustrate: the birth of the industry is commonly marked by the formation of Genentech in 1976, which was established by Professor

Herbert Boyer, from the University of California at San Francisco (UCSF), one of the inventors of the Cohen–Boyer gene-splicing technique, and Robert Swanson, a venture capitalist (Kenney 1986). The rapid "birth rate" of similar NBFs, such as Amgen, Biogen, Genetic Systems, and Immunogen, suggest that this new organizational form quickly gained legitimacy as the prominent adaptive form (Hybels & Popielarz 1996). By 1994, over 1200 such new companies were formed in the USA (Kornberg 1995), and the same form emerged simultaneously in many countries around the world, including Germany, Israel, Italy, Japan, Switzerland, and the UK.

Our understanding of organizational evolution and the emergence of new organizational forms may be enhanced by taking into account the complex interplay of the dual processes of (ecological) selection and (genealogical) replication. In a new form there is a selection of various elements from previously existing organizational forms, as a genealogical organizational "blueprint." These elements are transferred and modified into appropriate components of the new form. In this illustration, it is shown how a mixture of "ingredients" may be "inherited" from existing organizational forms and turned into a new hybrid form.

Fundamental questions about organizational change have been the object of substantial theoretical development from several perspectives. Researchers have sought to understand explanations for both why and how organizations change and new organizational forms emerge. In terms of "why" organizations change, scholars have identified changes in the social structure of societies, in environmental resources, or in technologies as constituting the grounds and creating the resource-space for new organizational forms (Stinchcombe 1965; Van de Ven *et al.* 1989; Romanelli 1991). For example, Chandler (1962) and Fligstein (1985) point to historical and economic changes that led to diversification in many large companies as fostering the emergence of multidivisional or M-form organizations. Ouchi and Jaeger (1978) argue that the Type Z organizational form, offering holistic concern for employees, emerged when social organizations such as churches and neighborhoods no longer satisfied individuals' needs for affiliation. Similarly, Powell (1990) proposes that network organizations based on trust, reputation, and friendship emerged in response to the need for long-term interdependent organizational exchanges whose commodity values are not easily measured.

In approaching the "how" question, several theories have been proposed to guide our understanding of the process through which organizations change and new organizational forms emerge. Two of the major theoretical approaches that have been used to study such questions are population ecology and organizational systematics. Population ecology theories (Aldrich & Pfeffer 1976; Hannan & Freeman 1977; Carroll 1984) introduce the natural selection process through which various organizational forms are selected or extinguished; organizational systematics theory (McKelvey 1982; Baum & Singh 1994) deals with genealogical processes of transmission and inheritance of organizational structures. These two approaches employ different foci and levels of analysis (Baum & Singh 1994). Population ecologists generally observe macro-level changes in populations of organizations and focus on the structure and integration of a hierarchy of jobs, work groups, organizations, populations, and communities. In contrast, the genealogical approach is concerned with the conservation and transfer of production processes, routines, skills, and knowledge at the micro-firm level.

It is suggested here that the ecological processes of selection and retention at the population level (Hannan & Freeman 1977) may be examined at the internal-firm level as well, by examining micro-level firm information related to selection and retention (i.e. replication) of routines and procedures from "parental" organizations (Romanelli 1991), as examples of a genealogical inheritance process. In addition, the successful emergence and evolution of a hybrid form may be importantly related to its ability to capture salient key features of its parents. The key features that are most strongly related to the emergence of a hybrid form will, of course, differ across organizational types and industries, depending on the nature of the parents and the intended purpose of the emergent hybrid. Hence, it is vital that key features be appropriately recognized and selected for their potential to affect the successful emergence of the hybrid form. This phenomenon is further demonstrated through an examination of the internal processes of a particular form of new organizational hybrid known as the "knowledge" firm.

In this new organizational form, advanced knowledge generated by scientific professionals is used in the creation of new products, such as in the biotechnology or information technology industries. Thus, the knowledge firm may be viewed as a hybrid of an established knowledge-creating organization – the research university – and an established production-oriented, market-driven enterprise – the large corporation. This is consistent with the observation by Powell and Owen-Smith (1998) that the boundaries between universities and firms in the life sciences are crumbling, with new organizational arrangements that blur the distinction between academic research and commercial development.

Despite the blurring of boundaries between universities and firms, the genealogical parents of knowledge firms are distinguished from each other in terms of their goals, labor, and production processes. Most importantly, in the research university, knowledge is an individual commodity that is generated by and resides with individual scholars. These individuals may choose to pass on their knowledge through teaching and publishing, but they remain the "owners" of their original ideas. In the industrial setting, on the other hand, knowledge is an organizational commodity (Nonaka 1994), in that the organization "owns" the knowledge that is produced by its actors, and the organization chooses how it will be used and marketed.

The challenge, therefore, to the new knowledge firms is to obtain from the knowledge creators (i.e. individual scientists who have been socialized in a research university framework) the commitment to produce organizational knowledge consistent with the market-oriented goals of the new hybrid form. In order to do this, the new knowledge firms must establish a context and incentives that enable and encourage individual scientists to willingly create "organizational knowledge" rather than "individual knowledge" (Nonaka 1994).

Challenges confronting NBFs

As Kornberg (1995, p. 95) cautions, "good science and good technology might not be sufficient to make a company profitable." To enhance their prospects for survival and success, and to compensate for the "liability of newness" (Stinchcombe 1965; Hannan & Freeman 1977, 1984), NBFs may seek to retain elements of their genealogical organizational "parents" – research universities and the large corporate pharmaceutical firms – that have already achieved institutional legitimacy. The process allows NBFs to borrow from both parents various routines and competency elements (McKelvey 1982; McKelvey & Aldrich 1983) appropriate to the new form.

The effort to inherit a "blueprint" from the parental organizations, however, generates potential incompatibilities for NBFs. As noted by

Kenney (1986, p. 176), "the norms of 'doing science' in the university are very different from those necessary for economic success." These potential incompatibilities manifest themselves in various aspects of the management of the scientific labor process. For example, while Teece (1992) has argued that research and development (R&D) may be more efficiently governed by hierarchies than by markets, governance, and control in a typical firm hierarchy, but is inconsistent with such procedures in a research university environment. Of particular concern are expectations and norms about autonomy and about information-sharing. In their study of the Danish biotechnology industry, Kreiner and Schultz (1993) found that managers may have little direct control over how, when, and with what consequences employees participate in networking activities. This dilemma is particularly acute with respect to soliciting external knowledge resources while simultaneously protecting their own knowledge resources from expropriation.

Powell, Koput and Smith-Doerr (1996) also studied networking relations among biotechnology firms and found that beneath the formal ties exists a "sea of informal relations of knowledge exchanges," similar to a university laboratory, where scientists enjoy autonomy, work on their own projects, and share their knowledge with the wider scientific community. Liebeskind *et al.* (1996), and Argyres and Liebeskind (1998), report similar findings: Argyres and Liebeskind (1998) observe that universities were created to uphold their social-contractual commitment to society to create and sustain an "intellectual commons" – a knowledge archive openly accessible to all members of society. The universities support the practice of "open science" in order to allow for the evaluation and potential replication of findings by other scientists, helping to ensure the quality of research and facilitation of further discoveries. As a result, scientists typically expect, and receive, greater autonomy in their choices of research topics than do their counterparts in large established firms; they publish widely and draw on their network of relations with university scientists for obtaining scientific know-how (Liebeskind *et al.* 1996). All of these activities may run counter to the market-driven needs of NBFs.

What mechanisms were established by NBFs in confronting the challenges of establishing legitimacy in the eyes of their most important capital – their scientists – in their effort to address the potential incompatibilities of professional norms and market demands?

NBF hybridization case study: new genetics

The analysis employs a case study of a large and successful NBF located in California, referred to by the pseudonym of "New Genetics." The intent in this case study example is to focus on the theoretical development of new organizational forms as hybrids from genealogical parents in general, and on the emergence of NBFs as a particular type of new organizational hybrid.

New Genetics is one of the first NBFs formed in the USA, established within the first five years of the industry formation by a leading scientist. The firm is located in California, the geographical area with the highest number of NBFs in the USA.[1] Since its founding, the firm has grown significantly on virtually every growth parameter: it has increased its product diversification and entered new technologies; it has substantially increased its workforce and enlarged its physical facilities; it has become vertically integrated, has launched international units, and has established several subsidiaries. Despite these dramatic changes, however, the firm has retained the unique features with which it was established, especially those pertaining to the internal scientific-labor processes drawn from its parental blueprints, as described below.

Data from qualitative interviews with scientists and top executives at New Genetics were collected in 1993 and supplemented with information collected in 1996. These data have been augmented by observations and analysis of internal documents of the firm and by descriptive information on internal processes from business journals.

Analytical framework: human resources management

As knowledge organizations, the way NBFs manage their human capital is extremely important to their success (Youndt *et al.* 1996). Yet, as proposed above, the two parental forms of NBFs are the research university and large pharmaceutical corporations whose procedural norms and routines related to their human capital may be sharply contrasting. The argument here is that a viable strategy for the hybrid NBF would be to capture and modify salient key features

---

[1] Of a total of 554 NBFs "born" between 1976 and 1990, 133 were located in California (Source: North Carolina Biotechnology Center 1991 (www.ncbiotech. org/news_and events/industry_news/companies_database_reorganized.htm)).

related to the labor process in such a way as to best accommodate the socialized expectations of its organizational participants as knowledge-creators, while attending to its market-oriented production goals. This is because, as studies in human resources management have shown, optimum effectiveness is achieved when there is a "fit" between organizational structures and practices, and the expectations of the organization's personnel (Ledford & Lawler 1994; Jackson & Schuler 1995).

Because of the centrality of human capital in knowledge firms, we place our analysis within a framework of the functions of human resources management. These basic functions are: personnel selection, work assignment, training, coordination and control, motivation and rewards, and person-organization "fit" (DeCenzo & Robbins 1996). As discussed below, several representations of human resources functions have been identified, as they are found in the parents and the hybrid organizational forms. They do not constitute an exhaustive list, but rather a set of illustrative examples that we believe demonstrate the hybridization process of selection and retention.

Human resources function: personnel selection
Project team development scientists in universities have independence in selecting their research team members, who are frequently based at other institutions. Although members may differ in seniority (and a senior scientist or a member with special expertise may be deferred to by others) the team structure is generally collaborative among equals. In the industrial setting, assignment of team members and projects is a managerial decision, and team structure is likely to be hierarchical.

At New Genetics, teamwork was encouraged to facilitate collaboration on creation of a new concept, and norms of academia and industry were both evident in team selection and structure. In recognition of scientists' norms of autonomy in determining collaborators, New Genetics allowed team leaders some flexibility in the team selection process. However, more consistent with industry practices, team leaders were constrained in their choice of team members since selections were generally restricted to firm personnel. For example, the process of team organization upon launching a new R&D project called for the head scientist to select the other scientists within the firm with whom he wanted to work. If the head scientist expressed a need to recruit an external scientist who possessed particular expertise, the head scientist – as in academia – would be involved in the search for the new external team member. Final approval of team composition, however, was retained by the firm's managers, reflecting in part the firm's concerns with privacy protection, as elaborated below.

In terms of team structure, New Genetics adopted a self-organized team structure, also more common in universities than in industry, with the understanding that heads of departments worked for the teams, which determined their own needs for equipment and other resources. Because of the trust and shared perspective required within the team, generated through continuous exchanges (Nonaka 1994), the use of self-organized project teams was considered an important organizing strategy to enhance organizational effectiveness and survival.

Human resources function: work assignment and training

Scientists in a university setting expect to develop their own research agenda, and determine what is, to them, important work irrespective of the economic implications of the outcome. Funding is commonly solicited from external sources, and constraints on project selection generally arise from the competition for scarce research funds. In industry, economic potential is the major factor influencing selection of projects, and funding for projects is internal, based on the organization's assessment of the market-based demand for the outcome.

Like any new firm, New Genetics' first strategic challenge was generating project ideas and deciding which projects to pursue. As a knowledge firm, New Genetics depended on its research scientists as the source of new ideas. This created a critical challenge for New Genetics, since it required the delicate act of increasing the scientists' awareness of the economic imperatives of their work, without dampening their creative enthusiasm and the norm of independence in the selection of research projects to pursue.

At New Genetics, this was accomplished by mimicking several aspects of the research proposal process of universities. For example, every year, all scientists were asked to write one or more short research proposals describing the projects they wished to develop. Although there was no limit placed on the number of proposals a scientist could submit, each proposal was required to contain an explanation of how the research could lead to a marketable product.

This was similar to the requirement of academic funding agencies that proposals contain a discussion of how the research would contribute to the scientist's body of knowledge.

In addition, recognizing that scientists may be less aware of the market constraints or the competitive conditions of their research interests, New Genetics created a position of "strategy executive" with responsibility for helping the scientists to evaluate the profit-potential of the products. This executive serves as a technical resource for gathering information from the environment about the potential competitiveness of their projects and disseminating it to New Genetics scientists. This is similar to the technical support provided by universities to enable scientists to comply with proposal-writing guidelines often imposed by external funding agencies, thus enhancing their potential to be awarded competitive grants.

These managerial procedures replicated the academic routine of writing scientific grant proposals for external funding, while modifying the scientists' behavior by instilling recognition of the market potential of scientific discovery. Thus, the firm institutionalized a new form of "doing science" – internal competition for scientific excellence, augmented by adjustments to market potential. Kornberg's (1995) study of two NBFs (DNAX and Aleza) also indicates recognition of the importance of scientific norms, describing the emphasis in recruitment at these NBFs of promises of a far greater free-choice research environment than is found in large pharmaceutical companies.

After generating a set of proposals from its scientists, New Genetics managers had to decide which of the proposals to approve. Whilst maintaining the model of a competitive process, New Genetics, in fact, approved many of the research proposals developed by its scientists. The firm followed this approach not necessarily because it was believed that approved proposals had equal commercial potential or because there was unlimited internal funding. Rather, this represented a calculated decision that the firm's prospects for success were improved by having more projects in the pipeline and by developing a diversified portfolio of research projects.

In this way, by opting for increased variation, New Genetics managers were able to respond both to the norms of scientific independence of their employees and to the processes enhancing organizational survival. This strategy is supported by findings from other knowledge firms (Quinn 1986; Nonaka 1994). For example, Miner

(1994) indicates that high-technology company managers who permit employees (scientists) to pursue individual projects have basically decided to strengthen the variation process. In accepting inconsistencies in research projects and local inefficiency, the managers sacrifice some retention of resources in return for possible benefits of increased variation, which has been recognized by Weick (1976) and McKelvey and Aldrich (1983) as a way to enhance organizational adaptability.

Human resources function: coordination and control (internal)

In the university setting, scientists are accustomed to enormous flexibility in terms of scheduling their work, from short-term daily work schedules to long-term project schedules, with few reporting and monitoring mechanisms (Latour & Woolgar 1986). In industrial settings such extreme flexibility is rare, and employees must conform to externally imposed and monitored time and scheduling.

At New Genetics and at other NBFs, recognition of the norm of scheduling autonomy held by scientists was reflected in attempts to allow similar flexibility, within limits of expectations for project-completion targets. Scientists were encouraged to follow the timetable convenient to them, including working nights and weekends, so long as the project was completed within the allotted period. This organizational strategy suggested an expectation that organizational effectiveness would be achieved through placing trust in scientists' personal judgment, rather than imposing external monitors, thereby enhancing their commitment and dedication to their research.

Human resources function: coordination and control (external)

Scientists in university settings consider a major aspect of their occupational role to be publishing their scientific work, as well as participation in seminars and scientific conferences. These channels reflect the expectation of an open exchange of information among scientists, following the notion of the "invisible college" (Crane 1972). Indeed, the exchange of ideas is embedded in the norms of the scientific community as a key element in the process through which scientific knowledge is produced and reproduced (Liebeskind *et al.* 1996). In contrast, such exchanges are not common in the industrial setting because of the dangers of expropriation of ideas by competitors.

New Genetics had to confront the scientific norm of open exchanges of knowledge across organizational boundaries, either via collaborations of interorganizational team members or via contacts through professional interactions, without loss of proprietary information. Although the firm's scientists were encouraged by the firm to participate in many scientific conferences and to engage in external collaborations, strict secrecy was maintained about current research endeavors. For example, the firm's scientists would not disclose to outsiders the identity of their university collaborators, out of fear that this information might lead competitors to learn about projects the firm had in the pipeline. Indeed, the intensity of the competition over ideas and research directions led some New Genetics scientists to generate "false searches" when they needed to search on a network database of scientific publications. Thus, in addition to searching for material on topics relevant to their work-in-progress, New Genetics scientists would generate numerous searches on irrelevant topics, to mislead "espionage" agents who monitored the searches of other NBFs to learn about the sort of research work carried out by competitors.

Further, New Genetics prohibited its scientists from sending out any work for publication prior to an internal review by the firm's chief scientist. One estimate held that the firm's researchers published only about 30% of the internal scientific work in academic journals and that most of the published information concerned basic science. In contrast, unpatented applied scientific work which might be expropriated by rival firms was not published. However, the firm did not restrict external scientific collaborations over time. That is, the NBF allowed joint scientific publications with external scientists but imposed a time tag that provided the firm with sufficient time to patent the knowledge and transfer it into the commercialization process.

This process served the dual purposes of accommodating, at least partially, the scientific norm of collaboration, while preserving important economic survival goals of the hybrid firm. Thus, it allows interorganizational scientific collaborations to produce knowledge needed for the firm, thereby acquiring external knowledge at a relatively low cost. For example, Liebeskind *et al.* (1996) demonstrate that, although there were ongoing joint interorganizational scientific collaborations, most patents assigned to the NBFs were not shared with external entities, universities, or firms.

Human resources function: motivation and rewards

A university setting offers rewards (rank and salary) that are strongly related to the scientist's publication rate and quality. Thus, the reward structure encourages commitment to one's own accomplishments, with the goal of attaining recognition within the scientific profession. In industry, however, it is increasingly common for rewards to be tied to firm performance. The mechanism of profit-sharing is designed to enhance the employees' interest in and commitment to the overall firm's performance as well as their individual performance.

New Genetics used a composite form of compensation to reward its scientists that would sufficiently motivate them for individual productivity while still being cost-effective for the firm. Thus, the firm recognized individual scientific excellence through salaries, incentive rewards for successful projects, and shared rights to patents. At the same time, a profit-sharing policy provided all scientists with stock options in the company (Burrill & Lee 1989), thereby enhancing their commitment to overall organizational excellence. Scientists interviewed at New Genetics universally declared that their income working in an NBF was substantially higher than that of their university counterparts and that their commitment to the firm was strengthened by this combination of rewards based on individual and firm accomplishments.

Human resources function and organizational culture: person – organization fit

The environment of most university settings is generally stable, encouraging a systematic, risk-averse, less time-bound pursuit of knowledge. In contrast, the environment of industry is more dynamic; hence, organizations are more susceptible to changes in the environment and must respond more rapidly. These demands result in a greater likelihood of an organizational culture that fosters the pursuit of higher-risk projects.

New Genetics had to establish an organizational culture that fostered research efforts consistent with its turbulent environment. This need was dramatically different from the more stable, often risk-averse, research environment of the university and was closer to the dynamic environment of industry in general, which is more susceptible to changes in the environment and must respond more rapidly. Smaller entrepreneurial firms such as New Genetics are especially vulnerable to environmental shifts and hence are at great risk of failure unless they adopt a high-risk, high-return strategy. Such a strategy is facilitated through an innovative organizational culture, fostered by the charismatic leadership of its founder.

New Genetics reflected such a culture, having been established by a leading PhD scientist, uniformly described as highly innovative and charismatic, who generated a sense of excitement about joint "science-making." This entrepreneurial culture persisted and has been reinforced and passed down to newer generations of scientists through organizational stories and rituals, even though New Genetics has grown rapidly and the founder has left the firm to establish another NBF. Scientists at New Genetics reported that it was the spirit of entrepreneurship possible in NBFs, in general, and at New Genetics in particular, which enticed them to quit permanent academic positions, despite the early high risk of firm failure.

Further, many New Genetics scientists remarked on the compelling intangible presence of its founder, even in his absence, and the strong trust they felt in his ability to create a successful firm. His portrait hung in every office of the firm. Managers who knew him universally remarked in the interviews about his unique abilities and original vision. New scientists in the firm who were interviewed unfailingly mentioned that, although they had never met the founder, his standard of excellence and excitement over scientific work were transmitted to them when they joined the firm.

These observations are consistent with the emphasis of Dodgson (1993) and Liebeskind and Oliver (1998) on the necessity to organizational survival of establishing a basis of commitment and trust that can transcend individual relationships as organizational personnel change over time. Thus, at New Genetics, the strong identification with the charismatic entrepreneur, along with the shared spirit of entrepreneurship, built a highly motivated and committed research team, strengthening the potential for organizational survival.

The analyses suggested above, of the hybrid form of NBFs, were based on the assumption that some organizational forms are based on characteristics adopted from different parental forms. Other emerging organizational forms are a result of the special features of the industry, the nature of the knowledge creation process, the relations between the actors in the industry, or the specific constraints that are challenging the product creation process. As indicated in Chapter 2, the university–industry co-dependence features are one of the specific characteristics of the biotechnology industry. This characteristic is associated with the establishment of a few interorganizational knowledge exchange organizational forms. Let us elaborate on some of these forms.

Biotechnology research consortia

Research consortia are not a new organizational form in the analytical sense, yet such structures emerged and became more prominent in the context of the biotechnology industry as a form for enhancing university–industry collaborations and developing knowledge creation.

The organization of science may be located within various science organizations. These include universities, R&D firms, strategic alliances, research collaborations, and technology-transfer modes. An R&D consortium is a relatively new form of science organization. This form is an ad hoc organization, in which representative participating actors operate simultaneously within the consortium, whilst being actors in their base organizations. This form is a synergic form, which is distinct from the existing "pure" forms of the university and the R&D firm. The consortium as a form also differs from individual-level technology-transfer agreements since it allows multiple actors to collaborate and learn from each other in dyadic or multiple structures in an open flexible forum while being protected by general contractual arrangements.

Generally speaking, an R&D consortium has several advantages over other forms of collaborations for exploration purposes. First, it offers all members an overarching nonspecific contractual environment for conducting joint learning. In addition, membership is stable, and reputation concerns operate as an incentive control for all members not to act in an opportunistic manner (Nooteboom 2002). Finally, the usually lengthy timeframe of a consortium and the joint participation of university laboratories and science firms may enhance network-based altruistic behavior and benevolence in the form of values, social norms of proper conduct, moral obligation, and bonds of kinship (Nooteboom 2002).

Thus, the resources, stability, bounded contractual environment, and the possible dense learning exchanges in an R&D consortium may be highly beneficial for learning exploration and exploitation.

A consortium, as a contractually bounded environment for collaborations, is expected to provide participants an opportunity to collaborate freely for learning. In this context, firm and university participants may join various learning environments, including seminars, informal, and formal collaborations, as well as consulting exchanges. Therefore, a wide range of collaborations is expected for each participant. Following Gilsing and Nooteboom (2005), the incentive governance of reputation should increase the protection from opportunism in collaborations. Congruently, since universities and industry operate jointly in the consortium we should expect that social norms of knowledge exchange and moral obligations toward the pursuit of science of academic scientists will generate bonds of kinship among the consortium members.

University scientists and industrial scientists operate within different institutional arrangements (Liebeskind *et al.* 1996; Oliver 2004). Merton (1973) defined academic science as "open science" since the aim of such science is to develop general knowledge that is publishable and thus open to the public. R&D firms, aiming at exploiting the economic potential of their inventions, are operating within the "closed science" arena, in which knowledge is bounded and publications are only a side product (Liebeskind *et al.* 1996). Transformations within the recent decade, when university-based technology-transfer units became the organizational actors aiming at the protection of the intellectual property rights of academic scientists, have blurred the difference between the two groups of scientists. Studying a consortium as a new form for the organization of science allows us to define actors by their roles and to clarify the features of this new organizational form of science. Actors who originate from two institutional environments (e.g. universities and R&D firms) may act in an indistinguishable manner within the consortium or may demonstrate an interest to maintain pooled resources that reflect upon the institutional norms of their base organizations. The degree to which these changes were institutionalized will have an impact on whether university and industrial scientists utilize the learning opportunities in similar or distinct manners.

Biotechnology incubators

Technological incubators are established as innovation-enhancers for startup firms. The concept of incubators was developed about three decades ago, and since then various countries have established technological business incubators in order to advance economic entrepreneurship, creation of venture capital, and advance innovative products and services. Incubators are a new organizational form that operates under an idea similar to the notion of the incubators that support young chicks in their initial phase of life. The underlying assumption of this new form is that innovative technological ideas need a nourishing supportive environment for the initial stages of the developing (Mian 1996). The concept of an "incubator" is a metaphor for an administrative–management–technological supportive environment in which a few new technology-based firms (NTBFs), following Mian (1996) are gathered together for a short period of time, during the transition from the idea stage to the startup phase, in order to develop the needed initial capabilities.

During the incubation period inexperienced startup entrepreneurs chosen for the incubators receive the supportive services and resources. The American National Business Incubation Association (NBIA) defines the central goal of an incubator as to facilitate the "production" of successful firms which are financially independent. Among the crucial services provided by the incubators are managerial counseling, technical support and facilitation in gathering venture capital, and exploring other financial sources for young firms.

Wiggins and Gibson (2003) describe business incubators as an organizational form established in the USA 30 years ago. By 2003 there were more than 800 of them in the USA, and most were non-profit entities and associated with universities. These scholars argue that in order to succeed, business incubators must accomplish five tasks, including: establishing clear metrics for success; providing entrepreneurial leadership; developing and delivering value-added services to member companies; developing a rational selection process for new companies; and ensuring that member companies gain access to necessary human and financial resources.

Based on the NBIA, many forms of incubators exist. They differ in the ownership structure, partnerships, regulation, management, and areas of specialization (Pace 2001). In addition, incubators vary in their goals, which include regional development, employment services, and university–industry technology transfer.

The need for technological business incubators as an organizational form may be explained through two concepts from organizational theory. Organizational theory suggests that new firms suffer from the liability of newness and liability of smallness (Hannan & Freeman 1989). These liabilities are associated with their limited ability to access resources as well as the lack of reputation and legitimacy. Network theory assumes that interorganizational exchanges enhance firms' success probabilities because of reduced uncertainties resulting from their dependence on resources that are helped by other organizations (Scott 1995). In addition, the exposure of firms to a larger pool of collaborative opportunities, established through the incubator management team, provides an opportunity to access important resources for the startup stages (Oviatt & McDougall 1995). The entrepreneurial context is based on richness of learning and collaborative embedded networks (Aldrich & Zimmer 1986), and thus the successful entrepreneurs are those who establish a wealth and breadth of networks needed for acquiring crucial resources for startups.

Social capital is another concept related to organizational theory that is of value in our analyses of incubators. Coleman (1988, p. 98) perceives social capital as a unique form of resources that is accessible to social actors, and includes special features of the social structure that allows for actions of actors. Thus, social capital is basically the resources which result from the social structure (Bourdieu & Wacquant 1992). The basic idea is that the contact networks of an individual are an important asset that can be exchanged with other returns (Burt 2005). A recent study distinguished between three forms of capital: organizational, human, and social, and tested their effect on innovative capabilities (Subramaniam & Youndt 2005). In their study they defined human capital as the overall skill, expertise, and knowledge-level of an organization's employees. Organizational capital was defined as the organization's ability to appropriate and store knowledge in physical organizational-level repositories such as databases, manuals, and patents, as well as in structures, processes, cultures, and ways of doing business. Social capital was defined as the organization's overall ability to share and leverage knowledge among and between networks of employees, customers, suppliers, and alliance partners.

In a recent article, Inkpen and Tsang (2005) distinguish between three types of networks: intracorporate networks, strategic alliances, and industrial districts, while using a social capital perspective. They claim that all these networks of exchange and learning are valuable for technology-transfer. Incubators can help small firms to establishing such networks.

Incubators are a new organizational form in which all of these networking forms are partially expressed, thus the incubator may be considered an organization with a hierarchal management body, while NTBFs are independent subunits. Therefore, incubators may generate the conditions facilitating knowledge-transfer through the various social capital dimensions and the three forms of networks, as suggested by Inkpen and Tsang (2005, p. 155).

In general, it has been argued that knowledge-transfer may be facilitated in the three modes of networks (Inkpen & Tsang 2005). In the intracorporate network, knowledge-transfer is facilitated by personal intramember transfer, decentralized network, low personnel turnover, shared vision and collective goals, and accommodation for local or national culture. In strategic alliances, knowledge-transfer is facililated by strong ties with repeated exchanges, multiple knowledge connections between partners, a non-competitive approach to knowledge-transfer, goal clarity, cultural diversity, and trust based on the shadow of the future. Finally, in industrial districts, knowledge-transfer is facilitated by proximity to other members, weak ties, stable personal relations, cooperative interactive logic, norms, and values that govern informal knowledge exchanges, and trust is enhanced through commercial transactions that are embedded in social ties. Knowledge-transfer exchanges are important for small firms, whereas developing the capabilities for such exchanges needs to be learned. Incubators can help their tenant small technological startups to develop their capabilities for learning by establishing strategic alliances and learning from proximate other members as is done in industrial districts.

What are the innovative dimensions of incubators? In a case study of a bio-incubator, Cooke *et al.* (2006) found that it was innovative in three ways. First, it involved an international comparative analysis of biotechnology incubators of its kind. Second, the incubator representatives were monitored and investigated by an academic partnership team, and, third, there was a stated aspiration by the incubator companies to engage in co-incubation across borders. Cooke *et al.* (2006) argue that a "co-incubation" is a new kind of boundary-crossing innovation in which advanced startup businesses are assisted to enter other national markets and/or benefit from specialized services or scientific, technological, or commercial knowledge absent in the home country but present in a partner country. This study shows that not only crossing industrial boundaries is important for innovation of incubators, but also that crossing international boundaries may be crucial for the innovativeness of biotechnology incubators.

University spin-offs

Entrepreneurial universities are associated with establishing various forms of spin-offs (Wright, Birley & Mosey 2004; Oliver 2007). Despite the importance of understanding the institutional shifts on the individual scientist and the entrepreneurial university levels, not much research has been conducted on this front. On this front, Owen-Smith and Powell (2003) have studied the decisions made by universities regarding patenting. Pirny, Surlemont and Nlemvo (2003) have constructed a typology of university spin-offs, and Etzkowitz (2002) introduced the notion of the triple helix (focussing on the inter-relations of universities and industry and government as the engine for innovation, as described above). University spin-offs are considered an important subset of startup firms because they are considered an economically and knowledge-intensively powerful set of high-technology companies (Shane and Stuart 2002).

University spin-offs are newly developing organizational phenomena in which universities establish startups that are based on scientific discoveries of their own scientists. There are various definitions for such spin-offs. Nicolaou and Birley (2003) define university spin-offs as the transfer of core technology from an academic institution into a new company, where the founding member(s) may include the academic(s) who may or may not be currently affiliated with the academic institution. This is a wide definition that allows for various degrees of involvement by the inventing scientist and the role of the university is not specified.

Another definition of university spin-offs is "New firms created to exploit commercially some knowledge, technology or research results developed within a university" (Pirnay, Surlemont & Nlemvo 2003, p. 355). Since the knowledge component is crucial here, and academic research involves a great deal of tacit knowledge (pieces of personal knowledge accumulated by the scientists through their academic activities), the degree to which the scientists are involved in the spin-off is crucial for its success leading to the emerging phenomena of "entrepreneurial scientists."

Understanding university spin-offs as a distinct organizational form needs to clarify the distinction between entrepreneurs and scientists. The entrepreneurship literature views entrepreneurs as economic actors who from the outset are executing their ideas with an eye on the market, and within the institutional context of a business and the marketplace. Scientists, by contrast, are socialized into, and operate within, a research community whose values are very different from that of the commercial world. For a university scientist to become an entrepreneur, let alone successfully launch and manage a venture, requires basic changes in attitudes, thinking, and relationships coupled with acquiring a wide range of managerial capabilities. Conversely, it seems difficult for economic entrepreneurs to turn into scientific entrepreneurs in order to exploit research innovations. This is because they lack the scientific know-how and networks that would allow them to evaluate prospects and further the realization of specific scientific ventures.

Thus, theoretical frameworks that apply to economic entrepreneurs are incomplete when it comes to understanding scientific entrepreneurship and we need to draw on the entrepreneurship literature and to ground this literature in a set of theories that are better suited for discerning the specifics of scientific entrepreneurship associated with university spin-offs.

Generally speaking, in this organizational form the entrepreneurial firms offer complementary assets for academic intellectual property to the traditional university–industry technology-transfer, in which universities license to biotechnology or pharmaceutical firms the rights to conduct R&D based on the scientific discoveries of the university scientists. Such choices made by the university reduce the risks associated with the failure of the scientific venture owing to the involvement of the inventing scientist.

Since university spin-offs, in all forms, represent a relatively new phenomenon, we have limited research that offers a longitudinal perspective on this complex organizational form. A life-cycle approach to university spin-off forms (Vohora, Wright & Lockett 2004) suggests that there are a number of distinct phases of development, and each venture must pass through the previous phase in order to progress to the next one. These phases include: research, opportunity framing, pre-organization, re-orientation, and sustainability. However, each phase involves an iterative nonlinear process of development in which information needs to be gathered as the needed resources are sought. In addition, these scholars argue that at the interstices between the phases, the ventures face "critical junctures" in terms of the resources and capabilities needed for moving to the following stage. The critical junctures are identified as: opportunity recognition, entrepreneurial commitment, venture credibility, and venture sustainability and returns. Thus, we learn from their study that the evolutionary growth path of university spin-offs is complex and modular, and that social capital, resources, and internal capabilities need to be acquired in order to enable the venture to generate revenues and compete effectively.

Despite the growing body of research on university spin-offs, there are only a few studies that focus on university-based spin-offs (Kirby 2006; Oliver 2007). University-based spin-offs represent a unique subset of university spin-offs that differs in characteristics and complexities from the "parent general form" of university spin-offs. They may be defined as "an entrepreneurial organizational form that is established by universities – mostly technology-transfer offices – in order to exploit the economic potential in academic discoveries of university scientists." This form differs from other forms of technology-transfer and spin-off ventures in that it represents an economic venture of a university and it assigns a significant and central role for the scientist-entrepreneur. Thus, the university is acting in a composite role of a venture capitalist, an entrepreneur, and a general and scientific manager. This is done usually in order to provide an "in-house" incubator for the university venture, aimed at bringing up the venture to the stage at which its market potential is exhibited. In university-based spin-offs the specialized technology-transfer officers lead the initial phases of the venture in full collaboration with the entrepreneurial scientist. Once any market potential has been exhibited the venture may be sold to an industrial firm wishing to bring the product into the market.

Discussion

This chapter started with an analysis of the organizational characteristics of the most evident new organizational form in the biotechnology industry, and moved to other, less dominant or unique, forms for learning and knowledge exchanges, such as consortia, incubators, and university spin-offs. As Lewin, Long and Carroll (1999) have observed, the transformation of organizational forms may be seen as the result of a confluence of major forces of environmental changes and significant organizational responses to the perceived shift in the "rugged landscape." The emergence of NBFs demonstrates how changes in environmental opportunities foster the creation of an organizational niche for innovative entrepreneurs to fill. In particular, NBFs have emerged as a response to opportunities presented by the discovery of new scientific technologies that created the basis for a new kind of marketable product. Two resources acted together in establishing the new form: venture capital provided the seed money for research laboratory-like new firms, and leading scientists oriented toward making science profitable have joined with research ideas, reputational scientific networks to recruit the needed intellectual capital, and current knowledge of the possibilities of the new technological development.

Population ecology studies have shown how organizations evolve and thrive by fitting into advantage niches through competition for resources (Hannan & Freeman 1984; Hannan & Carroll 1992). However, as noted by Aldrich and Pfeffer (1976), environmental selection is concerned not only with organizations as wholes, but also with particular structures and behavior within organizations. Further, the structures and behavior within new organizational forms are importantly related to the individuals who constitute the core of the firm, and, as both Selznick (1957) and Stinchcombe (1965) observe, organizations tend to take on the characteristics of people and environments that surround their early establishment. The analysis of the case study of New Genetics supports these arguments, by showing how both the scientists as a professional community, as well as the organizational genealogical parents – the university and market-oriented corporations – have contributed to the structure of the new form.

In essence, the hybrid form represents a selection of the features seen as advantages of the genealogical parents, and a modification where the features raise potential incompatibilities. The set of features recognized as important for selection and modification will, of course, differ according to the purpose and goals of the new organizational hybrid. For hybrid firms in the biotechnology industry, we have argued that the key features relate to the firm's human capital, namely, the management of the vital human resources of scientific labor.

All other forms introduced in this chapter are based on features that may enable and facilitate knowledge creation and knowledge-exchanges processes. While each of these forms may be applied to a special subset of organizations, this chapter has tried to highlight the advantages of these forms as it was exerted from their basic organizational elements and process assumptions.

4 | Scientific entrepreneurship

In order to have a full understanding of the arena of scientific technological innovation in general, and of biotechnology in particular, we have to place the role of basic research conducted in universities in context. Recent literature on national systems of innovation depicts intensive scientific collaborations between universities, industrial organizations, and government agencies (Etzkowitz & Leydesdorff 2000; Etzkowitz *et al.* 2000), and argues that university research may increasingly function as a locus of national knowledge-intensive networks. In addition, Hicks and Katz (1997) found that research in general is becoming more interdisciplinary and that research is increasingly conducted more in networks, both domestic and international.

At the same time, research on structural and procedural changes within universities raises the issue of the "second revolution" of universities. "The first academic revolution was the transformation of universities from institutions of cultural preservation to institutions for the creation of new knowledge. Putting that knowledge into use followed soon after. The second academic revolution was the translation of research into products and into new enterprises" (Etzkowitz & Webster 1998). This "second revolution" is based on large funding from the pharmaceutical industry, or smaller but more extensive precompetitive and contract research collaboration that industry and academia share.

These interinstitutional collaborations are coupled with the growth of commercialization of academic science and the translation of research findings into intellectual property (patents) – a marketable commodity (Djerassi 1993; Etzkowitz 1998; Etzkowitz & Webster 1998; Kleinman 1998; Lee 1996; Packer & Webster 1996). Along with the commodification of intellectual property rights, university cultures were claimed to be changing to resemble the private sector owing to an increased dependence on resources from the private sector (Hackett 1990).

Scientific academic entrepreneurship and entrepreneurial universities are growing phenomena, yet little do we know about them. Recently, Rothaermel, Agung and Jiang (2007) conducted an intensive and wide literature review based on 173 articles published in a variety of academic journals. They found four major research streams that emerged in the area of university entrepreneurship. These include entrepreneurial research university, productivity of technology-transfer offices, new firm creation, and the environmental context of this topic, including networks of innovation. They submit that this framework is useful in guiding future research on this topic, yet it is still complex and under-researched.

The increase in the commercialization of academic science is associated with the related, respective individual-level phenomenon of entrepreneurial scientists, where academic scientists participate in various ways in the commercialization of their scientific inventions. Some internal features of the scientific work associated with biotechnology are of significance in providing the contextual framework for the study of biotechnology-related scientific entrepreneurship. In the classification of science-based innovations (Senker & Faulkner 1992; Pisano 1994), the distinction between developed and developing science refers to the level of "maturity" of the scientific knowledge.

Biotechnology is defined as a developing science, in which the research and development (R&D) process is based on tacit knowledge with little a priori understanding, and the process is exploratory and based on "learning-by-doing," a tightly coupled and reciprocal research process that is heavily based on integrated teams of interdisciplinary experts (Pisano 1994; Cardinal, Alessandri & Turner 2001). The nature of the R&D process in biotechnology-related fields, which is significantly different from developed sciences such as chemistry, can also be related to the characteristics of scientific entrepreneurs who function within an exploratory, tacit, and limited knowledge base. This chapter will explore these complexities as embedded within the inherent conflict between entrepreneurship as an individualized behavior and biotechnology research as a collaborative process.

Biotechnology in Israel

Israel's biotechnology scientists provide the grounds for an interesting case study. According to Watzman and Avitzour (2001), Israel's academia produces 1700 graduates a year, in all levels within the life sciences, and it boasts one of the highest per-capita rates of publication in the world. Similar to patterns found in the US biotechnology industry (Zucker, Darby & Brewer 1998), the biotechnology industry in Israel was initially founded primarily by academic scientists. In 1990, Israel boasted only 30 biotechnology companies, employing 600 employees, but by 2000 there were 160 companies employing more than 4000 employees.

In order to ease the commercialization of academic research, the government set up three initiatives in the 1990s. These included: the creation of incubator units for fledgling companies; the supply of high-technology resources for academic and startup companies; and the creation of links between academia and industry. The survey used in the present chapter was one of the government's initiatives.

Entrepreneurial scientists

"Scientific entrepreneurship" or "entrepreneurial scientists" are conceptualizations that have not been commonly used in either the scientific literature or the entrepreneurship literature. An early reference to the phenomenon was made by the sociologist of science, Ben David (1971, p. 159), in his historical analysis of the changes in American universities that led to the "professionalization" of scientists, and the development of scientific entrepreneurs. Ben David's historical accounts show that the onset of professional training in American universities occurred around 1900, and the function of the universities was to train students to perform and apply research of the highest standards. Thus, they required the most up-to-date research laboratories in order to train graduate students as well as facilitate professors' research. According to the German model, the role of a research worker was not a central element of the German science organizations. Moreover, research that was directly paid for was not considered research "because it had none of the metaphysical pathos of the deepest expression of creative spirit" (Ben David 1971, p. 156). However, in the new American model, academic scientists enjoy autonomy in research, and act as members of the professional community and professional associations.

Under this view, there is no contradiction between creative accomplishment in research and the organization of research. As a result, organized and standardized research (including paid-for research) became normative in American universities, and led directly to the increase of entrepreneurial scientists and administrators (Ben David 1971, pp. 158–159). Thus, according to Ben David, the initial concept of "scientific entrepreneurship" refers to academic scientists, who conduct professional, large-scale research with graduate students, under professional administration, including "paid-for" research (e.g. invited research by and with industry).

More recent literature introduces new accounts of "entrepreneurial scientists." In this context, we witness research on academic scientists who establish knowledge firms (Antonelli 1999), or on university "star" scientists who work collaboratively with firm scientists (Zucker, Darby & Armstrong 2002). Even though Zucker, Darby and Armstrong (2002) did not refer to the "star" scientists as entrepreneurs, such stars may be classified as entrepreneurs since the study found an interesting link between the scientific publications of star scientists and firms' successes. The joint publication these scientists had with firms' scientists increased the number and citation rate for firms' patents and contributed to firms' successes. Another study (Zucker & Darby 1997) found that "star" bioscientists had a central role in determining when and where new biotechnology firms (NBFs) were formed and the degree of their success.

An alternative account of scientific entrepreneurship (Oliver & Ramati 2003), refers to scientists who acknowledge the commercial value of their academic scientific research, act in various ways to economically legitimize it and commoditize it, and facilitate its commercialization. Accordingly, a modern process that aims to capture the value of intellectual property rights is the process of claiming patents over scientific inventions in order to license the rights to future use of these inventions by interested parties (Oliver & Liebeskind 2003). Claiming for patents rights over academic research can serve as another feature of entrepreneurial scientists. Historically, for the past 25 years, there has been a steep increase in patenting activity by US universities and publicly funded research institutes (Eisenberg 1996; Henderson, Jaffe & Trajtenberg 1998; Eisenberg & Nelson 2002; Mowery *et al.* 2001; Mowery, Sampat & Ziedonis 2002). This trend has been stimulated mainly by the passage of the Bayh–Dole Act in 1980 and the Federal Technology Transfer Act in 1986, which devolved the right to patent the fruits of federally funded research from the federal government to recipient institutions. European countries follow the same pattern. A recent study found that the share of public research organizations (universities and public research laboratories) in patent application has been increasing from 1975 to 1998 (Nesta & Mangematin 2002). These changes are also evident in Israeli academic institutions, and we have increasing numbers of patents' claims assigned to universities.[1]

Scientific collaborations in biotechnology

Biotechnology is considered an industry that is clearly science-based (Meyer-Krahmer & Schmoch 1998). As a result, academic scientists are highly involved in collaborative work with the industry (Liebeskind *et al.* 1996). These collaborations are added to the traditional normative scientific collaborations that exist between scientists working in academia (Merton 1968; Crane 1968, 1972; Friedkin 1978).

Owing to the multidisciplinary nature of biotechnology research, coupled with a need for various kinds of resources (i.e. funding, equipment, technological know-how, and materials), scientific collaborations in biotechnology require collaborations across various institutional settings and disciplines – including between scientists within the same university, between scientists in different universities, and between academic and industrial scientists (for some examples, *see* Powell & Brantley 1992; Liebeskind *et al.* 1996; Powell, Koput & Smith-Doerr 1996; Powell *et al.* 1999; Zucker & Darby 1997; Liebeskind & Oliver 1998; Oliver & Liebeskind 1998; Oliver 2001; Hagedoorn 2002; Zucker, Darby & Torero 2002). These scientific collaborations are perceived as "learning-intensive" opportunities and may be derived from network centrality (Powell, Koput & Smith-Doerr 1996) or location in crowded technological segments (Stuart 1998), but are also a factor of the scientists' characteristics (Zucker, Darby & Torero 2002). Since biotechnology is characterized as a developing science in which knowledge is not yet well defined (Pisano 1994; Cardinal, Alessandri & Turner 2001), these collaborations allow for codifying and internalizing complementary knowledge, and

---

[1] The four major universities are assignees to over 1450 patents in the US patent database, with about 620 to the Weizmann Institute, 408 to Yissum at the Hebrew University, 232 to Ramot at Tel Aviv University, and 190 to Technion.

for its transformation into new knowledge. Therefore, scientific collaborations add to scientific capability building of the scientists in a relatively economic fashion. This scientific capability building results not only from the explicit learning opportunities in every kind of collaboration, but is also impelled by the interdisciplinary structure of biotechnology collaborations. The advantage of interdisciplinary collaborations lies in their ability to enhance the interplay between tacit and explicit knowledge (Nonaka 1994), from various scientific areas that are considered central features and requirements in individual and organizational learning processes.

Because of the "newness" of the topics covered in this study, the nature of the research is exploratory. One inquiry relates to the relations between intellectual property rights (in the form of patents over scientific inventions) and various forms of scientific collaborations.

Merton (1968) refers to the "Matthew effect" that claims that "those who have more get more." This hypothesis was corroborated in various studies of social processes within which science and scientists develop. For example, Foschi (1991) found that high-status scientists were judged more successful than lower-status scientists, even if their findings were exactly the same. In the context of the present chapter, the question is: "Would those who have more protected intellectual property rights (patents) participate also in more scientific collaborations?"

This chapter asks the general question, namely: "What are the relations between scientists' background characteristics, the existence of scientific collaborations of various kinds and protected scientific inventions in the form of patents?" More specifically, it aims at understanding the impact of scientific capital (various ranges of specializations), intellectual capital (patents), academic tenure, research settings (institutional affiliation), and valorization of human capital (laboratory size) on the accumulation of learning enhancing collaborations of various kinds. Or, in a hypothesis format: the number of scientific specializations, technologies used, areas of interest, laboratory size, and patents play a role in the propensity of the laboratory to valorize.

Another direction of exploration in this chapter focusses on identifying classifying variables that introduce significant differences between various subgroups among the sample of entrepreneurial scientists. Finally, the chapter introduces some descriptive features of the top inventors among the entrepreneurial scientists, and suggests three general compositions for this phenomenon.

Data and variables

Data

The study concentrates on biotechnology-related scientists who are actively searching for new collaborations. These scientists, from academic and nonacademic settings in Israel, have replied to a survey that was conducted by a national committee in order to compile a database for national and international collaboration searches by biotechnology firms. In this respect, all scientists in the sample may be considered "entrepreneurial scientists" as they expressed an active interest in enlarging the scope and the exposure of their research into commercial domains through collaborations by responding to the survey. These scientists also become potential "technology-transfer" agents since the survey aimed at providing information to biotechnology and pharmaceutical firms on the research interests and activities of biotechnology-related scientists in Israel, and thus generating potential for university–industry technology-transfer.

The data were collected in 1994 through mailed questionnaires that were sent to all scientists in Israel who were interested in biotechnology-related research. The data-collecting agency was a private research firm employed by the National Biotechnology Committee. This committee was nominated by the Ministry of Industry and Trade, and was mandated to explore the potential of the biotechnology industry and to enhance biotechnology R&D in universities and industry. This particular scientists' database was finally compiled in 1998 in order to allow interested Israeli and international industrial parties to search for information about relevant collaborators. The database became available to interested Israeli and international parties. The data were in text format, and were coded, entered, and analyzed in order to correspond to the research focus.

The secondary use of the data results in non-optimal variables and scope of measurement. On the other hand, the data have several advantages. First, since the data were not collected as a designed research but rather as an instrumental tool for interested scientists, the response of the scientists was based on strong self-interest.

In addition, the self-interest assumption led to an expectation of more accurate and reliable data since no researcher, knowing his responses are about to be used as public data, will risk partial or false information. The database included originally 306 scientists in universities, industry, and governmental research centers in Israel and from which 291 cases were used in the final analyses owing to missing data. No information could be obtained about the response rate and sample biases. However, owing to the instrumental nature of the data, and the "selection effect" in the response to the survey, it is reasonable to assume that all respondents who were seeking industrial collaborations may be considered "entrepreneurial scientists" at various levels. To this information, patent data, extracted from the US patent database, were added for each scientist in the survey.

Variables

Five continuous dependent variables were used as proxies for various forms of innovation and technology-transfer: the number of academic collaborations the scientist currently has, the number of industrial collaborations the scientist already has, the number of local collaborations in Israel (both with academia and with industry), the number of current international collaborations (both with academia and with industry), and the number of total collaborations (composed of all kinds of collaborations).

The independent variables in the study include:

- *Laboratory size*: This was based on the combined number of students in the researcher's laboratory (master, doctoral, and postdoctoral students). This variable was used first as an aggregated variable, but due to the strong explanatory power of this measure, a distinction between the numbers of students in each of the three categories was made at later analyses.
- *Number of areas of interest specified by the scientist*: The list ranges up to six areas of interest and the variable is a count variable.
- *Number of scientific specializations specified by the scientist*: These include medicine, molecular biology, immunology, biochemistry, neurobiology, agriculture, ecology, marine biology, food, bioinformatics to name a few of the 25 areas specified in the study and the variable is a count variable.

- *Number of technologies used by the scientist*: These include 24 technologies, including molecular biology, genetic engineering, classic agriculture genetics, cell culture, ecology, immunological systems, computerized systems, and others. The variable is a count variable.
- *Number of biological systems studied by the scientist*: These include 12 systems among which are humans, mammals, fish, plants, fungi, viruses, and bacteria, and the variable is a count variable.
- *Academic age*: This is based on the number of years since the scientist was awarded his or her highest degree (95.4% of the sample had either PhD or MD degrees).
- *Number of patents on which the scientist is one of the inventors*: This variable was compiled from an external source – through searches in the US patent database, and added to the database. Further, some dummy variables were constructed based on the count variable (see below).
- *Institutional affiliation*: A dummy variable in which academic scientists are 1 ($n = 152$) and non-academic scientists are 0 ($n = 139$).

Dummy variables

Additional dummy variables were constructed for exploratory comparisons of averages between subgroups in the sample and were later used for *t*-test comparisons of significance in equality of means.

In general, and as expected, the patent distribution is skewed as the number of patents assigned to the scientists in the sample (until 2001) ranged from 0 to 26 (with a mean of 1.79 and a standard deviation (SD) of 4.2, whereas until 1994, the mean was 1.06 with an SD of 2.8). Therefore, a set of dummy variables was constructed based on the patent data.

The protection of scientific inventions through patents is an indication of interest in commercialization of the scientific invention, thus listed patents may serve as indicators of entrepreneurial aspirations.

Four dummy variables are various measures of entrepreneurship, and were generated based on classifications of the patent invention information (through searching the US patent database for all listed scientists) as follows:

1. *Entrepreneurs*: The first variable is a dummy variable that refers to scientists that are listed in the patent database as having at

least one patent invention until 1994 ($n = 102$), compared with scientists with no patented invention.

2. *Continuous entrepreneurs*: The second variable refers to all scientists who are listed in the patent database as having at least one patent invention since the survey was done in 1994, compared with other scientists who do not have any patented inventions since that time. This measure refers to scientists who have declared an interest in collaborations with the industry by answering the survey and have continued to claim rights to patents since the survey was conducted, thus they are classified as continuous entrepreneurs ($n = 74$ versus others $n = 217$).

3. *High-scope entrepreneurs*: A measure for high invention-scope and intense intellectual capital is introduced by using a dummy variable that refers to scientists who are inventors of at least three patents ($n = 52$, about 18% of the sample), compared with scientists who do not have more than two patents.

4. *Entrepreneurial university affiliation*: In order to explore the possible effect of the scientists' academic affiliation (entrepreneurial university effects), and explore the option that some universities enhance more scientific entrepreneurship, a dummy variable was constructed for comparisons between scientists affiliated with the two universities in which most patents were invented (the Hebrew University and the Weizmann Institute-combined $n = 90$) with the other four academic institutions in the survey (Technion, Tel Aviv University, Bar Ilan University, and Beer Sheva University – combined $n = 62$).

The following two variables were designed to distinguish between scientists from different scientific sectors, and between scientists with and without postdoctoral students.

5. *Academic institutional affiliation*: The sector affiliation of the scientist is a dummy variable that differentiates between scientists who are affiliated with academic institutions ($n = 152$) and scientists who work in biotechnology firms, hospitals, or in government research centers.

6. *Postdoctoral students*: The presence of postdoctoral students in the scientist's laboratory can serve as an indicator for advanced and frontier research. Therefore, a dummy variable that classifies the scientists in the sample as having at least one postdoctoral student working with them ($n = 102$) versus not having any postdoctoral students ($n = 189$) was constructed.

Results

Descriptive statistics

Table 4.1 provides some descriptive statistics of the variables in the study, including means, SDs, and a correlation matrix. From this table, we learn that scientists in the study have relatively high tenure (measured by number of years since being awarded the highest degree, mainly PhDs, average of 19.7), and have on the average one patent in which they are listed as inventors. The averages of the various kinds of collaborations show that most existing collaborations listed by the scientists in the survey are academic and international.

Four major points are worth highlighting: (1) Laboratory size is positively and significantly correlated with areas of interest (0.23), number of academic collaborations (0.44), local (0.26), international (0.40), and total (0.45) collaborations and with academic tenure (0.24). (2) The number of area interests of the scientist is positively and significantly correlated with the number of technologies used by the scientist (0.32). (3) The number of specializations of the scientist is correlated with the number of biological systems used by the scientist (0.29) and the number of technologies used in the scientist's laboratory (0.27). (4) The number of biological systems used by the scientist is positively correlated with the number of technologies used (0.31). Some indications for the association between being a generalist or specialist in science and the ability to provide complementary knowledge assets in collaborations appear in the correlations. Although being a generalist-scientist in technological specialization and interests is associated with collaborations, being a generalist-scientist in specializations and biological systems is not. This finding leads to the conclusion that not all facets of generalist-scientists are associated with collaborations.

Regressions

Some of the exploratory questions were tested with multiple regressions. Table 4.2 shows the results of multiple regressions of the number of various types of collaborations on the structural, personal, and scientific characteristics of the scientists in the sample. Since the

Table 4.1 *Correlation matrix of the variables in the study*

Variables		1	2	3	4	5	6	7	8	9	10	11	12
All collaborations	2.0 / 1.85		0.97**	0.24**	0.69**	0.78**	0.45**	−0.03	0.25**	0.00	0.02	0.19**	0.14*
Academic collaborations	1.86 / 1.79		X	−0.05	0.68**	0.75**	0.44**	−0.02	0.24**	−0.02	−0.00	0.19**	0.15*
Industrial collaborations	0.14 / 0.45			X	0.13*	0.22**	0.10	−0.03	0.07	0.09	0.08	0.05	−0.06
Local collaborations	0.91 / 1.16				X	0.09	0.26**	−0.02	0.10	−0.00	−0.04	0.04	0.11
International collaborations	1.09 / 1.34					X	0.40**	−0.02	0.26**	0.01	0.06	0.23**	0.09
Laboratory size	2.91 / 3.42						X	0.13*	0.23**	0.01	−0.12*	0.16**	0.24**
No. of patents	1.06 / 2.8							X	0.09	−0.01	−0.03	0.12*	0.16**
No. of areas of interest	3.64 / 1.24								X	0.17**	0.12*	0.32**	0.08
No. of specializations	4.24 / 1.36									X	0.29**	0.27**	−0.07

Table 4.1 (*cont.*)

Variables	1	2	3	4	5	6	7	8	9	10	11	12
No. of biological systems	2.99 1.53									X	0.31 **	−0.17 **
No. of technologies used	9.88 5.08										X	−0.05
Academic age	19.7 8.61											X

Note: The numbers in the first column are of means and standard deviations (SD) of each variable. The number of responses used in the analyses is 291 owing to missing data in some of the cases. The numbers above the diagonal are Pearson correlations when * <0.05 and ** <0.01. The numbers below the diagonal in the first column are means and SDs of each variable.

variable "laboratory size," which is a composite variable based on the total number of MA, PhD, and postdoctoral students working with the scientist, was one of the most significant variables in the regressions presented in Table 4.2, it was decided to sort the effects of number of students in each category on the dependent variables.

Therefore, Table 4.3 shows the results of multiple regressions of the number of various forms of collaborations on the personal, structural, and scientific characteristics of the scientists – with the distinctive number of students in each category.

The multiple regressions presented in Table 4.2 and Table 4.3 reveal a number of interesting findings that should be highlighted and discussed. First, the highest significant contribution to the explanation of the variance of the dependent variable (for all five dependent variables) in Table 4.2 is the laboratory size of the scientist. The larger the laboratory size, the more total, academic, international, local, and industrial collaborations the scientist has (significant beta values of 0.41, 0.40, 0.36, 0.24, and 0.12, respectively). Of all the scientific scope variables (e.g. areas of interest, of specialization, and numbers of technologies and biological systems), only the number of technologies used by the scientist has a low but significant effect on the number of academic and international collaborations, but not on the number of industrial or local collaborations. In addition, scope of interest has a significant low impact on the number of academic and international collaborations. The final finding, that the number of patents has a low negative effect on the number of academic and international collaborations, calls for further investigation and analysis.

Table 4.3 breaks the number of students working in the scientists' laboratories into all three categories, and enters them as distinct variables and controls for whether a scientist works in the academic or the nonacademic sector. The results show that the number of postdoctoral students in a scientist's laboratory has the most significant effect on the number of academic, local, international, and total collaborations the scientist has (significant positive beta values of 0.26, 0.19, 0.20, and 0.27, respectively). In addition, academic scientists have significantly more (although with low correlation, and a significant level of 0.10), academic and international collaborations. Other than these effects, the other effects in Table 4.3 are similar to these presented in Table 4.2.

Table 4.2 Multiple regressions of the number of various forms of collaborations on structural, personal, and scientific characteristics of scientists

Variables/dependent variable	No. of academic collaborations	No. of industrial collaborations	No. of local collaborations	No. of international collaborations	No. of total collaborations
Constant	0.32	0.00	0.44	-0.12	1.016
Laboratory size	0.40***	0.12*	0.24***	0.36***	0.41***
Number of areas of interest	0.13**	0.04	0.05	0.15**	0.14**
Number of specializations	-0.08	0.06	-0.01	-0.08	-0.06
Number of technologies used	0.11*	-0.02	0.00	0.13**	0.10*
Number of biological systems used	0.03	0.06	-0.01	0.06	0.04
Academic age	0.07	-0.07	0.06	0.02	0.05
Number of patents	-0.11**	-0.04	-0.07	-0.10*	-0.12**
Adjusted R^2	0.222	0.007	0.052	0.203	0.234

$n = 291$
***$p < 0.01$
** $p < 0.05$
* $p < 0.10$

Table 4.3 *Multiple regressions of the number of various forms of collaborations on structural, personal, and scientific characteristics of the scientists – with distinct number of students in each category*

Variables/dependent variable	No. of academic collaborations	No. of industrial collaborations	No. of local collaborations	No. of international collaborations	No. of total collaborations
Constant	0.12	0.00	0.35	−0.27	0.00
No. of MA students	0.12*	0.03	0.07	0.11*	0.12**
No. of PhD students	0.07	0.01	0.03	0.06	0.07
No. of postdoctoral students	0.26***	0.08	0.19**	0.20***	0.27***
Number of areas of interest	0.14**	0.05	0.05	0.16**	0.14**
Number of specializations	−0.07	0.07	0.00	−0.06	−0.05
Number of technologies used	0.10*	0.07	0.01	0.12**	0.10
Number of biological systems used	0.05	−0.02	0.00	0.08	0.06
Academic age	0.05	−0.08	0.06	−0.01	0.03
Academician	0.13*	0.06	0.02	0.17*	0.14**
No. of patents	−0.10*	−0.03	−0.06	−0.09*	−0.11*
Adjusted R^2	0.229	0.00	0.049	0.213	0.244

$n = 291$
*** $p < 0.01$
** $p < 0.05$
* $p < 0.10$

Difference between subgroups

In order to further explore possible distinctive classifications of entrepreneurial scientists, *t*-test analyses were conducted to compare the significance of the differences of the averages of scientists in various subgroups. The comparisons are based on a set of dummy variables constructed through the data (as defined and described above). Below, the most significant differences that are of interest are reported for each of the six dummy variables constructed to reflect the possible context of entrepreneurial scientists. Findings show that:

- *Entrepreneurs*: Scientists who had at least one patent before 1994 ($n = 102$) in comparison with scientists who had no patents, have significantly more international collaborations (average of 1.23 versus 1.04); more doctoral students (average of 1.74 versus 1.13 for scientists with no patents); they have higher academic tenure (average of 21.69 versus 18.97); and specify more areas of interest (average of 3.9 versus 3.5) as well as use of technologies in their laboratories (average of 11.23 versus 9.39). All other variables did not show significant differences between the two groups.

- *Continuous entrepreneurs*: Scientists who had additional patents after 1994 or had patented inventions only after the survey was conducted (in 1994) were classified as recent entrepreneurs. The comparison between the recent entrepreneurs (those who had patents after 1994) and those who did not have any patents after 1994 (but may or may not have patents prior to 1994), shows some interesting results. The significant differences found for this classification of subgroups are in the number of industrial collaborations (the recent entrepreneurs have a significantly higher average of industrial collaborations – average 0.216 versus 0.115); have more postdoctoral, doctoral, and MA students (0.96 versus 0.48; 2.15 versus 1.00; 1.69 versus 0.82, respectively); and expressed significantly more areas of interest in the survey (an average of 3.97 versus 3.52). All other variables did not show significant differences between the two groups.

- *High-scope entrepreneurs*: Scientists who had more than two patents had significantly more postdoctoral students (average of

0.98 versus average of 0.52); had more doctoral students (average of 2.10 versus average of 1.12); and more MA students (average of 1.5 versus average of 0.94). In addition, they had a higher tenure (average of 22.25 versus average of 19.14); and listed more areas of interest (average of 4.02 versus average of 3.55). All other variables did not show significant differences between the two groups.

- *Entrepreneurial university affiliation*: Among the academic scientists subsample, scientists affiliated with the two more entrepreneurial academic institutions in Israel (in terms of the total number of patents listed per institution – the Hebrew University and the Weizmann Institute, $n = 90$) were compared with scientists from all other four academic institutions in the sample ($n = 62$). The findings show that significant differences are found between scientists from the entrepreneurial universities and scientists from the other universities. Scientists from the Hebrew University and the Weizmann Institute had more international collaborations (average of 1.7 versus average of 1.24); had more postdoctoral students (1.11 versus 0.65) and more doctoral students (2.34 versus 1.8); and had a higher academic tenure (23.62 versus 20.51). All other variables did not show significant differences between the two groups.

- *Academic institutional affiliation*: In the comparison between scientists working in academic institutions and scientists in government research centers, in industry, or in hospitals, significant differences in which the academic scientists had higher averages were found for the total number of collaborations, a significantly higher average of 2.57 versus 1.38; significantly more academic collaborations – average of 2.41 versus 1.27; and more international collaborations, having a significantly higher average of 1.48 versus 0.66. In addition, it was found that scientists working in academic institutions had higher tenure (defined as number of years since acquiring the highest degree) (22.7 versus 16.4 on average); and had listed fewer biological systems with which they were working (3.24 for industrial and government scientists versus 2.76 for scientists in academic institutions). All other variables did not show significant differences between the two groups.

- *Postdoctoral students*: The highest number of significant differences was found between scientists who had postdoctoral students working with them and those who did not have postdoctoral students working with them. These scientists were assigned as inventors on significantly higher numbers of patents (an average of 2.64 versus an average of 1.33); had significantly more total collaborations (an average of 2.97 versus 1.48); had more academic, international, and local collaborations (average of 2.80 versus 1.36; 1.75 versus 0.74; 1.22 versus 0.75, respectively); had more doctoral and MA students (an average of 2.61 versus 0.58 and 1.87 versus 0.59, respectively). In addition, they had higher academic tenure and classified themselves as working with significantly more technologies (averages of 22.09 versus 18.4 and 11.18 versus 9.19, respectively). All other variables did not show significant differences between the two groups.

Characteristics of top entrepreneurial scientists

This chapter has focussed on an effort to explore general features of entrepreneurial scientists and their relations to other variables. In addition to the statistical analysis, we now discuss some qualitative insights into the characteristics of entrepreneurial scientists.

Table 4.4 introduces accounts of the distribution of characteristics of the "top patent inventors" focussing on scientists who have more than 10 patents on which they are listed as inventors. With these accounts, we may distinguish between a few "models" of entrepreneurial scientists, as well as some general features of the whole group. As a group, we can see that 12 out of 17 scientists within this group received their PhDs before 1980, and 13 of them received their degrees from either the Hebrew University or the Weizmann Institute (only one received his degree in the USA). Most top entrepreneurial scientists are males: only one scientist in this group is a female professor. In addition, all scientists are extensively involved in scientific publications (except for two industrial scientists, for whom no data could be obtained through the Science Citation Index, due to the inability to specify their organizational affiliation. For all other scientists, the search was based on the name and institutional affiliation as it appeared in the original database). In addition, all academic scientists have students at various levels working with them, including post-doctoral students. Finally, most of the academic professors have academic collaborations conducted in conjunction with industrial collaborations.

Table 4.4 *Top entrepreneurial scientists (inventing above 10 patents by 2002), by their major characteristics*

ID	PhD – year and institution	Appointment(s)	Organization	Field of activity	Biological systems	Technology applied	MS Student	PhD Student	Post doctoral student	Aca. coll.	Industry collaborations	No. of patents	No. of publications
1	1969 Hebrew University Israel	Professor of Chemistry; Consultant to a firm	Hebrew University	Biochem; Chemistry; Pharmacology	Human; Mammals	Molecular design; Peptide tech.; Prot. engine.	3	5	2	2	1	13	138
8	1968 Hebrew University Israel	Professor	Hebrew University	Agriculture; Ecology; Mol. biology; Plant pathology	Bacteria; Fungi	Cell separation; Gene expres; Transgenic plants	3	6	2	3	1	11	244
11	1961 Columbia University USA	Professor	Tel Aviv University	Molecular microbiology; Biotechnology; Nutrition	Bacteria	Cloning; Fermentation; Waste treatments	2	2	1	3	0	22	141
14	1981 Technion, Israel	Associate Professor Head of Department	Ben Gurion University	Bio-engineering; Biomaterials	Algae; Human	Drug delivery systems; Fermentation; Hormones	8	2	2	4	0	11	9
16	Weizmann Institute, Israel	Chairman and CEO of a biotechnology firm		Medicine; Chemistry; Molecular biology; Pharmacology	Human; Mammals	Cell markers; Drug delivery systems; Tissue culture	–	–	–	0	0	16	81/44 at the university

Table 4.4 (*cont.*)

ID	PhD – year and institution	Appointment(s)	Organization	Field of activity	Biological systems	Technology applied	MS Student	PhD Student	Post doctoral student	Aca. coll.	Industry collaborations	No. of patents	No. of publications
17	1982 Weizmann Institute, Israel	Senior VP of a biotechnology firm		Biotechnology; Biochemistry; Cell biology; Immunology	Bacteria; Mammals	Cloning; Fermentation; Growth fact; rDNA	1	1	0	0	0	21	105
43	1975 Wiezmann Institute, Israel	Professor	Weizmann Institute	Biochemist; Immunology; Molecular biology; Virology	Bacteria; Cell cultures; Viruses	Cell culture; Cloning; rDNA	1	2	1	0	2	20	111
51	1974 Hebrew University, Israel	Head of Government Research Institute		Agriculture; Developmental biology; Genetics; Physiology	Higher plants	Plant breeding; Tissue culture	–	–	–	0	9	11	46
67	1976 Weizmann Institute, Israel	Professor and Head of Department	Hebrew University	Biochemistry; Cell biology; Molecular biology	Bacteria; Human; Mammals; Phage	Cloning; DNA probes; rDNA; RNA technology	1	5	4	4	0	10	192

Table 4.4 (*cont.*)

ID	PhD – year and institution	Appointment(s)	Organization	Field of activity	Biological systems	Technology applied	MS Student	PhD Student	Post doctoral student	Aca. coll.	Industry collaborations	No. of patents	No. of publications
69	1954 Hebrew University, Israel	Professor	Weizmann Institute	Biochemistry; Immunology; Molecular biology	Bacteria; Human; Mammals; Viruses	Cell separation; Chemotherapy; Cloning; Oncogenes	0	4	4	6	0	14	44
124	1972, MD Hebrew University, Israel	Head of Department, Hospital, and the Hebrew University Medical School	Hadassah Hospital	Cell biology; Hematology; Molecular biology; Oncology	Cell cultures; Human; Viruses	Cell markers; Chemotherapy; Cloning; Gene therapy; MAbs	1	2	2	2	2	12	469
149	1966 MD, PhD Hebrew University, Israel	Professor	Technion	Bioengineering; Biophysics; Membrane biology	Cell Cultures; Mammals; Murine	Biosensors; Cell cultures; Tissue cultures; Transporters	0	3	0	0	0	18	63
165	1988 Tel Aviv University, Israel	Professor	Tel Aviv University	Chemistry; Marine biology; Natural products	Algae; Higher plants; Marine organisms	Chemotherapy; NMR	3	3	1	3	1	13	219

Table 4.4 (*cont.*)

ID	PhD – year and institution	Appointment(s)	Organization	Field of activity	Biological systems	Technology applied	MS Student	PhD Student	Post doctoral student	Aca. coll.	Industry collaborations	No. of patents	No. of publications
176	1971 Hebrew University, Israel	Professor	Hebrew University	Biochemistry; Biophysics; Drug delivery	Cell cultures; Mammals	Drug delivery; Drug targeting; MAbs; Peptide technology	2	6	4	4	0	26	217
184	1974 Hebrew University, Israel	Professor	Weizmann Institute	Immunology; Molecular biology	Bacteria; Cell cultures; Mammals	Cell cultures; Cloning; DNA probes; MAbs	0	4	2	0	0	25	157
266	1971 Weizmann Institute, Israel	VP Biotechnology firm		Biochemistry; Cell biology; Diagnostics; Immunology	Bacteria; Cell cultures	Biosensors; Cell markers; MAbs; Tissue culture	0	0	0	0	0	27	N/A
309	1976 Tel Aviv University, Israel	Head of Department, Biotechnology firm		Hematology; Molecular biology; Virology	Bacteria; Human; Viruses; Yeast	Cloning; DNA probes; Drug delivery systems; rDNA; PCR	0	0	0	0	0	26	N/A

The following profiles of entrepreneurial scientists may be drawn, based on the distributions in Table 4.4.

- *The "Inventor–Publisher" entrepreneurial scientist (e.g. #1, #8, #67, #176)*: This profile entails mainly the university scientist who has a high publication rate as well as a high intellectual property protection rate (in terms of patent invention), and has been working in academia for between 25 and 35 years, has more academic than industrial collaborations, and has between 8 and 12 students at various levels working with them.
- *The "Inventor–Limited Publisher" entrepreneurial scientist (e.g. #16, #149)*: These scientists can be heavily involved in collaborations with the industry (from personal records, it was evident that the academic progress of one of them was slower than other scientists in the same university owing to his heavy involvement with industrial collaborations. The slower academic progress can result from being perceived by the university as conducting limited-quality research and thus leading to a slower promotion rate of the scientist. Another barrier to promotion may result from the fact that findings of contracted research with the industry usually cannot be published without permission from the collaborating or contracting biotechnology firm in Israel. Withholding publications till patent submission or until various testing of the discovery are applied can result in delayed publications or lower rate of related publications. Such instances were disclosed through interviews with academic scientists who had research contractual arrangements with biotechnology firms.
- *The "Fast tracker all in all" entrepreneurial scientist (e.g. #165)*: These scientists are new entrants to the academic world, but have a strong emphasis on entrepreneurial science, focussing on simultaneously heavy publishing and heavy inventing and patenting, and thus acting on both the "open science" and the "privatized science" fronts (Henderson, Jaffe & Trajtenberg 1998; Oliver & Liebeskind 2003).

Discussion

The explorative directions of this study included the effort to analytically distinguish some features of scientific entrepreneurship as they were composed through the database of collaboration-seeking scientists. Within this frame of research, it was important to identify the independent variables – of intellectual capital and institutional characteristics – that could explain the variance within various forms of existing scientific collaborations.

The chapter focussed on the relations between scientists' background characteristics, the existence of scientific collaborations of various kinds, and protected scientific inventions in the form of patents. The structure of these relations can provide partial illumination to the construct of scientific entrepreneurship. The most significant evidence seems to show that among the entrepreneurial scientists in the sample those who had the higher rate of collaborations seem to have larger laboratories with students of all levels. But the most significant variable within the composition of the laboratory researchers is the number of postdoctoral students. This is an element worthy of additional discussion. Larger academic research laboratories, and especially when postdoctoral students are present, signify the valorization of scientific human capital since they provide a source of "in-house" learning for the scientist and the students. Postdoctoral students who usually arrive at the laboratory from other institutions have the ability of enlarging the pool of "in-house" research capabilities and knowledge base within the laboratory. A larger number of postdoctoral students in a scientist's laboratory also contribute to increased attractiveness and credibility, factors which are associated with scientific prestige. These "signals" of scientific quality may be generators for potential future collaborations with the industry as well as for other types of collaborations. To sum up, evidence showed that the distinction between lower levels of research students and postdoctoral students is important in predicting collaborations (except for industrial collaborations). Although MA and doctoral students provide research capabilities, postdoctoral students may bring new knowledge and capability resources to the scientist's laboratory.

Of course, we may argue for the opposite direction in the more precise logic of explanation. This argument claims that scientists who had higher scientific prestige, advanced and versatile knowledge, and large research funds tend to have larger laboratories. In Israel, the salaries and fellowships of the students in a scientist's laboratory are paid mostly through the various research grants that the scientist has managed to raise. In this context, Merton's (1968) Matthew effect, claiming that those who have more (in terms of plausible research funds in this case) will have more (advanced, especially postdoctoral students in this case), and will have even more (collaborations in this case) is nicely validated. An additional corroboration is provided by the finding presented earlier indicating that "high-scope" entrepreneurs (with more than two patents) have significantly more students at all levels, in addition to longer tenures and areas of interest, as well as by the finding showing that having at least one postdoctoral student is associated with significantly more patents.

Another interesting finding is that none of the independent variables in the study contribute to the explanation of industrial collaborations. This evidence shows that at the time of the survey, most scientists in Israel had few or no industrial collaborations, and the intellectual capital and institutional variables were best associated with the normative science of academic collaborations. Since that time, the National Biotechnology Committee in Israel has managed to convince the government to invest in biotechnology technology-transfer programs in the form of consortia and incubators, and without doubt there are currently more university–industry collaborations.

Some indication for this change is evident from the finding that the scientists with significantly more industrial collaborations were those who continued submitting patent applications since the survey was conducted in 1994, in comparison with those having no additional patents between the years 1994 and 2002. Thus, the subcategory of "recent entrepreneurship" was significantly associated with industrial collaborations as well as with significantly more students in each level and more areas of interest, leading to the observation that recent entrepreneurs tend to form more industrial collaborations.

Another expectation of the study was that diversity or generalization measures of the laboratory would be associated with higher rates of collaborations. This expectation was not met by the findings except for the weak association between number of areas of interest of the scientist and the number of technologies used in the scientist's laboratory. These findings may reflect the fact that the scientists with fewer collaborations tend to develop "in-house" diversified capabilities, and thus have fewer existing collaborations. Thus, being a generalist may be associated with more independent research. This finding may be in line with the fact that the number of patents assigned to the scientist has a negative (low but statistically significant) impact on the number of academic, international, and total collaborations, whereas it has no significant association in the bivariate correlation table. The fact that although intellectual property and institutional variables were controlled for, the zero association turns in three (out of five) regressions to negative and significant correlation, indicates that in regard to patents, Merton's (1968) "Matthew effect" does not appear to be valid. These findings may lead to a few inter-pretations. They may indicate that scientists who have experienced the process of securing intellectual property rights through patent protec-tion tend to collaborate less and promote more secrecy regarding their laboratory research (e.g. Arundel 2001; Liebeskind 2001). It could also mean that the more secured intellectual property rights the scientist has, the more the gains from royalties the scientist may receive can allow them to be less dependent upon external collaborations. Another option refers to virtues which may be associated with secured intellectual property rights – namely that the more patents a scientist has, the higher their ability to secure fewer but larger-in-scope collaborations which can fund the scientist's laboratory expenses.

Finally, an explanation may follow the direction offered by Zucker, Darby and Torero (2002), and Nesta and Mangematin (2002), who contend that patenting of biotechnology academic research produces knowledge that encourages firm creation by scientists. Thus, the negative correlation between patents and collaborations may be explained by an unaccounted-for variable – firm formation. Since the separate analysis of academic-only scientists found the same results, it may be the case that scientists with high rates of patents are involved in the founding of NBFs and therefore undertake less collaboration. With the lack of longitudinal data, all the above explanations are plausible, yet only further research using longitudinal dynamic data will be able to specify the direction of relations.

The exploration phase also asked whether there are different clas-sifications for scientific entrepreneurship, and if so, what do they represent. The study suggested various classifications based on col-laborations, patents, institutional membership, and the composition of publications and patents. All these directions seem to be uniquely associated with some characteristics which lead to the expectations of differential forms of scientific entrepreneurship.

5 | Science and discoveries in the context of private and public knowledge creation and learning

THIS CHAPTER WAS WRITTEN WITH
JULIA PORTER LIEBESKIND

Issues of knowledge creation, discoveries, and inventions, as well as scientific entrepreneurship, are embedded in the institutional environment. Universities, scientists, and networks of collaboration are shaped to a great degree by the norms and regulations of the institutional environment in which they operate.

In this chapter, we explore the effects of institutional context on the conduct and on the outcomes of scientific research through the lens of property rights arrangements. Using the example of the allocation of property rights of two breakthrough inventions in biotechnology, we ask whether the absence of narrowly defined property rights in these two inventions was a deterrent to the development of subsequent property rights in commercially valuable new inventions that employed them. In conjunction with this question, we open up new questions about the relationship between institutional policies regarding intellectual property rights and the progress and direction of academic research.

Introduction

For the past 30 years, there has been a steep increase in patenting activity by US universities and other publicly funded research institutes such as the National Institutes of Health (Eisenberg 1996; Henderson, Jaffe & Trajtenberg, 1998; Mowery *et al.* 2001; Owen-Smith 2003; Rothaermel, Agung & Jiang 2007). This trend has been stimulated by a number of factors, including: increased pressure on

Acknowledgement: We wish to thank Richard Nelson, Michele S. Garfinkel, and Allen Wagner for their most valuable comments and advice provided at various stages of this research. Mike Clark's web page and comments directed us to important sources of information regarding mAbs.

115

US public research organizations to increase the social returns from federally funded research; an increased emphasis on the definition and enforcement of intellectual property in the US courts; and, last but not least, the passing of the Bayh–Dole Act in 1980 and the Federal Technology Transfer Act in 1986, which devolved the right to patent the fruits of federally funded research from the federal government to recipient institutions (Eisenberg 1996; Henderson, Jaffe & Trajtenberg 1998; Mowery *et al.* 2001).[1]

In tandem with this increase in patenting inventions made within the realm of public research there has also emerged a norm of exclusive licensing of these inventions by public research institutions to businesses.[2] According to Eisenberg (1996), the practice of exclusive licensing is essentially mandated by current federal regulations. Whilst the Bayh–Dole Act itself did not provide specifically for exclusive licensing, subsequent federal legislation and executive orders now require the granting of exclusive licenses unless public research institutions can argue successfully in favor of broader licensing regimens, or for committing discoveries into the commons. These federal regulations are based on the premise that, without an exclusive license, a firm has few if any incentives to invest additional research and development (R&D) in order to bring a new invention to market (Eisenberg 1996; Mazzolini & Nelson 1998b). Since universities and other public research institutions are not equipped to undertake even the early-stage development of commercially promising inventions, technologies transferred from public research institutions to firms are necessarily only at an embryonic stage of development. Consequently, firms interested in commercializing such inventions need to commit substantial additional time and capital to further R&D. It is argued that firms will not be willing to undertake such investments unless they are assured that they will be protected from competition until their costs are recouped and some profit is earned. These arguments in favor of exclusive licensing are

---

[1] Prior to the Bayh–Dole Act in 1980, rights to patent federally funded research were retained by the federal government, and the patenting process was often cumbersome, time-consuming, and uncertain. Some government departments, however, did devolve wide-ranging rights to patent to some selected universities under Institutional Patent Agreements.

[2] Here we make a distinction that is commonly made in studies of science between "discovery" and "invention," an "invention" being practical in nature, a "knowing-how" rather than a "knowing-that." Only inventions are patentable.

parallel to arguments made in favor of patenting. That is, by granting either a patent (to a commercial inventor) or an exclusive license (to a commercial developer of a non-commercial inventor), society bears the temporary cost of monopoly pricing, but earns a longer-term social benefit from the invention itself.[3]

The growth of patenting and exclusive licensing by public research institutions has raised an intense debate about its costs and benefits.[4] Although it is not our purpose in this chapter to address this larger debate, we do undertake the task of demonstrating that some types of

---

[3] This argument is one that is well-established in contract economics. According to established models, patents induce investment in both discovery and commercialization by protecting investors from competition until their expenses and a reasonable profit are recouped (Mazzolini & Nelson 1998a). In these models, the social cost of a patent is that the patent owner earns monopoly rents for the life of the patent; the social benefit is that a valuable invention is made available to society, increasing social welfare. It is this argument that, in large part, motivated the passing of the Bayh–Dole Act in 1980 (Eisenberg 1996). Patenting is also argued to increase technological diffusion because patentees are required to publish their discoveries in such a way that others may readily put them into practice (Mazzolini & Nelson 1998a, 1998b).

[4] See, for example, Nelkin (1984), Eisenberg (1996), Argyres and Liebeskind (1998), Heller and Eisenberg (1998), Mazzolini and Nelson (1998a, 1998b), Eisenberg and Nelson (2002), and Nelson (2002). Whilst the argument over the costs and benefits of patenting the fruits of public research has been intense, there are few empirical data available to inform policy (Mazzolini & Nelson 1998a; Mowery, Sampat & Ziedonis 2002). There is certainly evidence that there has been a significant increase in patenting and licensing activity by US universities since the 1960s. One study, by Henderson, Jaffe and Trajtenberg (1998) shows that universities significantly increased their "propensity to patent" inventions between 1965 and 1988, even though the basic rate of invention apparently did not increase during the same period. They report a 15-fold increase in university patenting during this period, during which total US patenting rose by only 50 percent. Mowery *et al.* (2001) analyze the effects of the Bayh–Dole Act on patenting and licensing activity at three major US research universities: Columbia, Stanford, and the University of California. Their data show that the rate of patenting and licensing and licensing revenues at all three institutions increased rapidly between 1975 and 1995. For instance, at the University of California, invention disclosures tripled between 1975 and 1995; patenting increased almost five-fold; and license agreements increased more that ten-fold. At Stanford, invention disclosures also tripled between 1975 and 1995; patenting also tripled; and license agreements quadrupled. Most interesting from the point of view of the topic of the present study is the rate of exclusive licensing. The authors found that among these three institutions, the proportion of total licenses that were granted on an exclusive basis was about 60 percent at Columbia and Stanford, and over 90 percent at the University of California, for the period 1986–1990.

inventions made in public research institutions may not be best exploited from a social welfare point of view by the usual mechanisms of patenting and exclusive licensing. We demonstrate this argument by use of two case studies of pioneering inventions in biotechnology that were made within the sphere of public research: monoclonal antibodies (mAbs) and recombinant DNA (rDNA). These two inventions are interesting for three reasons.[5]

First, most commercial applications of biotechnology lie within the pharmaceutical industry, where intellectual property rights play a key role in the development and commercialization of final products, and in determining firm profits (Cohen, Nelson & Walsh 2000). The commercial importance of pharmaceutical patents has flowed back into public science, with biotechnology accounting for the majority of patenting activities by universities and other public research institutions (Henderson, Jaffe & Trajtenberg 1998; Cohen, Nelson & Walsh 2002).

Second, both of the inventions we investigate were "research tools;" that is, they were not "final products" but technologies which enabled the development of final products. In addition, both inventions involved technologies that were highly extensible, having uses in a number of different product areas. Thus, it might be argued that these technologies are "non-rivalrous" in their use – that is, they have the nature of a public good, in which use of that good by one party does not reduce its value to other users (Arrow 1962). For such goods, it may be argued that their greatest value is achieved not by exclusive patenting, but by diffusing them broadly, so that all their potential uses are exploited.

Third, and finally, both of these inventions were made before the current norms of patenting and exclusive licensing were put into place. Furthermore, monoclonal antibody technology was developed in Britain (by Köhler and Milstein in 1975, working at the laboratories of the Medical Research Council (MRC) in Cambridge).[6] Possibly for one or both of these reasons neither of these inventions was managed in terms of intellectual property according to current federal

---

[5] New biotechnologies include three distinct techniques: fermentation technologies engineering, recombinant DNA and hybridoma; (*see* Tansey and Catterall 1995).

[6] Current practice in terms of patenting and licensing in the UK is similar to that in the USA.

regulations. The mAbs technology was not patented at all. The second invention – rDNA technology, developed by Cohen and Boyer at Stanford University in 1973 – was patented, but licensed very broadly, and at low cost to commercial users.

As we recount, the development and diffusion of these two inventions was pivotal in stimulating both the early development and the subsequent growth of the biotechnology industry. On the commercial side of the public/private boundary, our data show that both of these inventions contributed to the generation of a multitude of subsequent "downstream" inventions that were themselves patented. This finding suggests that the absence of narrowly defined property rights in these two inventions was not a deterrent to the development of subsequent property rights in commercially valuable new inventions which employed them. This evidence is consistent with the argument that at least some discoveries made in basic science are non-rivalrous in use, and that patenting and exclusive licensing are not always necessary to stimulate subsequent development and commercialization (Nelson 2002; Mazzolini & Nelson 1998a, 1998b). We also show that the two inventions were widely used to inform subsequent scholarly research. Publication is an important measure of innovation diffusion, both within the research community and in the process of technology-transfer to industry (Agrawal & Henderson 2002; Cohen, Nelson & Walsh 2002). Our findings also raise the question of how the development of the entire field of biotechnology might have evolved (or not) had these two inventions been managed on an exclusive basis by a single commercial entity, as they would be under current norms of intellectual property management.

This chapter is organized as follows. In the next section, 'The two inventions: science and intellectual property rights,' we briefly describe the histories of the two inventions and then describe in some detail how the intellectual property rights for each invention evolved. Interestingly, both of these inventions stimulated a public discourse and debate over property rights; we report some aspects of these debates to illustrate concerns over disposition of property rights to public science. Then, in 'Innovation diffusion: patenting, publications, and commercialization,' we discuss the contribution of the two inventions to the development of the biotechnology industry, and provide data on the effects of these discoveries on subsequent patenting and research activity. The chapter then provides a discussion and concludes.

The two inventions: science and intellectual property rights

rDNA

Invention

Recombinant DNA (rDNA) is a genetic engineering procedure that serves to join together DNA segments from different origins (species or subspecies) to create new life forms. It was discovered in 1973 by Dr Herbert Boyer, a biochemist from the University of California at San Francisco (UCSF), and Dr Stanley Cohen, from Stanford University. The two researchers met in an Hawaiian delicatessen and worked out an experiment that would use an enzyme discovered by Boyer and a genetic delivery device (plasmid) discovered by Cohen. In this experiment, the researchers cut and pasted a gene from one organism to another in order to manufacture ("express") a specific protein (Robbins-Roth 2000; Hughes 2001).

Intellectual property rights

The patenting of rDNA may be said to have come about by pure chance. In the fall of 1973, Cohen and Boyer published their groundbreaking findings in the scientific journal, *Proceedings of the National Academy of Science* (Cohen *et al.* 1973). The article was noticed by a reporter from the *New York Times* who then wrote a column in 1974 on its implications for genetic engineering.[7] In turn, this article was noticed by a public relations specialist at Stanford University, who brought the paper to the attention of Niels Reimers, the head of Stanford's technology-licensing group. Stanford University had a long history of being interested and involved in university–industry technology-transfer, and the technology-licensing group was actively engaged in searching out discoveries on the Stanford campus which might be successfully commercialized. According to his own account, Reimers sought out Cohen, whom he knew, and said:

"Stan, this looks like it's interesting and important work" and he said "Yes ... but no patents. This is something that is going to go out broadly." I said "Well, it certainly will, but if we apply for a patent on it ... we might be able to get an exclusive license to a company to develop a recombinant

---

[7] "Animal Gene Shifted to Bacteria" by Victor McElheny, *New York Times*, 20 May, 1974.

insulin and so on. You can't get drugs developed today without some proprietary protection ... we could get companies to follow safety guidelines [on genetic engineering] also, through the mechanism of the license." Stan finally agreed to cooperating. (Reimers 1997)

Later, Cohen persuaded Boyer to allow Stanford to patent the discovery, with an agreement that the two universities (Stanford and UCSF, where Boyer worked) would share any royalties from commercialization. In fact, the patent rights to the new technology were necessarily limited to only US rights because the discovery had already been published. Elsewhere in the world, published results cannot be patented subsequently; in the USA at that time published discoveries could still be patented so long as the patent was applied for within one year of publication. Stanford applied for the patent in 1974; the process patent was granted by the Patent and Trademark Office (PTO) in 1980, and the product patent (on the specific plasmid engineered by Cohen and Boyer) in 1982.

The proposal to patent rDNA was not without repercussions. One issue was the question of whether it was appropriate for a university to seek a patent on a basic scientific discovery. For instance, Reimers sent the patent proposal out for review before applying to the PTO, and one reviewer responded with the following remarks:

It is my view that this is a somewhat ill-conceived patent application that disregards ... the contributions of other scientists and is very basic in its concepts and applications. ... I am concerned that, given the fundamental nature of the work, and the number of scientists involved, either directly or indirectly, that this patent will not reflect favorably on the public service ideals of the University. (Reimers 1997)

One issue raised by this reviewer was the fact that only Cohen and Boyer were listed as inventors on the patent application. This attribution was disputed by a number of other scientists, including one of the co-authors on the original 1973 publication, Robert Helling, and another co-author on another paper that appeared in 1974 (Morrow *et al.*), John Morrow. Morrow hired lawyers and sued Stanford for unfair exclusion from the patent. Both of these claims to inventorship were later rejected by the patent examiner at the PTO. Despite this finding, another scientist working on gene-splicing at Stanford – Paul Berg – maintained in a recent interview that Morrow should have been named as an inventor:

John [Morrow] was resentful for a long, long period afterwards. He was screwed out of any benefits from that [discovery], or the recognition of it. (Berg 1997)

Berg also apparently had a number of conversations with Reimers about attribution of the fundamental discovery, because much of the original work on gene-splicing had been conducted in his own laboratory. Berg's complaint (and possibly Morrow's) illustrates the differences in norms, criteria and practices in attribution of credit within the scientific community, and the granting of patent rights by government.

A second consideration that the reviewer cited by Reimers is pointing to is the "basic" nature of the invention itself. Because rDNA technology facilitated the genetic engineering of new organisms it was essentially a process invention or a "tool" rather than a product. In addition, it had widespread applications. Hence, rDNA technology is what is commonly termed an "enabling technology." Although Reimers had originally conceived of granting an exclusive license to this technology, as his conversation with Cohen above indicates, he soon decided that the patent should be licensed in such a way that the technology would be widely diffused:

Typically, we license exclusively, because most university technology is undeveloped. . . . But when you've got a basic tool, such as this, you want to get it out broadly and nonexclusively. (Reimers 1997)

Despite this policy, Boyer reported that he received a certain amount of criticism from scientific colleagues about his agreement to patent the new technology (Boyer 1997). However, he attributed their concerns to a misperception that patenting would prevent their using the technology in research. Patents, however, only exclude others from putting a technology into practice in commerce; patented technologies may be used freely in research without a license and, indeed, the intention of the patent documents is to provide enough detail so that others may easily imitate new technologies. According to Boyer's accounts, the new technology was widely diffused within the community of molecular scientists within a year of its discovery, not least because of Cohen and Boyer's own willingness to distribute their plasmid (the specific cell they engineered in their experiment) essentially to any scientist who requested it.[8]

It is also important to note that the importance of rDNA as an enabling technology was not the only consideration in Reimer's

[8] *See* footnote 7.

decision to license it broadly. He was also apparently concerned that, unless the licenses were offered non-exclusively and at low cost, the validity of the patent itself might be in question because the patented technology concerned only the process of gene-splicing itself, and not the stage at which proteins were expressed from the newly engineered organisms.

Monoclonal antibodies

Invention
Antibodies are proteins made by the human immune system that recognize invading microbes, viruses, or tumor cells and stick to them. This sticking signals to the rest of the immune system a call to attack and destroy the invaders. Monoclonal antibodies (mAbs) were discovered in 1975 by Georges Köhler and Cesar Milstein at the Medical Research Council (MRC) Laboratory of Molecular Biology in Cambridge, UK. The MRC is somewhat similar to the National Institutes of Health in the USA: it both funds research in universities and has its own research laboratories. Hence, as in the case of rDNA, the research that led to the discovery of mAbs was conducted within the sphere of public research (Cambrosio & Keating 1995; Milstein 2000; Robbins-Roth 2000).

Köhler and Milstein were looking for a method of reproducing specific antibodies *in vitro* in order to further their research on the characteristics of the antibodies themselves. They fused rodent antibody-producing cells with immortal tumor cells (myelomas) from the bone marrow of mice to produce a fused cell, which they called a "hybridoma." A hybridoma has the ability of the cancer cell to reproduce almost indefinitely, plus the ability of the immune cell to make antibodies. These fused cells may then be screened to isolate those hybridomas producing antibodies of a determined antigen-specificity and required affinity. Given the right nutrients, these specific hybridomas will grow and divide almost indefinitely, enabling the mass production of antibodies of a single type (i.e. mAbs). For this breakthrough the scientists won the Nobel Prize in Medicine in 1984.

Intellectual property rights
Unlike rDNA, the technology for mAbs was never patented by the inventing scientists. As in the case of rDNA, however, there was

a considerable amount of debate about how the property rights to this technology should be disposed. One account is provided by Milstein himself in an article in *Immunology Today* (Milstein 2000). In this article, Milstein records that he recognized that he and Köhler had developed a new process for making mAbs in large quantities, something that had not been achieved previously although it had been attempted by a number of other scientists (Cambrosio & Keating 1995). He recognized that the new technology was potentially patentable and sent a copy of the preprint of the first article describing the invention to the headquarters of the MRC, which passed it along to the organization responsible for patenting inventions in public research, the National Research and Development Corporation (NRDC). In a now-famous decision, the NRDC concluded that the invention was not patentable. On 7 October 1976, the NRDC wrote a letter to the MRC stating their reasons for this decision, as follows:

Although they [i.e. Köhler and Milstein] also suggest that the cultures which they have developed, or rather similar cultures, could be valuable for medical and industrial use, I think this statement should be taken as a matter of a long-term potential, rather than immediate application. . . . It is certainly difficult for us to identify any immediate practical applications that could be pursued as commercial venture . . . In summary, therefore, unless further work indicates a diagnostic application or industrial end product that we can protect, despite the disclosure of the *Nature* chapter, we would not suggest taking any further action ourselves.[9]

What is notable here is that the decision not to patent is based on the fact that the invention could not be shown to have utility (i.e. usefulness in commercial application). The reasons given by the NRDC make no mention of the issue of patenting an extensible technology, as was important in the rDNA decision.

   In a subsequent evaluation of the decision not to patent mAbs, it was concluded, "No-one, including Dr. Milstein, really appreciated the full commercial potential of a piece of outstanding academic work" (Tansey & Catterall 1995). Milstein himself has observed:

Today, it is difficult to appreciate the atmosphere prevalent at the time. Scientists working for the MRC and other publicly funded research

---

[9] *Technology Transfer in Britain*, p. 9 – cited from the original letter – the original letter may be found also at: www.path.cam.ac.uk/~mrc7/mab25yrs/index.html

institutions had no particular interest in patenting issues, and certainly no incentive to patent their inventions. ... At the time, there was no technology transfer office in the NRDC. (Milstein 2000, p. 363)

On another occasion, Milstein remarked:

Then, of course, there is the issue of the ownership and the patenting and what you call the scandal and the controversial issue of why the patent was not taken. Not less interesting perhaps at the time is what was the patenting atmosphere in this country and indeed elsewhere, particularly in the emerging field of biotechnology, and I am not referring to whether we thought it was good patenting or whether it was bad, whether discoveries should be given to the world of patents were morally justified or not, but rather what was the attitude towards genetic engineering patents themselves and what were the conditions, the incentives, the involvement of scientists themselves, or indeed research institutions, in Britain for patenting issues. (Tansey & Catterall 1995, p. 7)

According to Milstein, the two scientists felt reluctant to discuss the technological applications in their first publication after its discovery:

We felt somewhat shy, as if we were blowing our own trumpet too much by putting that sentence at the end. In the end we decided we should because we were convinced that that was going to be true. ... We were rather shy about the issue of patenting therefore. (Tansey & Catterall 1995, p. 8)

Milstein himself was apparently relieved at the NRDC decision to not seek a patent on mAbs. Under the European patenting system, patents are granted not to those who are first to invent, as is the case in the USA, but to those who are first to file for a patent. This means that any research being done on a process or product, which might qualify for a patent but is not yet at a sufficient stage of development to qualify for a patent, must be done in secrecy, otherwise a patent may be granted to a competitor, even if they are not the original inventor. Thus, had the NRDC been interested in pursuing a patent claim, Köhler and Milstein would have needed to conduct further research required for the patent in secrecy, rather than being able to conduct their research according to the academic norm of "open science" (Merton 1973, 1977).

However, only two years after this decision by the NRDC not to patent mAbs, scientists at the Wistar Institute in Philadelphia applied for two US patents on hybridomas they had developed – using melanoma cell lines given them by Köhler and Milstein. Milstein publicly opposed the granting of these patents for two reasons. First, he claimed that they were based on obvious developments from public knowledge – that is, the original invention that he and Köhler had developed. Second, he claimed that they were based not on a practiced application of mAbs, but on an idea of how to make a practical application. That is, the invention had not been proven to work in practice (Milstein 2000).[10] It is noteworthy that Milstein did not object to the fact that he and Köhler had supplied the myeloma cell line used by the Wistar Institute scientists in their patent claims. Apparently, Köhler and Milstein actively promoted diffusion of their technology by sharing their cell line with a number of other scientists, without placing legal restrictions on their use (Cambrosio & Keating 1995), similar to the diffusion efforts of Cohen and Boyer with rDNA technology.

Echoing the debate at Stanford, Milstein has also questioned whether it is appropriate for scientists to pursue patenting of inventions developed with public funds:

Within our laboratory, we established a set of principles. The public interest should come first, the scientific interest of the inventors – second, and making money should be considered only in the light of the first two priorities. (Milstein 2000, p. 363)

In his own laboratory, Milstein has favored a policy of broad licensing of patented inventions, similar to the approach taken by Reimers at Stanford for licensing rDNA.

---

[10] (i) In order to qualify for a patent, an invention must be shown to satisfy five criteria, as follows (Merges *et al.* 1997): *Patentability:* The subject matter must be an invention or subject that it has been agreed can qualify for a patent. (e.g. new life forms created by genetic engineering were only recently determined to be patentable; ideas are not patentable under any circumstances, only technologies). (ii) *Novelty:* The invention must be the first invention of its type. The applicant must show that there is no "prior art" (i.e. prior identical invention) in either the public domain, or patented by any other party. (iii) *Utility:* An invention must be determined to be "useful" to qualify for a patent. (iv) *Non-obviousness:* The invention must be shown to be not of a nature such that a person of ordinary skill could produce it. (v) *Enablement:* The patent documents must provide sufficient information to enable others to practice the invention. That is, the invention must be put into the commons as a practicable technology. This means that many inventions require considerable further development after they are originally invented.

Innovation diffusion: patenting, publications, and commercialization

Patenting and commercialization

Since 1975 an entire industry has developed based on biotechnology, especially on the two technologies discussed in this chapter. Between 1975 and 2000, more than 3500 surviving new biotechnology firms (NBFs) were founded worldwide; of these, 2400 were located in the USA and a further 600 in the UK.[11] Many of these firms depend directly on public science for key research activities, including: the transfer of highly trained, and often highly productive, scientists from the public research sector (e.g. Kenney 1986; Liebeskind *et al.* 1996; Zucker, Darby & Armstrong 2002); licensing of patents from universities and other public research institutions (Kenney 1986; Mowery *et al.* 2001); and ongoing research agreements with public research scientists, either by funding research programs, consultancies, or joint in-house research efforts (Kenney 1986; Liebeskind *et al.* 1996; Powell, Koput & Smith-Doerr 1996; Powell 1998). Patents have played a very important role in the founding and funding of NBFs; they are often unable to obtain funding from venture capitalists or other sources unless they can demonstrate that they can obtain, or develop, a patent portfolio. One reason for this is that most of the biotechnology industry may be considered a subfield of the pharmaceutical industry, where patents are a key to profitability (Cohen, Nelson & Walsh 2000). Patents are also important to other applications of biotechnology, such as plant breeding, animal breeding, and chemical applications.

Although patents may be important to the production of products in the pharmaceutical and related areas, it is possible that the patenting and narrow licensing of research tools or enabling technologies such as the ones we study here could slow and/or narrow commercialization of public research. Specifically, if an important enabling technology is patented and licensed narrowly, or even exclusively, other firms wishing to use that technology in the development of their own products would need to seek a sublicense from

---

[11] These data are drawn from *The Biotechnology Directory*, 2001.

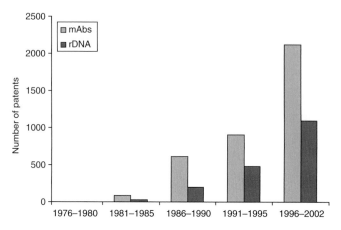

Figure 5.1 Number of patents in the US Patents and Trademark Office (PTO) database, by technology and year.

the primary licensee(s) in order to do so. This would create a situation in which, indeed, it may not be worthwhile for potential sublicensees to pursue product development, because the primary licensee(s) may be able to charge monopoly (or oligopoly) prices for use of their technology. In such cases, from a social welfare point of view, the enabling technology will be "under-used," relative to its potential value (Mazzolini & Nelson 1998a, 1998b). Thus, for such technologies, the exclusive licensing provisions of federal regulations may have the opposite effect than that intended; that is, they may choke off commercialization, rather than promote it. Indeed, Mazzolini and Nelson (1998a, 1998b) and Nelson (2002) have argued that, for certain classes of inventions such as the ones we examine here, patents and/or exclusive licenses are unnecessary as incentives for commercialization.

Our data provide some considerable support for the argument that non-patenting of enabling technologies does not inhibit their use in commercial applications. These are given in Figure 5.1. The figure shows the number of patented products that were developed using either rDNA or mAbs between 1976 and 2002. The counts were derived by searching the United States Patent and Trademark Office (PTO) database for patents that cited either of the two technologies in their patent claims section. For rDNA, we used the phrases "rDNA"

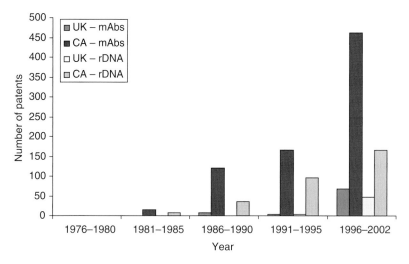

Figure 5.2 Number of patents in the US Patents and Trademark Office (PTO) database, by technology, year, and country or state.

or "recombinant DNA" in our search; for mAbs, we used the phrases "MAbs" or "monoclonal antibodies."

Figure 5.1 shows that, in all, more than 3600 new products were developed and patented based on the mAbs technology, and over 1800 new products were developed and patented using rDNA technology from their date of invention until March 2002. Furthermore, the figure shows that use of these technologies has increased steadily and significantly since their discovery in the 1970s; the number of products patented between 1996 and 2002 was more than twice the number of products patented between 1991 and 1995. Had these two technologies been patented and narrowly licensed, it is unlikely that such extensive subsequent development would have taken place or indeed could have taken place.

In Figure 5.2 we present similar data for the two largest geographical centers of the biotechnology industry: California and the UK. Again, these data show a continuous and significant increase in the development of patented products using the two technologies. Interestingly, for the mAbs technology, which was developed in the UK, the number of subsequent patents based on mAbs was significantly higher for inventors in California than inventors in the UK (as was the number of subsequent patents based on rDNA.) This shows that spillovers from this technology were not confined locally, as has been shown by other studies (e.g. Zucker, Darby & Brewer 1998). We discuss the diffusion of the mAbs technology to the USA further below.

With regard to the biotechnology industry, both technologies are broadly diffused. First, rDNA is used in the production of almost all proteins that are produced in the biotechnology industry, because gene-splicing is a necessary step in creating cells that will express proteins in sufficient quantities to produce therapeutic compounds such as growth factors, hormones, and immunomodulation compounds (e.g. interleukins).

Genetic engineering is also widely used for developing new drug-delivery systems and in veterinary applications, as well as in the production of hosts of other products, such as new plant and animal species, and new organisms used in the food, waste disposal, energy, and mining industries (Bains 1998). In addition, over 350 new biotechnology firms worldwide are specialized to genetic engineering technology.[12] With regard to mAbs, there are over 730 firms worldwide using the technology.[13] Today, mAbs are directed to many clinical markets, including cancer, cardiovascular diseases, inflammatory disorders, transplant rejection, and cancer (Robbins-Roth 2000, p. 56).

Other factors contributing to innovation diffusion

Whilst we have argued above that the nonpatenting (of mAbs) and the broad licensing (of rDNA) have been important to their diffusion and commercial exploitation, we should note here that their intellectual property regimens were only one of the factors that led to their important role in the development of the biotechnology industry: their extensive diffusion also called for other "public-spirited" actions. Even if an inventor licenses her technology broadly to other parties,

---

[12] These data were obtained by searching in *The Biotechnology Directory*, *2001* using the search terms "gene cloning," "gene transfer," and "protein engineering."

[13] These data were obtained by searching in *The Biotechnology Directory*, *2001* using the search terms "monoclonal antibodies" and "hybridomas."

or even publishes it without patenting, she may still prevent others from practicing the invention if she has exclusive ownership of complementary assets that are necessary to put the patent into use (Teece 1986). Specifically, in the case of microbiology, specialized assets such as cell lines, reagents, computer programs for analyzing molecules, or tacit know-how of experimental routines may be necessary for development and commercialization (Eisenberg 1996). Thus, whereas the patent (or other publication) may publish the *intellectual* property, other *real or intellectual* property may also be necessary for the invention to be put into use by others, either in public research or in commercial applications.

In the case of both rDNA and mAbs, the technologies were not only widely published in scientific journals, at presentations, specialized meetings, and in the case of rDNA, in the patent document, they were also diffused by the scientists sharing their actual research materials – that is, cell lines – with other parties. In the case of rDNA, not only was the process patented, the patented product (the new cell line) was also widely distributed by Cohen and Boyer (Hughes 2001). According to Cohen's own account, the rDNA invention was widely diffused within one year after its invention.

In similar fashion, Milstein went to considerable effort to popularize the use of mAbs technology in scientific research, not only by giving presentations and organizing special meetings, but also by distributing his line of myeloma cells to other scientists who requested it. The original diffusion of mAbs technology took place from Milstein's laboratory to those of other researchers with whom he was closely affiliated. For example, Georges Köhler had been visiting Milstein's laboratory from the Basel Institute of Immunology when the two invented the technology; he transferred the technology back to the Basel Institute at the end of his visit. Milstein also sent cell lines to laboratories at the University of Cologne, the Wistar Institute, and the University of Pennsylvania (Cambrosio & Keating 1995). The cell line was brought to the USA by Leonard Herzenberg of Stanford Medical School. Herzenberg had spent a sabbatical year during 1976–1977 in Milstein's laboratory, where he learned about the technology. Herzenberg did much to popularize the use of mAbs on his return, organizing a special meeting on the new technology at the National Cancer Institute, and distributing myeloma cell lines and mAbs essentially to anyone who asked for them. This latter approach by

Herzenberg reflected an ideal similar to that expressed by Milstein (2000):

When the first few [hybridomas] were made it created a situation of haves and have nots ... For the most part, everybody was playing very close to the bat. They gave their friends some antibodies, but they were not going to give the antibodies out. They were generally not going to make them publicly available. From our point of view, we thought very differently. (Cambrosio & Keating 1995, p. 94)

Soon, Herzenberg found the job of providing hybridomas too burdensome, and at this point, he entered into an agreement with Becton Dickinson to produce them commercially.

Early commercialization

As we have mentioned above, the inventions of rDNA and mAbs were key factors in the development of the biotechnology industry. Below we provide a brief discussion of the early stages of commercialization of the two technologies.

With regard to rDNA, the first dedicated biotechnology company ever founded – Genentech – was founded by Herbert Boyer, in collaboration with Bob Swanson, a venture capitalist. By his own account, Boyer became interested in the commercial application of rDNA technology early on (Boyer 1997). Before meeting up with Swanson, Boyer had approached at least one other drug company, but it was not interested. At the time of the invention of rDNA, Swanson was a venture capitalist working with Kleiner Perkins. Whilst he was experienced in funding new technology firms, Swanson was actively looking for new opportunities outside the established areas of venture capital lending at that time, which were mostly in the computer industry. He obtained a list of participants at an important biotechnology conference (held at Asilomar in 1975), and systematically contacted each one regarding possible commercialization of the science. When he reached Boyer, Boyer was receptive and invited him over to his office to talk. Eventually, the two men formed a partnership – Genentech – to commercialize the rDNA technology. Interestingly, Swanson approached Riemers and asked him to grant an exclusive license to Genentech for the entire rDNA technology; however, Reimers refused. Nonetheless, Genentech has developed a number of new patented products using the rDNA technology. However, Genentech did run into problems over property rights regarding rDNA: in the 1990s, the firm was sued by the University of California for illegally taking cell lines that were the real property of the university to its own laboratories. The case went to trial, but Genentech settled the suit (for $350 million) before the jury could return a verdict.

After the formation of Genentech, Swanson quit Kleiner Perkins and went to work for the firm full-time. Boyer, however, never conducted research directly for the new firm; instead, Genentech funded his laboratory at UCSF, and also entered into research contracts with other scientists at the City of Hope and Cal Tech, both in the Los Angeles area. Swanson and Boyer's first business plan was to produce human insulin, using rDNA. (At that time, human insulin was very scarce, and patients were obliged to use the less pure and effective bovine insulin.) The firm's research program first proved the usefulness of the rDNA technology, reproducing a smaller and simpler protein, somatostatin, and then moved on to successfully reproducing human insulin: the first major pharmaceutical product developed using biotechnology. In its early days, Genentech's research was financed by Kleiner Perkins. Later, the firm entered into a joint venture with Eli Lilly, which dominated the market for bovine insulin.

Although Boyer never conducted research directly for Genentech, he served as vice-president of the firm until 1990, and he still retains a seat on its board of directors. He has become wealthy from his shareholdings in the firm, despite his original lack of interest in benefiting from royalties from patenting the technology. Many other new biotechnology firms have been founded subsequently based on the rDNA technology, including industry giants Chiron and Amgen.

Unlike Boyer's involvement with Genentech, the two inventors of mAbs were reluctant to become involved with its commercialization. Köhler, by his own account, owns no patent rights to this day. In the Wellcome Witnesses seminar (1995) he was quoted as saying:

I am surprised at all the fuss over patenting and the discussion here. Scientists are not the persons who should patent; some other mechanism has to be found, and the pharmaceutical industry has the mechanisms.

Milstein was also reluctant to get involved with commercialization:

In 1980 Celltech was created, based on development that had been going on at LMB and my lab, and I was asked to be on the Council of Celltech and didn't want to do it but thought I ought to. But I couldn't accept the way

Celltech were doing things and the atmosphere, and I resigned a year later. In 1985 changes in the law were made and the labs and scientists not the NRDC were allowed to take out patents. There was a conflict between Celltech and LMB [the Laboratory of Molecular Biology at the MRC] and LMB broke away from Celltech and did not use them as patent agents. ... There should be rules based on: (1) the interest of the taxpayer, I mean responsibility to the public at large; (2) the interest of protecting the scientist; (3) making money must come last. This is the least important consideration. (Tansey & Catterall 1995, p. 30)

The early commercialization of mAbs technology took place in Switzerland and the USA. In Switzerland, Roche obtained access to the new technology through the Basel Institute of Immunology upon Köhler's return in 1976. Roche applied the invention to both diagnostic research and to isolating biologically interesting proteins such as interferon.[14] The technology was transferred to the USA by Dr. Leonard Herzenberg, who then transferred the technology to Becton Dickinson for the purpose of producing hybridomas for use in scientific research. The technology was also transferred from Herzenberg's laboratory to Dr. Royston at the University of California, San Diego. Royston and another scientist, Birndorf, then obtained venture capital funding and founded a new biotechnology firm, Hybritech, to exploit mAbs technology commercially. After Hybritech's founding, other new firms were also founded to exploit mAbs technology, including Centocor, IDEC Pharmaceuticals, Biotherapeutics, Genetic Systems, Invitron, Synbiotics, and Xoma. Other rDNA-based biotechnology firms such as Genentech and Cetus also developed in-house capabilities in mAbs technology to complement their rDNA technologies in new product development and production (Robbins-Roth 2000, p. 54).

Publishing and technological diffusion

As Agrawal and Henderson (2002) have shown, patenting and licensing is only one means by which innovations are diffused and transferred to commercial use. Another key mechanism in technology diffusion and transfer is publication. To measure publication of scientific articles reporting research on rDNA and mAbs, we use two

[14] Cited from the Roche website: www.roche.com/home/company/com_hist_intro/com_hist-1965.htm

approaches. First, using the website of the Science Citation Index (http://scientific.thomsonreuters.com/products/sci/) we measure the number of academic publications that have cited each of the three foundation articles describing the rDNA technology and the four foundation articles that describe the mAbs technology.[15] These data are shown in Table 5.1. The table shows that the three foundation articles for rDNA technology were cited 1102 times between date of publication and 2002; for the mAbs technology, the total number of citations is an amazing total of 14,207! These data demonstrate that these key articles have contributed greatly to subsequent research and development work in molecular biology.

Second, to demonstrate the diffusion of these two technologies in the research literature, we measured the number of articles that contain the words "rDNA" or "Recombinant DNA" and "MAbs" or "Monoclonal antibodies" in their abstracts up to the year 2001. The results are presented in Figure 5.3 and Figure 5.4. Figure 5.3 presents these data for all publications included in the MEDLINE database. The figure shows first that many more articles cited the mAbs technology than cited the rDNA technology. Apparently, the mAbs invention stimulated more research than did rDNA, for reasons we cannot explain here. (For instance, we cannot attribute this difference to differences in their intellectual property regimens, although rDNA certainly has had as much if not more impact in commercial applications to date.) The figures also show that rates of citation of mAbs technology in publications started to decline in 1994, apparently indicating its declining importance in research, if not in commercial applications.

Finally, in Figure 5.4 we present data on the number of articles in two top-ranked scientific journals – *Science* and *Proceedings of the Academy of Sciences* – that cite either of the two technologies. Again, the figure shows that rates of citation of the mAbs technology were far higher than rates of citation for rDNA. This figure also shows that rates of citation for both technologies increased fairly rapidly after their initial publication, but then declined. The decline in citations for the mAbs technology in these two top journals began in 1988,

---

[15] The three foundation articles for rDNA were identified by Hughes (2001). The four foundation articles for MAbs were identified by Cambrosio and Keating (1995).

Table 5.1 *Rate of citation of the foundation articles for rDNA and mAbs,* based on the website of the Science Citation Index from initial publication to 2002*

Number of article	Year of publication	Number of times cited
rDNA		
rDNA[1]	1973	668
rDNA[2]	1974	139
rDNA[3]	1974	295
mAbs		
mAbs[1]	1975	10,059
mAbs[2]	1976	1670
mAbs[3]	1977	1665
mAbs[4]	1977	813

* The foundation articles are as follows.

rDNA (Source: Hughes 2001):

[1]Cohen, S., Chang, A. C., Boyer, H. W. and Helling, R. B. (1973) Construction of biologically functional bacterial plasmids in vitro. *Proceedings of the National Academy of Sciences* 70, 3240–3244;

[2]Chang, A. C. and Cohen, S. (1974) Genome construction between bacterial species *in vitro*: replication and expression of Staphylococcus plasmid genes in *Escherichia coli*. *Proceedings of the National Academy of Sciences* 71, 1030–1034;

[3]Morrow, J. F., Cohen, S., Chang, A. C., Boyer, H., Goodman, H. M. and Helling, R. B. (1974) Replication and transcription of eukaryotic DNA in *Escherichia coli*. *Proceedings of the National Academy of Sciences* 71, 1743–1747.

mAbs (Source: Cambrosio & Keating 1995):

[1]Köhler, G. and Milstein, C. (1975) Continuous cultures of fused cells secreting antibody of predefined specificity. *Nature* 256, 495–497;

[2]Köhler, G. and Milstein, C. (1976) Derivation of specific antibody-producing tissue culture and tumor cell lines by cell fusion. *European Journal of Immunology* 6, 292–295;

[3]Galfre, G., Howe, S. C., Milstein, C., Butler, G. W. and Howard, J. C. (1977) Antibodies to major histocompatability antigens produced by hybrid cell lines. *Nature* 266, 550–552;

[4]Williams, A., Galfre, G. and Milstein, C. (1977). Analysis of cell surfaces by xenogenetic myeloma-hybrid antibodies: differentiation antigen of rat lymphocytes. *Cell* 12, 663–673.

whereas, for rDNA, it appears to have begun in 1984, showing possibly that research using these technologies by top-ranked scientists declined earlier than their use in more pedestrian scientific research, or in research directed toward commercial development.

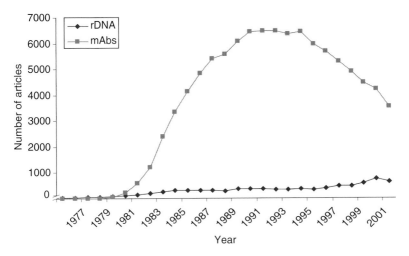

Figure 5.3 MEDLINE articles citing the two technologies, by year.

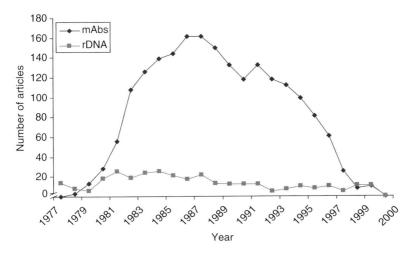

Figure 5.4 Articles published in *Science* and the *Proceedings of the Academy of Sciences*, by technology and year.

As in the case of patented products, it is important to note here that one reason that the two technologies diffused so rapidly in the world of scientific research – whether or not it was commercially motivated – is that Cohen and Boyer, and Köhler and Milstein, went to considerable efforts to promote their diffusion to other research scientists by giving presentations, training others, and sharing cell lines and other important research materials. Such cooperation would be unlikely in today's scientific community, where concerns over present and future intellectual property rights have made at least some scientists far more cautious about including others in their research teams, and far more restrictive in sharing information and research materials (Liebeksind & Oliver 1998).

Concluding remarks

In this chapter, we have offered some history and data on the property rights regimens and diffusion of two key inventions in biotechnology. The story of these two inventions has, however, been framed in the larger context of federal regulation and the development of broad norms about intellectual property regimens under which inventions developed in public science are claimed (using patents) and diffused (primarily through exclusive licensing). The two technologies that we have made the subject of this chapter were, unusually, not claimed or diffused in this way. The first of the two inventions, rDNA, occurred before the development of current US federal regulations; the second, mAbs, also occurred early in the history of this sub-field of molecular science, and took place in the UK. Hence, it might be argued that both inventions took place under an earlier regimen of "open science" (Merton 1973, 1977), rather than in the current climate of "contracted rights" and exchange (Liebeskind & Oliver 1998).

Although the regulatory environment of public science has changed, there has been a long debate, dating back at least 60 years, about how rights to the fruits of public science should be disposed (Eisenberg 1996). In our view, the data we present are supportive of the arguments made by Mazzolini and Nelson (1998a, 1998b) on this account: that any regulation of intellectual property in public science must, *inter alia*, take note of the technology in question. In the case of enabling technologies such as rDNA and mAbs, we consider it unlikely that such extensive development and diffusion would have taken place had these technologies been patented and exclusively, or narrowly, licensed. Meanwhile, the data we present on the degree of subsequent patenting using these technologies show that exclusive licensing was certainly not necessary to give firms an incentive to invest in their commercialization – a key argument that was invoked in developing the current federal regulations.

In addition to this evidence on intellectual property regimens, we also find it interesting and salient that both technologies were also diffused in terms of *real property* as their inventors went to considerable lengths to share cell lines and other research materials critical to putting them into practice. This behavior is consistent with the norms of open science, in which information and research materials flow freely and openly among scientists, and where intellectual property tends to be envisioned and enacted as a collective good, rather than as an individual one:

The distinctive anomalous character of intellectual property becoming fully established in the domain of science only by being openly given away (published) is linked with the normative requirement for scientists making use of the property to acknowledge (publish) the source. (Merton 1977, pp. 48–49)

The communal character of science is further reflected in the recognition by scientists of their dependency upon a cultural heritage to which they lay no differential claim. Newton's remark, "If I have seen further it is by standing on the shoulders of giants," expresses at once a sense of indebtedness to the common heritage and recognition of the essentially cooperative and (selectively) cumulated quality of science achievement. (Merton 1973, pp. 274–275)

As we have mentioned earlier in this chapter, we consider it unlikely that such a free sharing of such a valuable technology would take place today. The sense of an "open community" of scientific research has changed now that intellectual property rights have become a "taken for granted" norm in academic research, following the Bayh–Dole act of 1980 and the increasing role of industry in funding research at public institutions. This change in norms cannot be counted as other than a loss to the intellectual commons.

6 | The search for university–industry collaborations: linear and chaotic networking processes

Introduction

Recent organizational research focusses on issues of learning in networks (Oliver 2001; Beckman & Haunschild 2002; Hagedoorn & Duysters 2003; Hardy, Phillips & Lawrence 2003), all testing the degree to which organizational knowledge or decisions are based on learning gained through network-based exchanges. Since issues of technology-transfer and university–industry collaborations take an important role in explaining some of the learning features in knowledge intensive industries (Liebeskind *et al.* 1996; Powell, Koput & Smith-Doerr 1996; Owen-Smith *et al.* 2002), attention has been given to the issues of learning and knowledge-transfer across the different institutional contexts of academia and industry.

It is now well understood that biotechnology-related products are developed within interorganizational networks of universities, dedicated biotechnology firms, and large pharmaceutical firms (Liebeskind *et al.* 1996; Liebeskind & Oliver 1998; Oliver & Liebeskind 1998; Powell, Koput & Smith-Doerr 1996). The important role played by universities in biotechnology product development (Zucker, Darby & Brewer 1998) requires the establishment of collaborations between universities and biotechnology firms through which basic and applied science are transferred into products. These symbiotic interrelations result from the constant interdependence between the two types of institutions (Liebeskind *et al.* 1996; Oliver & Montgomery 2000). The motivations of the participants in university–industry alliances vary from needs for funding academic research to scientific reputation and better access to corporate R&D consulting options (Nelkin, Nelson & Kiernan 1987).

This chapter aims to explore the elements composing the processes through which research and development (R&D) collaborations between universities and industry are formed while acknowledging the complexities embedded in the process. The process of finding an industrial collaborating partner can be highly complex. First, the search process suffers from the limits of "bounded rationality" resulting from the wide range of opportunities and endless sources of information (Simon 1976). Second, a high level of complexity exists in specifying contractual arrangements for intellectual capital transactions (Powell 1990). Third, the environment of the biotechnology industry is characterized as extremely complex, dynamic, and hypercompetitive (Liebeskind *et al.* 1996). Owing to the lack of clear information about potential collaborators and their histories, the matching process is based greatly on trust (Powell 1990; Kornberg 1995; Oliver 1997; Liebeskind & Oliver 1998), which may lead to misjudgments (Lampel & Shapira 2001). These factors combined create a highly risky and complex environment for establishing university–industry R&D collaborations. Therefore the process of networking for R&D collaborative alliances may be compared to finding a needle in a haystack, where the needle is ambiguously defined and the haystack is highly complex, and it is attached to a viable outcome.

Networking for R&D collaborations

Recent research on alliance search processes found that firms apply a relatively uniform alliance-formation process (Mitsuhashi 2002). The process includes five stages: defining opportunities; identifying sets of prospective partners; making contact; proceeding with due diligence processes; and making deals. These stages are linearly structured in order to reduce uncertainties about partners' technological competences, partner future behavior, and the potential commercial success of the collaboration. In order to reduce opportunism and to establish trust, alliances are formed through consecutive meetings and contractual arrangements of nondisclosure agreements, and detailed due-diligence tests and other information on patents and publications and alliances' history.

Such rational decision-making processes are based on hierarchal stages of elimination of options, and result from a managerial rationale that aims to find the best solution to the problem. Simon (1976, p. 68) implicitly points out the major weakness of this format, namely, that it leads to a preference of a particular line of action, chosen only because it appears preferable. This kind of search process is directed toward risk-minimization, efficiency, and the achievement of the best economic return, and thus I refer to it as a "linear rational model."

Despite the simplifying and what is perceived as "risk-minimizing" power of the linear search process described by Mitsuhashi (2002), awareness of the many unknowns in networking for knowledge-based collaborations calls for the introduction of complexity approaches. The complexity paradigm, developed during the last decade, offers an interdisciplinary framework for studying complex interactions and emergent properties. Although it has been stated that the science of complexity in the study of organizations is still at its pre-paradigmatic stage (Anderson *et al.* 1999), it has recently started penetrating the social sciences (Anderson *et al.* 1999; Pigliucci 2000). Through the complexity paradigm "Science, it seems had finally cracked the next level of analysis, one that will replace the Cartesian approach and substitute a new, scientific holism for the old reductionism" (Pigliucci 2000, p. 62).

Chaos, usually a synonym for randomness or nondeterministic phenomena, refers in mathematic theory to deterministic phenomena with special properties that make outcome predictability very difficult. Complexity theory may also attempt to study chaotic systems (1) that are made of many interacting parts and (2) their interactions result in emergent properties which are not immediately reducible to a simple sum of the properties of the individual components (Pigliucci 2000, pp. 62–63). Complex adaptive systems exhibit surprising and non-linear behavior (Anderson 1999). Such adaptive systems are characterized by four elements:

- *Agents with schemata*: Scholars who view organizations as natural systems have shown that rules often do not govern actions (Meyer & Rowan 1977; Scott 1995). Agents in complex adaptive systems (CAS) need not be the prisoners of a fixed set of rules. "Because agents can possess multiple competing schemata at any one time, CAS models embody Campbell's idea that evolution occurs through a nested hierarchy of selective systems. Evolving actors develop various selective systems so that they can experiment and fail without being killed" (Anderson 1999).
- *Self-organizing networks sustained by importing energy*: Systems that consist of independent actors whose interactions are governed

by a system of recursively applied rules naturally generate stable structure. They self-organize, and regulatory processes emerge without the intervention of a central controller. Self-organization or "autogenesis" is the natural result of nonlinear interaction. Self-organization only occurs in open systems that import energy from the outside (Prigogine & Stengers 1984).

- *Co-evolution to the edge of chaos*: Consistent with the bounded rationality notion of March and Simon (1958), agents are unable to forecast the system-level consequences of their individual choices, and so they optimize their own fitness, not that of the organization.
- *Recombination and system evolution*: Simon (1996) has argued that adaptive entities contain an adaptive inner-environment based on nested hierarchies that contain other adaptive systems. These subsystems are themselves subject to evolutionary pressures. Every element can change over time, thus there is no way to predict the trajectory of the evolution of each subsystem – for example, in this chapter – the transfer collaboration.

A fundamental implication associated with the science of complexity is that order naturally emerges in systems no matter how simple, complex, nonlinear, or chaotic they are through self-organization (Lewin 1999). Following the basic assumption of cybernetics (Anderson 1999; Oliver & Montgomery 2001), when a system is open to receiving energy from the environment it will tend to create order. Without new energy a closed system will decay into maximum disorder and chaos. Lewin (1999, p. 215) argues that the implication of naturally evolving systems calls for new management logic which requires the facilitation of emerging processes, coupled with openness to bottom-up processes and acceptance of equifinality. The notion of *equifinality* (Meyer, Tsui & Hinings 1993), that states that under complexity assumptions there are many different routes which lead to the same equally viable outcome, is of value here. In contrast to rational theory, which seeks to maximize efficiency and make decisions based on linear rationality, complexity theory assumes equifinal processes.

Metaphor for collaboration searches

The literature on organizational metaphor is interdisciplinary in nature. It has roots in philosophy, linguistics, psychology, and anthropology.

More recently, organizational researchers have used metaphor in order to depict cognitive processes in an illustrative sense (Morgan, 1980, 1983; Grant & Oswick 1996). Metaphor serves as a cognitive tool that facilitates the ability to see the world in a different manner and encourages different ways of thinking (Lakoff & Johnson 1980; Barrett & Cooperrider 1990). Following Morgan's (1986) original metaphors of organizations as machines, organisms, brains, culture, political arena, psychological prisons, flow, and transformation, other organizational scholars have used this framework. Some examples include the brain (Broekstra 1996), embryos (Clegg & Gray 1996), and man (Doving 1996).

The use of metaphors as an analytical tool allows us to depict the cognitive perception of the emergence of collaborating networks as embedded in the social reality context of actors and their choices of action. For this purpose, two distinct metaphorical patterns for university–industry collaboration networking search are suggested: the "linear" and the "chaos" metaphors.

The chapter is organized as follows. First, descriptions of the method and the data used as illustrations for the metaphors and trends discussed in this chapter are provided. Next, the complex environment in which these networks emerge is described, highlighting the specific attributes which make the formation of these partnerships puzzling. Then, the reader is offered some examples from the author's field notes about central areas of ambiguity, illustrated by technology-transfer officers and scientists. Further, two "ideal-type" network search metaphors are presented, analyzed, and placed into context. Discussion of the implications of these models summarizes the chapter.

Methodology

This chapter is based on insights from a total of 35 in-depth interviews with: (1) 15 university and nine industry scientists; (2) nine TT officers; and (3) two university R&D vice-presidents, all involved in Israeli biotechnology R&D. Because little is known about the formation of technology-transfer collaborations, a case study approach to building theory was used, as suggested by Yin (1984) and Eisenhardt (1989).

Owing to confidentiality agreements with the interviewees, only limited information on them is provided. The interviews were conducted over two periods: 25 interviews were conducted during the academic year of 1996–1997 and 10 additional interviews were conducted during 2003–2004. The additional interviews were conducted on issues which needed further in-depth rich texts and scope of perceptions and experiences, and in order to test the degree to which the initial findings were supported by additional interviews reflecting a later period.

The interviewees were selected based on a snowball sampling method, and all interviews were conducted on-site in three universities and in three biotechnology firms. In two universities, the R&D vice-president was interviewed as well. Further, technology-transfer officers in the three universities were interviewed: two officers were interviewed in one university, three officers in the second, and four in the third. The technology-transfer officers were asked to suggest names of scientists who were involved in biotechnology-related technology-transfer for further interviews (15 university scientists altogether). The technology-transfer officers and the scientists related to the university–industry collaborations were asked about their industrial counterparts in past and current collaborations. In a sense, the sample is a stratified one in which only actors involved in biotechnology-related university–industry technology-transfer were selected. This theoretical sampling method (Eisenhardt 1989, p. 537) was chosen with the aim of increasing the likelihood that the chosen cases were likely to replicate or to extend the emergent theory. Obviously, the richness of the data in the interviews is only partially captured, yet a careful analytical effort was made to depict some of the most general trends that seemed to emerge.

Each interview lasted between one and four hours. The interviews were based on a semi-structured format and typically began with an invitation to describe the interviewee's professional background. The interviewees were then asked to concentrate mainly on the reasons, advantages versus risk, and processes which led in general to the formation of university–industry research collaborations. Both the scientists and the technology-transfer officers were asked to share their views on the search process for university–industry collaborations. In addition, the interviews focussed on issues of intellectual property rights, university policies, scientists' interests, and potential conflicts in building effective collaborations.

The analytical synthesis offered in the chapter is based on content analysis of the interviews in which cross-case patterns were sought (Eisenhardt 1989, p. 540). Eisenhardt (1989) suggests that such searching may be based on the selection of categories or dimensions which emerge as central in respondents' answers, and within-group similarities coupled with intergroup differences may be elicited. This tactic was applied in the present study and the content analysis focussed on the perceptions of scientists and technology-transfer officers about developing new university–industry collaborations. In addition, the analysis searched for the actors' interpretation of efficiency and effectiveness of various processes through which such collaborations may be formed.

After generating two lists of quotations, from the university scientists and the technology-transfer officers, these were sorted into general categories that reflected the largest areas of ambiguity and differential perceptions (a selection of the most distinct differential perceptions of the two groups is presented in Table 6.1). The analysis searched for common themes among the respondents of each group on a set of topics in which ambiguity seemed to be dominant. By use of a table format, in which the distinctive perceptions of scientists and technology-transfer officers were contrasted, it became apparent that the two groups had different perceptions of issues related to intellectual property rights, the issue of scientific secrecy, and arrangements of university–industry technology-transfer.

At this point, it must be stated that the argument presented in this chapter does not attempt to capture all the possible perception differences between technology-transfer officers and academic scientists (and does not argue that these are dominant differences), neither does it call for generalizability of the findings. Rather, the goal is to illustrate and contextualize some of the cognitive differences between scientists and technology-transfer officers. The differences reveal a paradox of opposing perspectives or seemingly irrational findings (Lewis 2000) – that, despite existing policies about technology-transfer in all universities in Israel, scientists and technology-transfer officers tend to apply different perceptions concerning the emergence of technology-transfer collaborations, and that scientists tend to act, at times, in what may be perceived as an irrational way. The effort to untangle this paradox will be presented further in the chapter.

Table 6.1 *Areas of differential perceptions*

Areas of ambiguity	Scientists	Technology-transfer officers and vice presidents for R&D
Intellectual property rights	It is hard to detect where an idea originates. If I am on leave from my university and work in a laboratory in another university with other scientists, or in a biotechnology firm, and together we discover something, it is not clear who owns this discovery. (Genetics professor, large research university) Some of the discoveries came from ideas I gathered in a consulting job and had nothing to do with my work at the university – don't they become my property? Why should I give all my property rights to the university? (Microbiology professor, small research university) What is knowledge? It is what we learn from our research work and what we learn from others. If I do not talk with others about my work I do not learn enough. I get wonderful ideas through conversations with others, even when they are in very different areas. Whose knowledge is it then? Mine? Theirs? Ours? What is the value of this knowledge if it serves only one person? (Microbiology professor, large research university)	There are ways in which scientists try to claim individual rights to their ideas and not share them with the university. They may have a joint appointment with another university, and claim the ideas originated in the other institution – in this case, the invention belongs to our share in the scientist's appointment. The other "trick" is to claim that the idea originated while the scientist was on sabbatical or on leave of absence at another institution – I don't allow this, and did not allow it since I got this position. I also don't allow scientists to initiate contracts on their own with external companies – it all has to go through the university. ... Our scientists may be consultants to other companies but cannot be partners. We also don't permit our scientists to receive options or stocks from companies beyond what is approved by the university. Otherwise, it will not be clear whose interests does the scientist comply with. The university is fairly liberal. It allows 40 percent of the patent rights to the scientist and if the university establishes a company in order to continue the development, the scientist gets stocks in that company. (Vice president for R&D, large research university)

Table 6.1 (*cont.*)

Areas of ambiguity	Scientists	Technology-transfer officers and vice presidents for R&D
	University scientists who are working under a contract with a biotechnology firm cannot publish without its permission. It is clear that the firm can withhold any publication if it thinks it discloses information the firm wishes to keep secret. In addition, if the scientist does not alert the firm to new ideas, he will not receive additional financial support for their laboratory. In many respects, the firm "owns" the scientist. (Chemistry professor, large research university)	The university "owns" all rights to the intellectual capital of its scientists. A scientist cannot claim for a patent on his own. The law indicates that all patents belong to the employer, and there is no scientist who can claim to have an idea that originated during his nonwork time. If one of our scientists decides to found a company in order to commercialize his ideas, the university will sue him – this is against the law. (Technology-transfer officer, large research university)
Dilemmas regarding scientific secrecy	My laboratory is fully funded by the investing company, but I keep my sovereignty by applying for other external grants so that, at any point, I'll be able to tell the company to go on without me if we disagree. I apply for federal grants rather than for additional industrial funding because you can't collaborate innocently with two competitors. (Molecular biology professor, large research university)	Curiosity and creativity are the essence of science and these should not be blocked by the search for profit. Only societies which encourage curiosity and the search for the truth will benefit from their scientists. Their scientists reward the society in return. ... Science also needs a free flow of information and suffers from the need to hold information in this competitive world. (Vice-president for R&D, large research university)

Table 6.1 (*cont.*)

Areas of ambiguity	Scientists	Technology-transfer officers and vice presidents for R&D
	In conferences, scientists like to talk and do talk among themselves. If they would not do that they would not be considered scientists. While they talk and share ideas it is possible to gather valuable information. However, in order to avoid industry norms of espionage, I do not go to conferences on a company's budget, and therefore, I do not spy for them – let them send their own spies. (Molecular biology professor, large research university) The biotechnology industry is paranoid since it is hard to write a patent, the market is very competitive, and it is easy to take someone's idea and with a slight change make claim for having independent rights to it. … We are instructed and are signed in our contract for secrecy of our work and ideas. However, I have the feeling that everyone in Israel knows what we are doing, since here everyone is a friend of everyone … When I talk about technical issues, I avoid disclosing any information regarding my specific work. I am much more careful when I go out to scientific conferences. We attend conferences, listen to papers, and look at poster sessions, but hardly talk. (PhD scientist, eight years with a large biotechnology company)	Of course, there are these "astronauts" who say, "We are working for academic freedom in intellectual work. We do not care for the money." I would say that 80 percent of our scientists are thinking this way. We have "lost" many patent claims in the past, since the knowledge leaked. No investor will invest in our ideas if there is no patent application. (Vice-president for R&D, large research university) In the past, academic freedom and contribution to the mankind were the ideal. Today, the approach is different: if the scientist did not apply for a patent, and disclosed his discoveries without protecting them, no company will invest in his research, and thus there will not be any contribution to the mankind. (Technology-transfer officer, small research university)

Table 6.1 (*cont.*)

Areas of ambiguity	Scientists	Technology-transfer officers and vice presidents for R&D
	There are the bureaucratic-scientists who care mainly for the rights to intellectual capital, and thus promote secrecy. But then they end up with 100 percent of zero. I believe that we need to raise the curiosity of others in our projects, we need to take the risks and try to convince future investors that we are on to something important even if we did not finish the testing and validation phases. (Microbiology professor, large research university)	
Arrangements of university–industry technology-transfer	Scientists are incapable of running all the needed diplomacy for negotiating their ideas with external partners. So they go to the technology-transfer office here for assistance. But, the administrative people don't always know what is the right thing to do, and don't make all the right decisions. There are many cases where if the university had applied for a patent, the university would have made a lot of money out of royalties. On the other hand, there are many companies which make millions of dollars with our ideas, and the university does not see a cent of it. (Biology professor, small research university)	Consulting differs from collaboration. In consulting, the initiative comes from the external entity, while in collaboration you transfer intellectual capital for ownership of future returns. Most scientists do not understand the difference between the two issues, and transfer important knowledge in consulting jobs. They are "suckers" since they deliver valuable information without realizing what they are doing. I try to educate them to understand this issue and avoid disclosing intellectual capital without returns. (Technology-transfer officer, small research university)

Table 6.1 (*cont.*)

Areas of ambiguity	Scientists	Technology-transfer officers and vice presidents for R&D
	How does our company get services from universities or research centers? It is all on the basis of interpersonal relations and who has the knowledge or the equipment. They come to us and explain what they need, and ask for a price offer. They provide a very general description, such as we need such and such fermentor, or such a germ. Then, once we agree to collaborate, they tell us more about the project. It is all based on trust, and on the assumption that if this trust is violated, everyone will know about it and will never ask for our collaboration again. (Microbiologist, large biotechnology firm) There are various informal collaborations between our university and the firm. We reciprocate help and advice. These collaborations are not captured in formal contracts. On the very informal level, we pick up the phone and consult with them. This is not knowledge-transfer or collaboration, but just professional aid. Both sides benefit from it. (Molecular biologist, small research university)	When negotiating a collaboration contract with a biotechnology firm, I try to keep the scientist in the background. It is like a good chess game, and you need only one good player on each side. If the scientists interfere, the contract can be harmed. They are so eager to start the collaboration, and are willing to give the other side valuable information before the agreements are signed. They are also ready to receive less for the collaboration than I aim for, so I prefer to keep them in the background and allow them to participate only when the contract is ready to be signed. (Technology-transfer officer, small research university)

University–industry R&D collaborations in the biotechnology industry

As indicated, the biotechnology industry consists of firms involved in the research, development, and commercialization of a variety of products in the area of human health, agriculture, chemical and food production, and waste management, in which newly developed biotechnologies are used. The industry is characterized by hyper-competition, uncertainty, appropriability, and intellectual resource immobility, as well as a high dependence on university-based intellectual capital (Liebeskind *et al.* 1996; Zucker *et al.* 1996; Liebeskind & Oliver 1998).

Consequently, academic scientists in biotechnology-related academic areas may experience conflicting demands. On the one hand, they are, more than ever before, experiencing a large pool of opportunities for R&D collaborations with biotechnology firms. These collaborations enable academic researchers to acquire learning capabilities in the search for new frontier knowledge, provide opportunities to participate in breaking new discoveries, and to take part in multi-institutional, multidisciplinary research through the process of converting basic science into applied and marketable products. Yet, these collaborations embody constraints resulting from the growing institutional and legalistic requirements for intellectual capital protection by universities and biotechnology firms (Liebeskind & Oliver 1998; Liebeskind 2000). These requirements lead to increased secrecy (Liebeskind 2000) in the form of concealing research results, postponing the publication of new discoveries pending on filing patent applications, and refraining from information exchange with other scientists (Liebeskind & Oliver 1998). At the same time, because of high laboratory costs, academic scientists are constantly searching for grants and R&D collaborations to support their ongoing and future research.

Owing to two "resource holes" – the lack of research funding needed for academic biotechnology research and the perceived inability and/or lack of interest of firms to conduct basic research – university–industry codependence emerges. Thus, various university–industry collaborations emerge frequently. These collaborations may be based on joint research in the university laboratories, in the firm's laboratory, consulting relations, joint seminars, fellowships for the professor's students, and other forms (Etzkowitz 1998, p. 9; Oliver 2004).

Technology-transfer and academic science

In general, universities have come to realize that biotechnology-related basic research cannot innovate without large funds for basic research. Since federal or academic research funds are not sufficient for maintaining a fully equipped laboratory, research funds are raised through R&D collaborations with the industry (Liebeskind *et al.* 1996; Kreiner & Schultz 1993). In this respect, biotechnology is unique. One of the university R&D vice-presidents defined these characteristics as leading to a more complex scientific area than other "high-technology" areas such as information technology (IT):

> Biotechnology, unlike the electronic industry, is an industry with many gray colors, not blacks and whites. It does not deal with a correct or wrong equation, but is based on a lengthy, expensive, and intensive research. There are so many unclear and ambiguous parameters, and it is impossible to control for all the unexpected.

Basic and applied research in biotechnology does not have linear and predictable outcomes (Pisano 1996). Although this kind of research has many applied results, which, after patenting, may yield a high rate of return in terms of royalties to universities (Liebeskind 2000), research universities do not always encourage their scientists to focus on the applied aspects of biotechnology-related fields. Instead, they usually continue encouraging basic research, which builds reputation and facilitates success in raising funds from academic or national sources. Lee (1998) shows through a survey study of a large sample of university professors how university–industry R&D collaborations are perceived as likely to interfere with academic freedom to pursue long-term fundamental research.

Since universities became aware of the financial potential of the discoveries of their scientists they have become a major player in the commercial and patenting arena (Owen-Smith 2003). With heavy patenting policies following the Bayh–Dole Act in 1980 (Public Law 96–517) that gave universities rights to seek patents for discoveries made by scientists with support of federal funds, universities vigorously began to claim rights to their intellectual capital, whilst sharing a portion of their revenues from licensing their patents with the inventor scientist. In addition, overheads and potential royalties from such transfers have become a significant fraction in university budgets

(Liebeskind 2000). However, realizing that the financial potential in scientific discoveries may lead to increased secrecy in academic research, inappropriate licensing agreements, and conflicts of interests among universities, their scientists, students, and industrial research sponsors (Nelson 1998; Liebeskind 2000), Israeli universities also apply for patents in the US and elsewhere. Based on the US patent database, within the years between 1996 and 2002, 336 patents were assigned to Israeli universities and research institutes, based on inventions of Israeli academic scientists.

All seven universities in Israel have established technology-transfer offices and are seeking profits and royalties through patenting and contracting for scientific collaborations. Although university policies try to explicitly note rules for allocating royalties in this shifting academic terrain, in which the demarcation between basic and applied research is blurred and scientific entrepreneurship is on the rise (Etzkowitz 1998), much control remains at the scientists' level and the range of scientists' choices is evident (Owen-Smith & Powell 2001a). The blurring and reforming boundaries (or lack of them) between university and industrial research may lead to areas of ambiguity. For example, the distinction between contractual collaboration and consultation is blurred when the focus is on the flow of intellectual capital across institutional boundaries. Intellectual capital can be fully transmitted under either a collaborative or consultative governance form, and it is hard to specify the type and volume of knowledge that is transferred in each form of contract. More precisely, the boundaries of the transaction are not specified solely by the contractual agreement. The owner of this knowledge – the scientist – creates the limits of the transaction through his or her own interpersonal negotiations with industrial partners. Thus, the scientist remains quite flexible while the university administration does not have full ability to monitor all actions taken by the scientist. The university can rely only on the structure of the incentive system offered by the university, for intellectual property rights, to motivate scientists to secure the rights to their intellectual property. By forbidding direct contracting between scientists and industrial partners, the university administration places limits on the "free" transfer of intellectual capital. However, academic scientists still enjoy the freedom of publishing prior to patenting, exchanging open information about their scientific work, or disclosing their intellectual property to firms without securing returns (Liebeskind & Oliver 1998; Owen-Smith & Powell 2001b).

The industry seeks informal exchanges with academic scientists. Industrial scientists interviewed enjoy almost limitless research conference attendance. The following quotation depicts well the description that repeatedly appeared in the interviews of industrial scientists:

When I go to conferences, I don't know too many people, but it is known that it is easy to get tips from university scientists. We can ask them everything, and they tell freely everything they know – it is a pure pleasure. Those who come from the industry do not talk much, and avoid answering questions. When you are a university scientist – if you don't talk, you don't exist. If you don't publish you don't exist – so you want to talk. In the industry, the contrary is true – if you do talk, you don't exist. (Male PhD scientist, five years with the company)

At these conferences, industrial scientists are instructed to gather scientific information needed for the firm's ongoing exploratory research without disclosing any confidential firm information. In addition, on their return from conferences, firm scientists are asked to write conference reports in which all new-learned scientific developments are disclosed in detail. Often, academic scientists, who are constantly searching for industrial collaborations, find themselves exchanging ideas as if they were operating within the "open science" domain. In this respect, industrial scientists take the role of "informational sensors" and "knowledge explorers" within the academic scientific networks. These networks are mostly embedded in norms of the free flow of scientific information and scientific collegiality of the commons (Crane 1972; Eisenberg 1987; Liebeskind & Oliver 1998).

University scientists indicate in various ways that what is valued by their institutional environment is "basic scientific work," whilst applied scientific research is not expected to be conducted by university scientists (Merton 1968). This message is conveyed by the university promotion system: "No one will get a PhD degree in our institution for an applied dissertation", or, "My colleague wants to get promoted to a full professor and thus he tends to avoid any contact with me till he'll get it," describes an industrial scientist, or in the words of a university scientist who also works as a chief scientist of a biotechnology firm: "My colleagues at the university are very angry with my association with the industry – they always act as if

I am working most of the time at the company, although they all know that I am there only two days a week, yet they feel as if I betrayed them."

The attractive research support offered by the industry leads many university scientists to reassess the classic university ideal model of basic scientific research and free flow of information exchange (Merton 1968; Eisenberg 1987; Liebeskind & Oliver 1998; Etzkowitz 1999; Owen-Smith & Powell 2001b; Liebeskind 2000) and switch to applied research, which embodies potential for R&D collaborations. The following quotation is illustrative:

There is very little applied science in universities. They dislike it very much – it is not "Kosher." However, since there is not enough funding for basic research, the university scientists understand today that without applied research, they will be stuck. No research will progress." (Chemistry professor, male, large research university)

University scientists trust that by choosing to stay in the academic setting they can benefit from the distinct incentives of autonomy and academic flexibility. Yet, being committed to industry-funded R&D collaborations creates some potential hazards for university scientists related to loss of independence:

The university still delivers the message that they are interested mainly in the production of good basic scientific research, and not so much with the patenting of discoveries. It needs to maintain its reputation. The reputation is to be the first in the scientific community. However, this is not what most scientists are doing. Basic research will never bring enough funding needed for maintaining our laboratories so most scientists are directed more toward applied research since this is where the money is. Yet, this is a double-edged sword. When you are funded by the industry there are restrictions placed on your research. You cannot collaborate with other scientists on the same projects, you need to get firm approval for any research you wish to publish or present, and your students may not be able to publish their research without firm approval. Also, getting out of a bad contract with the industry is very complex and costly." (Genetics professor, large research university)

Additional risks are embedded in such commitment to the industry. Scientists indicate that, in R&D collaborations, funding continuity is at risk since there is a constant threat that funding will be cut off, sometimes at very short notice if, or when, the firm decides to abandon the research direction it is working on. Although collaborations with industry are governed by detailed contracts, many university scientists seem to be doubtful regarding the ability of such contracts to control explicitly for all possible contingencies. After a few years of R&D collaborations, some of the scientists interviewed have realized that the contracts they signed were disproportionately attentive to the firms' need to capture rights of their future intellectual capital. The contracts thus constrained their future scientific work in a sophisticated way, which excluded them from other possible collaborations. As a result, scientists experienced frustration and a sense of helplessness.

Technology-transfer officers

Technology-transfer officers are usually university unit's employees. Their role is designed to maximize securing returns for scientists' intellectual property rights, to the university and to scientists. Most technology-transfer officers have some background in science or law, or both, and are responsible for two main activities: securing patent rights of academic scientists and dealing with royalties, and facilitating the searching and contracting for R&D collaborations between academic scientists and research-oriented firms in areas such as biotechnology, nanotechnology, and micro-electronics (Seitzer 1999). Technology-transfer officers in Israel are members of the Association of Technology Managers (AUTM), which is a nonprofit, professional society founded in 1991 with over 1800 members working in 250 academic institutions and an equal number of companies.

The scientists interviewed admitted that without the aid of technology-transfer officers, many good ideas are "cherry-picked" by industry without any return to the university. Yet, technology-transfer officers often follow their universities' interests rather than those of the scientists, resulting in conflict between technology-transfer officers and university scientists (Rhoades & Slaughter 1991). In many interviews, technology-transfer officers were described as incapable of finding and/or contracting for needed R&D collaborations the scientists were looking for, and as not being able to understand the needs of scientists. Often, technology-transfer officers are perceived as being profit-driven whilst negotiating contracts in which scientists are not allowed to intervene.

The differences in interests reflect also on different perceptions and cognitions regarding a larger array of issues. Table 6.1 captures some

Table 6.2 *Comparison between the two models for university–industry technology R&D collaborations*

	The "linear" model	The "chaos" model
Understanding success	Forward – linearly related to rational planning	May be understood only backward – when departing from final outcome
Central role in the search process	Technology-transfer officer as the professional	Scientist as the source of knowledge
Technology-transfer professionals	Initiate the search process and the contract; the centralized responsible party	Needed only for the finalization of the contractual stage after the scientist sets all terms
Rationality	Bureaucratic top-down rationality	Bottom-up probability-maximizing rationality
Serendipity	Should be avoided as much as possible	Is the key to success
The nature of risk	Minimized risk – all precautions taken into account and mainly precontract secrecy	Calculated risk – aimed at increasing options for finding fit collaborations
Goals	Efficiency through rational elimination processes – finding the best collaboration	Survival – finding a "good-enough" collaboration
Trust	Initial lack of interpersonal trust; organizational-level trust disaggregated to the scientist level	Initial interpersonal trust; scientist-level trust aggregated to the organizational level
Knowledge base	Personalized and compartmentalized	Mainly tacit – becomes explicit through cognitive interpersonal interactions
Sharing pre-contract research information	Should be avoided or shared under legal contracts	Should be shared based on the judgment of the scientist; tends to be informally shared, and is the key to successful collaborations
Intellectual capital ownership	Belongs to the organization in which the scientist works as a return for enabling and facilitating scientific research	Belongs to the scientist who pays his dues to the employing organization

illustrations for areas of differential perceptions and ambiguity. The quotations in the table show that the issue of the rights to intellectual property seems very clear to technology-transfer officers, but is more ambiguous for university scientists. At the same time, the issue of maintaining secrecy over research projects and findings is central in the perception of technology-transfer officers and university R&D vice-presidents, whereas it does not seem to be such a crucial problem for university scientists. Lastly, the illustrative quotations show that scientists perceive R&D collaborative arrangements as being built upon trust, informal and evolutionary arrangements, and reciprocity resulting from joint interests and differential needs. At the same time, technology-transfer officers perceive R&D collaborations as based on sophisticated strategic negotiation, strict guidelines, and constraining formal arrangements.

Search processes for university–industry R&D collaborations

As mentioned above, the search for R&D collaborations between academic scientists and industry in the area of biotechnology is highly complex owing to the high number of firms conducting biotechnology R&D, the multiple mechanisms of information gathering, and the partiality of relevant information. In addition to the complexities, contracting the "wrong marriage" may be highly costly, since much is at stake. At the least, the "costs" of such collaborations may amount to unwanted loss of time and delayed scientific progress, which can jeopardize a whole research project and sometimes even the career of the scientist. More costly may be a contract in which untrustworthy partners may turn to act opportunistically, disclose vital secret research information, or hold up the research progress by creating bureaucratic and financial hurdles. Efforts to change the contract terms at a later stage can result in high liabilities for the scientist. However, as stated above, the need to search for industrial collaborations is unavoidable for many academic scientists in biotechnology. Thus, despite the high perceived and possible risks, many scientists in universities are continually seeking industrial collaborations.

Is there is a good *model for networking* for such collaborations? This was the central focus of the research question. Previous research studied various structures of the transfer processes, focussing mainly on variations within firms involved in the transfer process (Harmon, Ardichvili & Cardozo 1997), but without examining the search process from the university side. The interviews revealed many perceptions and experiences. Analytically, they may be classified into two distinct "ideal-type" metaphors or models for searching and establishing R&D collaborations. I title them the "linear" and the "chaos" search models. Both models are directed toward networking for university–industry R&D collaborations, but they differ in their basic assumptions, goals, and perception of rationality. In reality, neither model is likely to exist in its pure form, but rather various modes of mixed models exist. In the next section, we characterize the main dimensions of the models and classify their basic assumptions and internal logic.

The linear model of networking for R&D collaborations

The linear model operates linearly toward success and efficiency. It aims to be purely rational as it makes all effort to promote planning, risk management, and focussed operations. This can best be achieved by decoupling the search and contracting phases from the scientist and allowing the technology-transfer officer to act in the service of the academic scientist. Thus, clear hierarchy and differential responsibilities for top professional officials form the skeleton of this model. Only such distinction of roles can assure rationality of decision-making processes and calculated management of risk resulting from opportunism, mistakes, or incompetencies. Rationality is bureaucratic as it is imposed by the technology-transfer professional. The rationality of the search process is linear as are linear decision-making processes (March & Simon 1958). The goal is to detect the best collaboration through an exhaustive search process in which all possible options are evaluated, and the elimination of options results from formally established criteria. Therefore, serendipity has no place in the linear model, and precontract knowledge or information exchanges are not allowed for. Serendipitous searches for collaborations are not wise since they lack systematic logic and are associated with limited exploration that may result in a nonoptimal collaboration.

The linear model also assumes that collaborations should be formed and contracted for by the specialized positions within the hierarchy, rather than placing these responsibilities on the shoulders of the scientists. In this respect, the process is mechanical and only when the "best" collaboration has been selected and is "safely" protected by contractual agreements is the scientist allowed to move from the background to the foreground and enter the "operational" level of the R&D collaboration.

Lack of initial trust is the basic assumption in the linear model. Trust is defined as "the willingness of a party to be vulnerable to the actions of another party, based on the expectations that the other will perform a particular action important to the trustor, irrespective of the ability to monitor or control that other party" (Mayer, Davis & Schoorman 1995: 712). However, the exchanges that deal with future transactions of knowledge are not easily captured within formal contracts (Liebeskind & Oliver 1998) and thus require some levels of trust even within formal contracting procedures. The collaboration contract aims at specifying the actor's expected future behavior assuming both sides operate professionally out of intrinsic interests and do not wish to risk their reputations by acting in an untrustworthy manner (Oliver 1997). Of the three types of trust specified by Zucker (1986): characteristic, process, and institutional, institutional-based trust is the most prominent in this model. This results from the fact that the scientist who would play the active role in the R&D collaboration is in the background during the process of the collaboration formation. The formal agreements are contracted between the university and the firm, and assume that the firm's reputation and the university's research distinction would act as reputation facilitators and precursors for future trustworthy behavior and lack of opportunistic acts. Thus, it is the trustworthiness of the institution that is disaggregated to the level of each collaboration (Oliver 1997).

Knowledge and knowledge-ownership are assumed to be clearly defined and secured in the linear model. Thus, the focus is on the transfer of the knowledge commodity rather than on the collaborative process as a knowledge-generator mechanism. In this respect, knowledge is assumed to be stable and static. The linear model assumes the ability to compartmentalize the independent and unique knowledge contribution of both sides of the collaboration, and thereafter the ability to specify the conditions under which the knowledge is handled.

One of the assumptions of the linear model is that scientific intellectual capital – the knowledge base of the scientists – belongs to the employing institution. This knowledge is an organizational commodity and thus should not be exchanged or shared prior to the formal contractual agreement. The bounding of knowledge-sharing is directed toward the minimization of risks from appropriation of knowledge or other opportunistic behavior. Thus, very limited pre-contracting knowledge exchanges should take place.

The chaos model of networking for R&D collaborations

The chaos model is less ambitious as it strives to find a "good-enough" collaboration rather than full efficiency or optimal success – finding the best collaboration. This means that operating out of this model's image requires more risk-taking and flexibility in order to assure a successful collaboration, even at the risk of reduced efficiency and rationality.

The four elements suggested by Anderson (1999) are highly relevant to the "chaos model" of networking. First, academic scientists are agents who are capable of operating without fixed rules, and who can apply nested selective systems toward their search process. Second, the encounters with industrial counterparts emerge as "self-organized systems" in which stable structure of interactions may emerge based on recursively applied rules of scientific collaboration and trust-worthiness, without the intervention of the administrative bodies. Third, since scientists acting as their own agents aim to optimize their own fitness they do not always comply with the university system-level instructions. The fourth element refers to the wide range of nested "weak ties" (in which contacts of contacts may evolve as a potential collaboration) in the scientific or the industrial, or both, networks. These multiple networks compose subsystems which permit multiple evolutions of collaboration options to evolve, yet it is hard to predict how they may change over time and which subsystems will prevail.

The chaos model of networking assumes the need to maintain an inflow of resources into the system (Anderson 1999). Order – in this case, a formal collaboration – will be created only when there is a free flow of ideas and information between the university scientist and other scientists (including industrial scientists). In fact, this order may only be established when there are preorder, precontract exchanges of information and ideas. Through open exchange of information and tacit knowledge the interest of the two parties in collaboration emerges, and this is how synergistic good ideas can evolve.

Operational success may be understood only through tracing backward once the collaboration has been formed. The scientist is the central actor in this model as he is the source of the knowledge, and thus the information needed for making the decisions about possible collaborations. The technology-transfer officer is needed for facilitation in the final stages of contracting, especially when additional professionals such as lawyers are needed. In the chaos model, the process of forming R&D collaborations is not rational, in the sense of full control and efficiency, and thus does not focus on eliminating options whilst promoting other options using rational evaluation measures. Rather, the chaos process allows for multiple coevolving of possibilities for collaborations. The key words in understanding this process are *serendipity* and *self-organizing* and *self-reference* (Bergmann Lichtenstein 2000). Serendipity in science is considered one of the forces leading to many break-through discoveries. Several scientists interviewed mentioned that they believe that basic biological research should not be directed only toward explicitly stated goals. Rather, the ambiguous and unfocussed search for discoveries seemed to have, in their view, the greater potential for making major discoveries.

Combining the "chaos model" with the notion of serendipity leads us to view the formation of collaboration as probabilistic. The probability of encountering the expected partner increases if the environment provides the needed facilities for the right encounters. Similar to laboratory experiments in the biological sciences, patterns are discovered when opportunities for random encounters of elements are increased. The model assumes that there is no one best outcome, but that there are many good outcomes that need to be discovered randomly when the specialized environment is provided.

The study of complex systems has identified self-organization as a consistent pattern identifying change (Bergmann Lichtenstein 2000, p. 128). Since there is no equilibrium in a nonlinear system, increased learning is enhanced through self-organization. The formation of university–industry R&D collaborations provides another illustration of how these systems of collaboration shape and reshape using self-organization assumptions. In self-organizing systems it is of interest to managers to support such self-referenced learning collaborations (Bergmann Lichtenstein 2000, p. 129).

Redundancy and "waste" in exchanging proprietary scientific information are not only allowed but, rather, are encouraged by the chaos model. Consequently, risk-taking in terms of exchanges of proprietary information is the only possible facilitator for the inception of collaborations, and is calculated as an important element of the model in the search for a "good match" rather than for the "best match."

Since the scientist is now in the foreground, the assumption of trust, rather than lack of trust, is the leading force in the informal encounters. Trust emerges from the joint interests of both sides and the interpersonal "chemistry" formed between two scientists. The similarity is based on shared norms and professional language, and has been referred to as characteristic-based trust (Zucker 1986; Oliver 1997). This kind of trust facilitates the inception of the collaboration. The formal procedures taken at later stages are built on this characteristic-based trust, but may insensitively harm it by imposing process-based or institution-based trust prematurely. If the formal procedures are carefully established after characteristic-based trust has developed, the agent-level, characteristic- and process-based trust may be aggregated to the organizational level.

Knowledge in this model is assumed to be specific or tacit, and it can become explicit only through socializing with other specializing persons possessing complementary knowledge (Nonaka 1994; Nonaka & Konno 1998). Only through interpersonal cognitive and social interactions of tacit knowledge bases can knowledge become externalized, and problems specified and resolved. New ideas are generated through the combination of individual knowledge followed by a stage of internalization of the knowledge at the individual and the organizational levels. These precontractual interactions are possible mainly under the "chaos model" that accounts for possible nonlinear embedded, yet unanticipated, gains to both sides of the collaboration.

Knowledge *per se* has no value as it becomes valuable only when there is an organic match between the appropriate "seller" and "buyer" in the transaction. Therefore, knowledge is distributed relatively openly until the "right" match is found.

Precollaborative encounters need a facilitating environment. A semi-specialized, nonformalized environment provides the "habitat" for an organic synthesis of knowledge and information belonging to the possible alliances of buyers and sellers. "Free-flowing" information exchanges during the precontractual stage provide the facilitating environment for encounters, without the need of a governing "visible hand." Only after the first-stage encounters are formed may the collaboration be formalized by the specialized professionals (contract lawyers and technology-transfer officers). An interesting question that emerged in interviews was: "Why do scientists in biotechnology-related areas tend to exchange more information than needed in their encounters with possible collaborators and tend to ignore the instructions of technology-transfer officers for secrecy?"

One possible answer is embedded in the nature of scientific community norms which call for "open science." This behavior may also result from the scientists' need for independence, which may lead to a conflict of interest between technology-transfer officers and scientists. Another explanation rests in a deeper observation offered by the scientists interviewed, and it refers to the isomorphism between the nature of the scientific process and the search process for collaborations. The nature of learning in biotechnology is based on underlying relatively thin theoretical and practical knowledge (Pisano 1996) and thus "learning-by-doing" rather than "learning-before-doing" is the central mode in which research is conducted. Pisano (1996) describes in detail how biotechnology-related research differs from chemical research. Biotechnology research involves "more art than science" (Pisano 1996, p. 1108) and is based on only a few general theories or "rules of thumb" to guide process search or selection. Pisano's observation that "You just can't tell ahead of time what is going to work" reflects the chaotic nature of the scientific process. The factors affecting processes are not well understood and make it difficult to anticipate the outcomes. In addition, unlike chemistry research (and probably other advanced research areas), "biotechnology research cannot isolate, analyze and characterize each reaction in the process" (Pisano 1996, p. 1108). The lack of precision ability results from the fact that the process is composed of thousands of reactions which may occur inside a host cell. Another difference between chemistry and biotechnology relates to the scaling-up problem in biotechnology. Owing to the complex nature of the research, "Researchers generally do not know ahead of time which environmental variables may be relevant, nor can they fully anticipate the impact of those which are identified" (Pisano 1996, p. 1109).

The above description shows that biotechnology research is chaotic in nature, in large part because of the slim body of existing knowledge, the limited ability to characterize intermediate and final products, and the lack of knowledge about how the environment will affect the scaling-up process. In the words of a scientist in a research university:

In my lab, it is almost impossible to predict what would lead to an outcome. I only know what can probably be the best environment that may lead to the outcome, and then I have to allow for the process to evolve. This is very similar to how I find collaborations. I go to conferences or meetings with people who have interest in my field and talk with them informally. Through these discussions, we learn about alternative options for continuing the research, and gather information on whom in the industry may be a relevant partner. My most advanced collaboration with a Swedish biotechnology firm resulted from a simple discussion over dinner at a house of a Hollywood actress who decided to devote her money to find a cure for diabetes, which is my research area.

Isomorphism between cognitive practices of research conduct and the perception of a search process leads to different metaphors for networking. Biotechnology scientists who experience chaos and complexity in their daily experiences in the laboratory find it artificial and ineffective to apply simple linear tools to the process of searching for collaborations. As their daily experience is based on ambiguity and serendipity, their collaboration-searching experience is no different. In an environment where it is impossible to control for, predict, or anticipate outcomes the "learning-by-doing" element of the process is the only one that can bring about exploration. This explains why biotechnology scientists tend to talk beyond the secrecy instructions, share new, not yet patented ideas with others, and talk with a large variety of scientists from different scientific disciplines.

Discussion and conclusion

The basic argument introduced in this chapter calls for absorbing the notion of *equifinality* (Meyer, Tsui & Hinings 1993) of processes, which assumes that there are many ways to reach goals. The "chaos model" is highly infused with values, and strives for survival rather than for efficiency. The model assumes that "order" exists in a complex structure and may be reached by free flow of resources such as information. This model does not assume forward-linear rationality, but implies a very minimalist model of rationality based on probability-maximizing parameters. A successful end to the search process indicates a new kind of rationality. This rationality does not result from linearity of decision-making, but, rather, from the evolution of nested subsystems of networks in which many choices are allowed to develop simultaneously through exchange of information. Thus, we are not observing a preprescribed process in which each step reduces the number of options existing in the previous step of the process. Instead, we have a nonshaped and nonpredictable process in which many options are allowed to develop simultaneously, without a formal structure, until a successful collaboration emerges. The process does not consider risk-taking and inefficiency as negative aspects, but rather as factors inherent in the nature of the process. The final achieved goal is not preconceived in an economic-rational process, but results from the higher probabilities associated with the search within unlimited options.

In biotechnology research, we have two scientific communities – university and industrial scientists. They share common norms and language, on one hand, but different environmental demands and constraints, on the other. These two communities are governed by two sets of administrative bodies which act as boundary spanners for the two scientific communities. However, interpersonal networks of scientists transact the formal boundaries of the two institutional forms in informal, "clan-" type (Ouchi 1980) networks (Powell 1990; Kreiner & Schultz 1993; Liebeskind *et al.* 1996; Oliver 1997). Even among strangers, the norms of these networks may permit a faster and more efficient "marriage" if the environment is assembled in a manner which increases the probabilities for encounters. Such an environment should be based on normative commitment, monitored through expectations of trustworthiness, allowing for the risk of information exchange, and encompassing a variety of scientists with related interests joining together in informal exchanges. As Koput (1997, p. 538) argued, "impressionistic decision processes are characterized by high commitment, close market relations, decisions by hunches, and a strong can-do attitude."

The aim of this chapter was to highlight the complexity of alternative models for intellectual capital networking, to illustrate different metaphors of networking, and to minimize the perception of a simple linear process in the formation of R&D collaborations. Thus, technology-transfer officers do have an important role in advancing academic research, but this should not undermine the significant role of the scientists involved. This call emerges from Granovetter's (1985) notion of embeddedness, which highlights the fact that economic exchanges are embedded in social relations. In this view, university–industry transactions are not atomized and separate from other transactions, but, rather, are embedded in forceful social and scientific networks. Thus, scientists' embeddedness in social, scientific, and reputation networks is valued and utilized in the "chaos model," whilst quite abandoned by the "linear model."

The above theoretical construction calls for additional research on the conditions under which each model is prominent in university–industry exchanges. We also need to explore the degree to which the use of these models lead to short- and long-term success in finding a collaboration and successfully continuing it throughout the project and into new projects.

Endnote

One university R&D vice-president (a full professor of microbiology) finds that the current state of affairs is leading to an undesirable outcome: "In the long run, universities will become research subsidiaries of industrial companies." This will give them all the needed funding, but will take away the spirit of free creativity essentially needed for good basic science. This view brings us back to the original role of basic scientists in society. The beneficiaries of this free flow would include the scientists, science, and society at large. Basic science cannot grow and progress within the constraints of industrial settings, yet it cannot survive without their financial support. The dilemma has yet to be resolved.

7 | Trust in collaborations and the social structure of academic research

Previous research provided some tangible evidence that commercial interests have the potential to, and in fact sometimes do, have an effect on the nature of trust in academic science. By offering a wide range of evidence found in the area of academic biotechnology research, we can examine how the success of commercially oriented collaborative research calls for a number of different forms of trustworthy behavior on the part of collaborators. The argument is that owing to the recombination of commercial interests into academic research a broader form of trust is required to support the research relationship than is required to support the normal academic relationship.

In academic science, trust, in the form of scientific credibility and accountability, plays a crucial and essential role. Trust relations in academia are built on networks of trust relations in which personal experience, reputation and gossip, and institutional norms are the factors which enhance trustworthy behavior. When an established social system is altered because of changes in norms of interests of some of its members it is important to revisit the role of trust in scientific exchanges and the emerged new structure of social and scientific exchanges in academic science. In a previous study Liebeskind and Oliver (1998) suggested that the increasing commercial value of scientific discoveries in molecular biology led to changes in the social structure of this academic field. Our observations were supported with findings from fieldwork and interviews gathered in Israel, the UK, and the USA since 1989. The interviews were with research scientists in the area of molecular biology in universities and biotechnology firms, as well as with technology-transfer officers, top university administrators, and corporate managers.

This chapter is based on some of the arguments and evidence that were introduced by Liebeskind and Oliver (1998), and on additional material gathered at later stages. The idea that led to the writing of the chapter was associated with an interesting observation encountered during fieldwork. It was decided that beyond the large-scale quantitative dataset that was available, interviews with scientists and managers of biotechnology firms would provide a better understanding of the complex learning process within and between organizations. Therefore, some interviews were conducted in a few leading biotechnology firms. The interviews were targeted at understanding the process of conducting scientific inquiry in biotechnology firms, the searching procedures used for finding collaborations, and the ways in which collaborations were constructed. At that time, most of the scientists had only graduated from universities and many of their collaborations were with their networks of academic advisors and colleagues. They seemed to have established very informal settings of scientific exchanges and collaborations, both within different laboratories in their firm, and with their academic counterparts. Examples of conflicts of interest between the different scientists did not seem to emerge during the interviews and the general sense was of a joint challenge, in which both sides (academic and industrial scientists) benefit from these informal learning and research exchanges, without strong interference from their organizations (either the university or the new biotechnology firm (NBF)).

A few years later, some of these scientists were revisited in order to learn more on some of their collaborations. It was hard to miss the major differences between the two timepoints of our interviews. At the second visit, the firms were larger in terms of employees, number of buildings and facilities, they had higher revenues, and some had products. Most notable, too, were the new bureaucratic procedures, intellectual property policies, and a strong sense of secrecy. At one firm, the entry to the buildings was securely gated and no unguided entry was allowed. In addition, as visitors, we had to complete forms with personal information, and we were then escorted to the person we were interviewing. At one firm we were directed first to the office of the firm's attorney, who asked us to sign a nondisclosure contract in which we had to state that we would not use any information divulged in the interview for any purposes, and would retain confidentiality regarding the interviewee and the firm. This formal procedure felt very odd and out of place. As organizational scholars, not only was our basic understanding of biotechnology quite limited, but we had not even considered asking any questions during the interviews about the details of the conduct of science by the interviewee or about the details of the scientific work conducted at the firm.[1]

After signing the nondisclosure contract we were escorted to the scientist we were to interview. He was very hospitable and spent over two hours with us, talking freely on everything we asked about. Yet, when we were to leave another person was assigned to escort us to the exit making sure we left the facility straight after the interview.

In another instance, when a scientist was interviewed a second time, it was possible to trace some significant changes in the system of trust, informal collaborations, and intellectual property right policies. During the first interview, the scientist told us about the various informal collaborations that the firm had with university scientists (without disclosing names of scientists or universities). At the second interview, a few years later, the scientist told us that universities were starting to create hurdles that prevented many scientists from collaborating with the firm. He told us a story about one university scientist who had an invention that was compatible with the research directions of the firm. The scientist wanted to collaborate with the firm on his invention and contacted the technology-transfer office of his university in order to arrange and negotiate an agreement for joint research with the firm.[2] However, the negotiations between the NBF and the technology-transfer office failed, and the technology-transfer office refused to sign the contract with the firm. The NBF scientists described the reaction of the university scientist as one of deep

---

[1] Until that point, I have never encountered any sense of lack of trust or suspicions during my interviews. As a practical mode of scientific conduct, I have always started each interview with a clear self-introduction and details of the major interest of our study. I also used to ask for the interviewee' consent to be interviewed and stated explicitly the promise to keep all the information confidential, avoiding any information in our publications that may disclose the identity of the respondent. We also retained permission to keep notes and/or tape-record the interview and asked the respondent to feel free to ask us to stop the tape should she/he feel uncomfortable with being recorded. It was my conviction that these practices established a clear atmosphere of trustworthiness during the interview, and indeed, never did I encounter a sense of luck of trust or a refusal to be interviewed. At times interviewees did ask us stop the tape, but they usually did not mind that we would keep taking notes. More so, interviewees were always happy to participate in a continuous interview, and agreed that we could come back to them any time in the future.

[2] At the early stage of interviews, I do not recall issues related to constraints set by technology-transfer offices in universities.

frustration. The university scientist was eager to move his invention further into the development phase, something that he was unable to do in his university laboratory and that needed the firm's laboratories, scientists, and capabilities to assist. He was described as someone who did not worry about intellectual property rights or about the potential profits associated with the discovery. His wish was modest and limited to the advancement of his scientific learning and fulfillment of his academic curiosity. All he wanted was to see whether his discovery could develop into a potential product. After the negotiations with the technology-transfer office failed, he contacted the firm directly and asked that they collaborate with him informally, without the formal contract with the technology-transfer office. The firm scientist checked with his legal department, which forbade him from even meeting the scientist again.

This example was a clear indication of a major shift in scientific norms or collaborations which resulted from the transformation of interests. The transformation led to an increased emphasis on the use of contracts to define the scope and conduct of academic scientific collaborations of all types, including teamwork, consulting, transfer of research materials, and preliminary evaluation of research results. As we have heard from many scientists, both in academia and in industry:

I never enter into a research relationship without signing a contract governing research materials and confidentiality. These days everyone signs these agreements before they collaborate. It is just the way that research is done.

The norms of conducting research collaborations have shifted throughout the years from the "handshake" type of informal agreements to "contract" types of formal agreements. The formalization of exchange relations was associated with the notion of the role and the structure of trust. An unsurprising observation was the locked research laboratories' quarters to which nonrelated scientists (even from the same firm) were declined entry. Magnetic card-keys were given to each scientist and these provided the security that only authorized scientists could enter certain laboratories. Even at a university, we heard, entry to some laboratories was restricted only to those scientists who were involved in a project. The gates within what used to be "open science," and the open flow of trustworthy learning exchanges, were gradually blocked by interests, policies, and locks.

Trust and credibility in academic scientific research

Trust is perceived as a condition that may or may not exist between two or more social actors, and that trusting may engender trustworthy behavior in the trustee (Dasgupta 1988; Gambetta 1988; Luhman 1988; Coleman 1990; Kramer, Brewer & Hanna 1996).

Three main conditions may result in trust: social process, calculation, and shared values. Process-based trust builds over time and is developed as actors acquire information on the past behavior of the other actors, which facilitates their decision to trust or distrust (Zucker 1986). In another study, Gulati (1998) found that in strategic alliances, past alliances and familiarity breed trust relations.

Calculative trust is based on estimates of the other motives and interests (Dasgupta 1988; Coleman 1990). The gains and the losses for being trustworthy are calculated against the costs that may result from untrustworthy behavior. In academic science, the gains for being trustworthy may be tangible, such as obtaining a faculty position or being allocated to prestigious and important committees, or may be intangible, such as general satisfaction from conducting research in a "trustworthy manner" or a sense of affiliation with the prestigious members of the scientific community.

Value-based trust is predicated on the understanding that actors share norms of trustworthiness behavior in relation to particular types of exchanges (Fukuyama 1995). Since it is based on familiarity and values, it is influenced by informal social structures and formal institutions (Zucker 1986; Fukuyama 1995). Khodyakov (2007) identified social control strategies that are based on common norms and facilitate trust relations.

The conduct and process of academic science is one area of human activities in which trust is of great importance. The process of scientific research focusses on relations between phenomena in a systematic method that gathers data through observations or experimentation. The goal of scientific research is to produce new "facts" or knowledge that are perceived as scientific discoveries, and which may increase the knowledge base of society (Latour & Woolgar 1986). The issue of credibility and trust in validity of others' scientific findings is a most central one in the development of science. The absence of trust would force each scientist to seek reproduction of previous research in order to check the discoveries of other scientists, and thus scientific progress will be hampered. In the words of Latour and Woolgar (1979, pp. 202–203):

For a working scientist, the most vital question is "is he reliable enough to be believed? Can I trust him/his claims? Is he going to provide me with hard facts?" Scientists are thus interested in one another ... because each needs the other in order to increase his own production of credible information.

Publications in academic science are important, since published ideas may be subjected to the criticism and scrutiny of other scientists (Dasgupta & David 1987). Publications are a result of a set of activities such as informal conversations between consulting scientists, collaborators, or simply colleagues, of formal presentations at seminars or conferences, and of working papers, journals, and book publications. Credibility and trust in academic science is produced through social exchange and is considered a commodity. Credibility also determines the pattern of the exchange and the willingness of one scientist to exchange ideas with another scientist. Thus, publications and credibility in academic science are interwoven.

   Reputation is another important aspect of exchanges in academic science. Credibility in a scientist is influenced by a reputation for competences in conducting careful and thorough research, and for research relations with students, colleagues, and collaborators. New and unexpected research results are more likely to be considered credible if the scientist has established a reputation as a competent and careful scientist. In this line, a scientist's reputation for allocating proper and fair credit to other scientists will credit them more for ownership for new ideas. When science is conducted in teams, any team member has the skills and ability to determine the accuracy of research and the fairness of allocation of credits (Latour & Woolgar 1979). Another excerpt is of value here:

Evaluative comments made by scientists make no distinction between scientists as people and their scientific claims...both reward and credibility originate essentially from peers' comments about other scientists ... The credibility of the professor and the proposal are identical. (Latour & Woolgar 1979, p. 202)

The structure of trust relationships in academic science

Based on Coleman's (1990) classification the structure of trust relationships in academic science can take three forms: interpersonal trust, intermediate trust, and institutional trust. These three forms of trust support academic credibility in different ways. These differences will be elaborated and illustrated as they are evident in academic science, based on field notes, interviews, and observations made over 15 years of study of related issues of learning and collaborations in biotechnology.

Interpersonal trust

Interpersonal trust is the most prevalent and fundamental form of trust in academic scientific research. Because most academic science in the biotechnology context (e.g. molecular biology, genetics, microbiology, chemistry, veterinary science, cell biology, and so on) is conducted in research teams (both intra-disciplinary and interdisciplinary), researchers learn about one another's conduct, competences, interests, and personality during their joint working. Thus, the joint research conduct includes a joint screening process in which team members establish and assign to others credibility and accountability in scientific research. Over time, this process leads to the development of interpersonal trust and distrust relations, and these are developed through what Zucker (1986) has noted as "process-based trust." Since the flow of information and learning exchanges during teamwork in science is crucial for the development of science, establishing interpersonal trust is critical.

The process-based element of trust relations is also relevant to the dynamic nature of mobility of scientists, either from academic research to industry-based research (either after graduation or when acting as entrepreneurial scientists). As scientists move between university and industry, or between biotechnology firms, the trust-based information they retain may also be transmitted to others. Thus, information on the trustworthiness and research credibility of scientists may be echoed by other scientists while they are moving from one research setting to another. Of course, encounters between scientists at conferences, workshops, and colloquia, and even interpersonal meetings, are occasions during which such information may be transmitted easily and this leads us to the type of trust that is based on *intermediacy*.

Intermediate trust

The interpersonal level of trust may be characterized as a transferable commodity through intermediate agents. Thus, a scientist in one laboratory who encounters another scientist whilst working in another laboratory may become an intermediate agent if: (1) she is considered trustworthy and credible by her research team members and (2) if she experiences and also expresses to her research team members a high level of interpersonal trust with the "new" scientist.

Just as interpersonal trust is a critical factor in scientific research, intermediate trust is highly important. This critical value results from the fact that each research team relies on information produced by others (Latour & Woolgar 1979).

Thus, the power of the social activity of "gossiping" is crucial in engendering intermediate trust, as gossip provides intermediate information about others' scientific credibility. The gossip mechanism is especially valuable when interpersonal scientific experiences are efficiently transferred within the informal networks of scientific community. Of course, interpersonal level of trust also has the ability to reshape the scientific networks as scientists consider others' opinions as valuable information before they enter new research exchanges and collaborations. Thus, intermediate trust may shape new collaborations in a speedy manner or prevent the establishment of other collaborations.

Institutional trust

The above-mentioned interpersonal and intermediate trust relations are operating within the institutional environment of any organization in which research is conducted.

Thus there is a variety of institutional arrangements, formal and informal, which govern scientific exchanges and are also associated with the development or erosion of trust in scientific research.

Two central elements are introduced in this context by Liebeskind and Oliver (1998, pp. 123–124):

First, the credibility of individual scientists is supported by the public granting organizations that support academic research, and by universities. The public funding of academic scientific research is understood to promote unbiased and open research, in contrast to private funding which is argued to induce partiality and secrecy. .... Public research funding is typically given only to scientists who produce and publish credible research findings ... Also, promotion and tenure in a university is granted primarily on the basis of peer reviewed (i.e. credible) publications, also promulgating the practice of "open science" and thereby, the production of credible scientific information. ... Moreover, because universities and public granting organizations are the sole suppliers of support for traditional academic science, scientists' actions are directed towards meeting the requirements of these institutions.

Second, informal processes of socialization and social control also support credibility. Entry into the community of academic research scientists requires a lengthy process of education and socialization, which engenders cohesion of beliefs and behavior, and binds scientists together into one "invisible collage" of shared values and understanding ... Also because the scientific research community is a bounded community, in which the identity of each individual is known to others, and within which information is freely exchanged, gossip can serve to condition scientists' behavior towards accepted norms or professional conduct.

Biotechnology and intellectual property

As mentioned already, the biotechnology industry is based on the commercialization of molecular biology applications and inventions. The actual commercialization could not have taken place unless firms were able to define and own property rights to commercially valuable discoveries in the form of patents. Without a patent, a firm has no incentive to invest in the development and commercialization of new products, because other firms would be able to imitate it without cost to themselves (Arrow 1962). A patent protects the firm's intellectual property rights and disallows imitation by competitors.

In the USA, the patentability of biotechnology products was established in a series of landmark court cases during the late 1970s and the early 1980s (Eisenberg 1987). Meanwhile, in 1980 the US Congress passed a law, commonly known as the Bayh–Dole Act, which allowed universities to patent biotechnology and other discoveries made by their faculties, and to license these patents to commercial firms. The intention of this legislation was to promote the commercialization of scientific research for the benefits of society. However, it was also recognized that allowing the privatization of knowledge generated in universities might undermine the objectivity of university research, divert faculty attention away from fundamental research, and interfere with the open exchange of research findings (Bok 1981; Nelkin 1984). Despite these concerns, the patenting of university research in the USA has proceeded rapidly (Henderson, Jaffe & Trajtenberg 1994). Most large US research universities started claiming ownership of patentable inventions made by their faculties, and licensing these patents to firms (Argyres & Liebeskind 1998). In Israel, patentable discoveries of faculty scientists are owned by the university and the scientist has rights to 33 percent of the royalties, while another portion (33 percent) of the funds are directed to the scientists' laboratory. Many universities have also established in-house, spin-off commercial entities to directly exploit the potential of the patentable discoveries of their faculty scientists (Oliver 2007).

Commercial considerations have also led to the use of other forms of intellectual property contracts in molecular biology, especially research material transfer agreements (RMTAs) and confidentiality agreements. RMTAs are used to govern the exchange of cell lines, reagents, and other research materials from one scientist to another; typically, they disallow any patent rights to discoveries made by non-owners' use. Confidentiality agreements are used to prevent collaborators on commercially valuable research projects from discussing their research with outsiders, in order to protect the patentability of discoveries that have not yet been made.

Previous chapters in this book have argued that as the commercial potential in biotechnology grown, university research in biotechnology is becoming increasingly influenced by intellectual property concerns. First of all, the value of intellectual property rights in biotechnology is now well established. Because secured intellectual property rights are so critical for the commercialization process, biotechnology firms today conduct only research which offers the prospect of patentable products, and many firms enter into research collaborations only if they are governed by agreements assuring that they will receive patent rights to any inventions made during the collaboration. In addition, and equally important, there has been an increasing involvement of university researchers with biotechnology firms. Eisenberg (1987, p. 195) noted that "Scientists working in biotechnology related fields are increasingly likely to be concerned simultaneously with the norms and rewards of research science and the rules and incentives created by intellectual property laws."

The transformation of trust relationships among academic scientists

The combination of commercial emphasis on securing intellectual property rights in biotechnology coupled with the widespread involvement of individual faculty members with biotechnology firms (Zucker, Darby & Armstrong 2002; Oliver 2004), has significantly affected the nature of relationships between academic scientists in molecular biology because their interests have changed from "normal" academic science, which cannot be exchanged for monetary value (Latour & Woolgar 1979, p. 229), to commercial-type research.

In the emerging form of commercial science in universities, scientists are no longer exclusively employed by the government as it becomes possible for them to exchange their knowledge for monetary capital in the direct form of patent royalties and research grants or in the indirect form of obtaining access to otherwise proprietary research materials, data, methods, and technologies which may be used to increase future research funding or income.

The potential monetary value in scientific exchanges can change scientist's interests in a few ways.

- *Publicity*: In "normal academic research," scientists build credibility through publication and garner resources from claiming priority (Merton 1973; Latour & Woolgar 1979; David 1992). Therefore, any valid research finding will be publicized as soon as possible. In commercial research, publication may result in a loss of valuable intellectual property, because once information has been released into the commons (i.e. published in scientific journals or presented in conferences) it cannot be patented (Nelson 2004). As a result, if a firm wants to obtain patent rights to discoveries made by a university scientist, the scientist must withhold information for a period of time until the discovery is submitted as a patent application. The important question here regards the degree to which commercial interests increase the period of secrecy relative to normal science, which is also characterized by a certain level of secrecy. During interviews with university technology-transfer officers and with university scientists, it was learned that firms require university scientists to withhold information about commercially funded research and bind them in formal agreements that prevent them from discussing related research information with colleagues and other scientists. To protect the principle of publicity, universities typically disallow firms from binding their faculties to secrecy agreements for lengthy time periods, yet academic scientists are not always immune to inducements to secrecy. At the early stages of university–industry technology-transfer in molecular biology, a scientist in an Israeli university was interviewed who claimed that a rigid contract of collaboration with a biotechnology firm prevented them from not only publishing research without permission of the firm, but also from planning future collaborations with colleagues since they were also bound by a contract with another firm. Another university scientist interviewed had kept one of their research projects entirely secret for a long period in order to preserve the commercial value of the findings. Aspects of secrecy may lead to double scientific standards in the university laboratory. For example, a scientist interviewed recently had two distinct sets of research projects. One set of projects was based on research conducted during the day in the university laboratory and with students. This research resulted in conference presentations, publications, and masters and PhD degree theses. The other set of projects was conducted during the late afternoon and evening, again in the laboratory, but alone without even a laboratory assistant. These studies had direct commercial value and were conducted for the scientist's entrepreneurial role. The knowledge from these studies was a part of the university spin-off startup that was being established and which was based on the scientist's scientific discoveries. Concerns for secrecy and the need to protect intellectual property rights meant that the scientist did not allow students to enter the laboratory where the commercial research was conducted.

- *Credits*: Commercial interests may also alter scientists' interest in the credit given to others who contributed work during the research process. In normal academic science, giving credit to others is considered an act that reflects upon the seriousness and complexity of the research. Such individual credit may also be exchanged for research grants and other resources necessary to produce more discoveries (Merton 1973; Latour & Woolgar 1979) or may add to the reputation of the credited scientist. In this vein, researchers who do not share credit fairly with their collaborators will be identified through informal information exchanges and gossiping, and may be boycotted in the future. In the new science, in which commercial interests take an important role in scientific activities, the costs of hoarding credit may be reduced because academic collaborators may be replaced by commercial collaborators. At the same time, the benefits of hoarding credit are increased since doing this gives rights for financial returns that are given from licensing to fewer rights-holders.

- *Delay in research and publication*: Intellectual property consider-ations also carry possible long-term future outcomes to the scientist. Working on a proprietary project may prevent the scientist from exchange of project-related information for a long period owing to contract clauses. In this context, the scientist may be prevented from conducting a specific line of research with collaborators for lengthy time-periods. Alternatively, scientists may be asked by technology-transfer officers or firms with whom they collaborate to withhold publication until a patent claim has been filed or until the commercial research has advanced beyond the risk of appropriation.

- *Contractual constraints*: The shift to commercial interests in normal science leads to an increasing emphasis on the use of contracts to define the scope and conduct of academic scientific collaborations of all types, including research teams, transfer of materials, and evaluation of research results. These contractual arrangements are also applied to basic academic research, which is conducted under contract with biotechnology firms and imposes limitations and constraints on the flexible and informal flow of scientific work.

The above-mentioned are examples of how formal, legally enforceable contracts are precise and restrictive. Thus the wide-ranging trust that was once necessary to support research collaborations in the past is not sufficient any more.

Commercial interests and the nature of trust in academic science and in collaborations

Not only do changes of interests in academic science result in struc-tural changes in the conduct of scientific work and collaborations, but they also have implications concerning the depth and extent of trust needed for research collaborations. Under the new "regimen" it is no longer sufficient for one scientist to trust the credibility of another. The secrecy needed for commercially oriented science means that secretive behavior by collaborators is much needed. Academic scien-tists have now learned to be very careful with what they disclose to colleagues and to industry scientists. By the same token, industrial scientists in biotechnology maintain that it used to be easy to learn from their academic counterparts about research ideas and findings in the early stages of the industry, but now academic scientists are also keeping secret their commercially oriented research.

Commercial interests have additional implications besides the change in the structure of trust relations. For example, commercial interests may shift scientists from dealing with "interesting research questions" to research questions of possible commercial value. These changes may have long-term implications on the structure of science and on the areas that are more intensely covered because of their commercial potential (such as finding therapeutic cures or diagnostic tools for diseases of wealthy nations, even if they amount to a small fraction of the world's population, rather than finding cures for diseases of the poor or those without medical insurance, even if they comprise a large fraction of the world's population).

Another important implication is that under the new regimen, commercially oriented collaborative research calls for a *broader and deeper* form of trust. This is a *broader and deeper* trust than that needed to support scientific collaborations in normal academic research relations (Liebeskind & Oliver 1998), and it results from the increased incentives for opportunistic and unethical scientific conduct that are found in commercially oriented research. Liebeskind and Oliver (1998) provide an example in which credit was hoarded in molecular biology. This relates to the famous Robert Gallo of the National Cancer Institute, who claimed that he discovered the AIDS virus and thus should hold the exclusive royalty rights for any diagnostic tests for the disease. However, the virus was already isolated by a group of scientists at the Institut Pasteur in France. In this example there were direct economic incentives involved in the interest to hoard credit. However, there are many others in which the wish to hold proprietary rights for even potential commercial value to research materials, data, or findings will lead scientists to hoard credit. In such cases, the risk of being exploited may harm research assistants, graduate students, or junior faculty members, who depend on senior scientists for academic advancement and resources for research.

A more recent example is of great interest in this context. On 19 September 2006, some US and Israeli newspapers published the coverage[3] of a court ruling on the lawsuit of the Weizmann Institute against ImClone, concerning appropriation of the Weizmann Institute's inventions in the development of a blockbuster cancer drug, Erbitux® (cetuximab).

The ruling was a blow to ImClone Systems Inc., and a triumph for a prominent Israeli research institution. The judge ruled that three scientists from Israel were the true inventors of a process used in the delivery of the blockbuster cancer drug. The US District Judge, Naomi Reice Buchwald, directed the US Patent and Trademark Office to replace the seven names on the controversial patent with those of Professor Michael Sela, Dr. Esther Aboud-Pirak, and Dr. Esther Hurwitz. The three scientists made the pioneering discovery at the Weizmann Institute of Science in Rehobot, Israel, in the late 1980s.

In a 140-page opinion, Judge Buchwald indicated that it was not a close call because the events described by the researchers and their experts were "strongly corroborated" by documents, whereas the version presented by the defendants was not. She also found that the plaintiff's witnesses were "as a whole, far more credible than the defendant's witnesses."

The key issue in the court case concerned the discovery, made by the three Weizmann researchers in the late-1980s using an antibody provided by Professor Joseph Schlessinger, who was previously a Weizmann researcher and who was working at a predecessor of Aventis. He is now Chair of Pharmacology at the Yale School of Medicine.

Judge Buchwald noted that *Scientist* magazine has said Schlessinger's publications are among the most-cited papers in the world. Schlessinger testified that he had been nominated for a Nobel Prize. On behalf of the Weizmann Institute research team was Professor Sela (82), a former president of Weizmann. Along with others, he invented Copaxone® (glatiramer acetate), the most widely used drug for treating multiple sclerosis. Professor Sela testified that he and the other researchers cared most about their work and left the pursuit of patents to others. The following citations are based on the *Israelinsider*

---

[3] Many newspapers published articles on this event. For example: www.townhall.com/News/NewsArticle.aspx?ContentGuid=5e0be7ad-5180–4f1b-88b9-e58679556811&page=full&comments=true; and the full court transcript coverage (140 pages): www.nysd.uscourts.gov/rulings/03CV08484_opinion_091806.pdf

newspaper. On 19 September Professor Sela of the Weizmann Institute said:

"I don't mind if I don't take a patent, unless it's stolen from me. Then I have to react," he said. "At the beginning, when I first saw it, I was in a state of shock. I mean, money is not important, but my name and my science, my honor demanded I should be replaced."[4]

The judge said that the Weizmann scientists were not included as inventors on the patent even though they conducted all of the experiments relating to mixing the antibody and chemotherapy drugs, while:

"Schlessinger in no way directed the research of the Weizmann scientists and had absolutely no interaction with them during the course of their experimentation."[5]

Fortune[6] magazine indicated that the former colleague of the Weizmann team, Joseph Schlessinger, "shanghaied" the idea and brought it to a corporate predecessor of Sanofi-Aventis, which then secretly applied for a patent on it. Whilst the application was pending, Aventis licensed the rights exclusively to ImClone.

At the time of publication, it was unclear when the patent credit names would be formally changed. Appeals on the judge's ruling could be filed.

The invention that resulted in the patent was a finding that a particular antibody, such as that in Erbitux®, may be combined with chemotherapy to fight the growth of cancer in a manner that has more success against some cancers than some other methods. The judge said that the predecessor company to Aventis, and later ImClone, copied the text and figures from a paper drafted by the Weizmann scientists into their patent applications. Judge Buchwald also said that the Weizmann researchers did not learn that Aventis and ImClone were pursuing patents until 12 years after the first patent application and only 14 months before the patent was issued. The lawsuit was brought in 2003.

Fortune magazine also adds that, from the judge's perspective, the balance of proof wasn't even close. As Judge Buchwald put it, "The Weizmann scientists have presented documentary evidence

---

[4] http://web.israelinsider.com/Articles/Business/9474.htm
[5] http://web.israelinsider.com/Articles/Business/9474.htm
[6] Nicholas Varchaver, 19 September 2006: 5:02 PM EDT

substantiating each step of the inventive process, in stark contrast to the dearth of evidence supporting the named inventors' version of events." The judge went on to describe the plaintiff's corroborating evidence as "overwhelming" and of "extraordinary breadth." By contrast, "Schlessinger's explanation. . .can most generously be described as strained," Judge Buchwald wrote, in her opinion.

Elsewhere, the judge commented that, "This exchange represents one of many instances in which Schlessinger exhibited great reluctance to acknowledge a fact that he perceived to be injurious to the defendant's case." In various places, her opinion dismissed his testimony as "not credible," "contorted," "incredible," and "wholly unsubstantiated by any contemporaneous records."

Another newspaper[7] cited Nicholas Groombridge, who argued the case for Yeda (the technology-transfer office of the Weizmann Institute), praised the decision, said it would be welcomed by the scientists, and said:

"People that devote their lives to science – what they care about more than anything else is recognition. They will be really, really happy to feel they have finally gotten public recognition."

This case has many implications for ImClone, for other firms attempting to develop similar drugs, for future court cases, and for universities conducting research and protecting inventions. Yet, the case, in the context of the present chapter, shows how trust-based exchanges between scientists have turned into an infringement of intellectual property rights. One of the Weizmann scientists in this case was interviewed by the author and claimed that the original publication was given to Professor Schlessinger under the expectation that he would provide feedback and comments on the publication, as is normal within the scientific community. Because of their previous collaborations, and exchanges of ideas and materials, there was no perception of a risk of appropriation and the information was given without any formal or informal contract. The information on the patent filing did not reach the Weizmann team for many years, and they learned about it only by chance.

---

[7] *International Herald Tribune,* Israelis win ruling on patent for cancer drug, 19 September 2006.

This complex case of a dispute over intellectual property rights provides a good summary for the claim of this chapter. It shows that, once the interests for parts of the academic scientific community have changed, the structure of trust in these exchanges has shifted too, and acts of what is perceived as "knowledge appropriation" occurred. What was originally a research publication by the three Weizmann scientists, who did not even seek patent-filing at that time, was filed as a patent by a previous colleague under his name (and without the names of the original inventors). This colleague accessed the article at a pre-publication stage under the normal scientific exchanges of "open science". Yet, he worked at that time in an NBF that was, by its nature, seeking commercial benefits. We can see from the claims made by Professor Sela that although he wanted to be credited properly for his science, the other side wanted to be credited (improperly in this example) for the commercial potential of this knowledge. This extreme case shows how trustworthy norms of credits in knowledge exchanges (between two well-known distinguished academic scientists, as in this example) might turn into bold appropriation when interests change.

8 | *Organizational learning and strategic alliances: recombination and duality of competition and collaboration*

Complexity in the concepts of competition and collaboration, and the network form of organization

The core argument in this chapter is that the study of interorganizational networks for learning and knowledge creation requires the adoption of a *duality* framework – collaboration or competition and the application of a *prism-like methodology*. By *duality* is meant "the quality or state of being dual or having a dual nature."[1] Using the concept of duality does not necessarily mean claiming that all network-based knowledge relations include competition or that competition excludes network-based knowledge relations. It simply implies that our understanding of collaboration and competition in knowledge-intensive industries, such as biotechnology,[2] may be enhanced by applying a method of observation that allows us to reveal the spectrum of relational forms that coexist in many network-based knowledge relations.[3] Thus, a *prism-like methodology* is suggested here, which may make it easier for us to seek the different "spectrums

---

[1] Source: *Webster's Revised Unabridged Dictionary*, © 1996, 1998 MICRA, Inc.

[2] As explained, the industry is composed of many types of organizational actors, including biotechnology firms, university scientists, large pharmaceutical organizations, governmental funding and research agencies, venture capitalists, hospitals, patent law firms, and others, which jointly offer the capabilities for producing biotechnology products. However, the chapter focusses mainly on alliances formed by biotechnology firms. In addition, there are many subareas in which biotechnology firms specialize (e.g. therapeutics, diagnostics, agriculture, food, veterinary science, and so on). Most of the arguments presented in this chapter refer to firms that operate within the same specialization.

[3] The concept of duality builds on previous research where it is claimed that: "The formation of a network is determined by the opposition of two forces. The first is the reproduction of network structure as a general social resource for network members. The second is the alteration of network structure by entrepreneurs for their own benefit (Walker, Kogut & Shan 1997). However, the research of Walker, Kogut and Shan (1997) is built on the notion that structure both enables and constrains entrepreneurial ambitions, while taking

of light" that exist in network-based knowledge relations. A "prism" is defined in optics as "a piece of translucent glass or crystal used to form a spectrum of light separated according to colors. Its cross-section is usually triangular. The light becomes separated because different wavelengths or frequencies are refracted (bent) by different amounts as they enter the prism obliquely and again as they leave it."[4] Although the prism concept is used mainly for metaphorical purposes, it corresponds nicely to the purpose of this chapter. The "spectrum of light" analogy of this metaphor refers to the fact that a full view of the "light ray" is composed of various collaborative and competitive features which coexist in many network-based knowledge relations. Thus, we need to use a "prism" approach to observe the sometimes hidden range of subcolors of competition and collaboration.

Despite the noted similarities, some other methodological implications are inconsistent with the formal structure of the prism. Unlike the prism, there is no assumption that all light rays can be separated, and if they are separated, they cannot necessarily be separated into the entire spectrum of colors. In addition, the spectrum of colors observed through use of the prism does not necessarily remain the same from one observation to another (in the order of the various relations or in translucency), reflecting the fact that competitive and collaborative relations are not always similar in all their stages or levels, or in the degree to which they are clearly visible to different observers. Lastly, there is no hierarchy or order assumed, as it is in the prism metaphor. Bearing these differences in mind, the prism metaphor will be used in the present chapter for observing instances of collaboration or competition dualities in network-based knowledge relations.

The chapter is organized as follows: first, the concepts of competition and collaboration within network-based knowledge creation relations are discussed, distinguishing between the two "pure" forms and arguing for the importance of using the duality perspective. Second, three interchangeable forms of competition and collaboration, as applied to interorganizational networks in knowledge-intensive industries, are suggested. Finally, the concept of externalities in economic actions is

---

an either/or approach for the reproduction or alteration of networks in the biotechnology industry.

[4] *The Columbia Encyclopedia*, 6th ed., 2001.

introduced, and then combined with the notion of positive outcomes of competition, and negative outcomes of collaboration in networks.

Network organizations (as an exclusive form of organizations) are defined by Podolny and Page (1998, p. 59) as "Any collection of actors (N greater than or equal to 2) that pursue repeated, enduring exchange relations with one another and, at the same time, lack a legitimate organizational authority to arbitrate and resolve disputes that may arise during the exchange." This form excludes pure market arrangements such as spot transactions or short-term contracts, and is distinct from market transactions that are non-enduring, and from hierarchies that have a legitimate authority to resolve disputes.

Most organizational researchers who study the biotechnology industry apply the perspective of the "network form" (Powell 1990), whereby network relations are perceived as the most central feature in moving the industry forward. The functional explanation for the emergence of the "network form" claims that the opportunities for innovation exist within firms as well as in their external networks, and the ability of an organization to learn results from its capacity to utilize both its own internal capabilities and the opportunities within its network through various forms of collaboration. Consequently by building on their embeddedness (Granovetter 1985), organizations can promote economies of development and production time (e.g. the ability to capitalize quickly on market opportunities resulting from network-based knowledge relations) and complex adaptation to market needs (Uzzi 1997, 1999). The search for knowledge and capabilities in networks stems from the environmental constraints that organizations have to cope with. In biotechnology, for example, many constraints, such as the cost of product development, the complexity of products and processes, the ambiguity of markets and products, stringent regulations, and the length of time to market, are thought to cause networks of collaborations to emerge.

Knowledge assets are becoming an important intangible asset for firms (Teece 1998), promoting increasing returns in the knowledge-intensive industries. The concept of *dynamic capabilities* refers to the capacity of the organization to sense opportunities and to reconfigure knowledge assets, competencies, and complementary assets and technologies to achieve substantial competitive advantage (Teece 1998, p. 73). McKelvey (1997) has argued further that the development of capabilities at the firm level is both a cause and an effect of the industry-level competitive process, generating the idea of co-evolution effects at multiple levels.

In studies of organizational learning, the "network forms" of organization have been described as a source of value for the firm (e.g. Ring, 1997; Kogut 2000). Knowledge-intensive industries may be expected to generate new forms of collaboration, in which network partnerships will be based on maximizing resource-utilization subject to the equitable distribution of returns rather than on individual firms maximizing their profits (Miles *et al.* 1998). The "learning-through-networks" approach focusses on the interorganizational network as a resource-generating entity that is able to enhance learning among collaborating firms by offering a greater variety of search routines and conveying more complex information. Todeva and Knoke (2005) argue that cooperative arrangements represent a new organizational formation that seeks to achieve organizational objectives better through collaboration than through competition. This view has become widely institutionalized through the work of Eisenhardt and Shoonhoven (1996), Hamel (1991), Koput and Powell (2002), Liebeskind *et al.* (1996), Powell (1990), Powell and Brantley (1992), Powell, Koput and Smith-Doerr (1996), Powell *et al.* (1999), Powell *et al.* (2005), Ring (1997), Stuart (1998), Teece and Pisano (1994), and Uzzi (1996, 1997, 1999), and others.

Despite the alleged advantages of collaboration, another stream of literature has questioned the advantages of networks. On this front, Osborn and Hagedoorn (1997, p. 270) question the efficiency of transferring and absorbing tacit knowledge among collaborating organizations. Further, firms in alliances may lose some of their interest in developing certain competencies and technologies (Hamel, Doz & Prahalad 1989), or they may reduce their revenues as a result of profit-sharing (Shan 1990). Risk is also associated with the incomplete nature of contractual arrangements and the resulting risk of opportunistic exploitation by partners (Hart, 1995; Das, Sen & Beal 1998).

Explanations for the failure of alliances vary. Studies based on game theory use arguments of opportunism, "tit-for-tat" behavior, or the learning-race approach in illustrating how and why alliances fail (Hamel, Doz & Prahalad 1989; Gulati, Khanna & Nohria 1994; Clark-Hill, Li & Davies 2003). Other studies focus on the lack of trust and information feedback that can account for the failure of alliances (Ring & Van de Ven 1994; Sydow 1997; Arino & de la Torre,1998; Liebeskind & Oliver, 1998).

In response to the alliance-embedded complexities listed above, recent studies have risen to the challenge needed to develop new theoretical perspectives that aim to capture the *paradox of cooperation and competition in alliances*, as in Clarke-Hill, Li and Davies (2003), or to map the character of the *interorganizational learning dilemma*, as in Larsson *et al.* (1998). These studies both emphasize the need for a synthesized multiparadigm if we are to understand the complex nature of alliances, and they apply theories of strategic alliances, organizational learning, collective action, and game theory. The literature notes that such synthesis is very limited (de Rond & Bouchikhi 2004).

The complexity involved in understanding network-based knowledge relations also lies in the conditioning effects of a firm's particular stage in its life-cycle. Specifically, it has been claimed that collaborations for learning are crucial in the exploration stages of the life-cycle (March 1991; Nooteboom 1999a, 1999b). At this stage, organizations are searching for knowledge and ideas for innovation and novel practices, and through various collaborations they manage to gain access to distributed intelligence across the boundaries of their own firm (Stark 2001, p. 77).

The exploration stage involves radical innovation whereby novel practices are introduced to the firm through its "entry ticket"[5] to learning networks. The process begins with general screening and the search for new knowledge, in which ideas are produced from new information to be found within networks. At this stage, interorganizational heterogeneity and diversity in capabilities and knowledge are required, so that different firms may access knowledge bases in a variety of networks assuming some form of reciprocity. As a result, if the invention occurs in organization A and its application is relevant to organization B, and its production occurs in organization C, then we can observe a fermentation of new ideas set off by this combinatory potential. In general, such an exchange structure will

---

[5] By "entry ticket" is meant the various conditions needed to "enter" the network of alliances. These are based on the firm's capabilities, managerial capabilities, networks and experience, and area of R&D specialization, as well as the quality of its scientists and their networks, and so on – elements that make biotechnology firms "worthy" of partnering in alliances. An initial alliance formed by a new biotechnology firm (NBF) marks its "entry ticket" to the network for exploration.

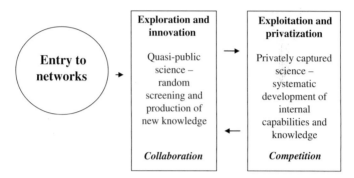

Figure 8.1 The dynamic symbiosis of collaboration and competition.
Source: Oliver 2004

generate a "semi-public knowledge base" model with blurred organizational boundaries, within which reciprocity allows for innovation.

However, the actual capture of value, which depends on rents from knowledge and discoveries, is essential to organizational survival. The exploitation stage that follows the exploration stage is based on tighter intra-firm networks and is needed to achieve productive efficiency (Nooteboom 1999a, p. 109). Since search behavior leads to the development of capabilities (Stuart & Podolny 1996), and endogenous relations are assumed to exist between capabilities and competition, it is posited that organizational capabilities shape the competitive environment (Henderson & Mitchell 1997; Huygens *et al.* 2001). Thus, the exploration–exploitation cycle generates an interesting dynamic: innovation and learning in knowledge-intensive organizations are induced by opportunities for collaboration from the semi-public interfirm knowledge base, whilst competition arises over the right to appropriate and privatize this knowledge and the growth of organizational capabilities reflected in the duality of collaboration and competition. This dynamic is depicted in Figure 8.1.

The duality of competition and collaboration in the context of interorganizational networks

Competition exists in situations in which a number of organizations are producing the same or related products (Callon 1998a, p. 44) and are thus all striving to get first to market and to capture both the consumer and the supplier niches. A more ecological and interactive perspective claims that "the competitive consequences of learning by one organization depend on learning by other organizations" (March 1991, p. 81). Since firms do not search in isolation from other firms (Stuart & Podolny 1996), "companies become rivals not simply because they operate in the same habitat, but because they influence each other's search behavior" (Huygens *et al.* 2001, p. 974).

On the other hand, collaboration occurs when firms work jointly on the development of products, where the distributed returns are sufficient for all the collaborating parties. Consequently, the difference between pure interorganizational competition and pure interorganizational collaboration lies in the context of *organizational boundaries*. In pure competition, the boundaries between the competing organizational systems are sharp and distinct. This springs from the tendency of organizations to capture value by attaining full control over their own product development process and thus, by excluding external collaborating partners, monopolizing the rights to and the rents of their internally developed product. The competition concerns the opportunity to become the first and sole beneficiary of a product domain and a captured market segment, through the internal exploitation of organizational capabilities and knowledge. Thus, in pure competition, information between organizations is not exchanged, joint research and development (R&D) does not exist, and manipulative acts intended to increase organizational competitiveness are the norm.

Conversely, pure collaboration may be defined as dense ties in interfirm collaborations which cross the firm boundaries for distributed intelligence (Powell 1990; Stark 2001) and shared complementary capabilities, assets, and interests without producing the same or related products.[6] In such conditions, the boundaries between organizations may become very blurred. In such boundary-crossing conditions, we can witness a free flow of information between collaborating organizations, which in turn enhances many joint projects where shared research findings, joint seminars, scientists' exchanges, and other joint activities are the norm. The exchanges are continuous and long-lasting and are based on trust and close relations between members of the exchanging organizations. Formal contracts may be signed, but there are many informal exchanges between research units in the organizations. Since knowledge resources are established

---

[6] This is generally the case with vertical integration alliances.

jointly by and for the collaborating organizations, they can all benefit from such resources while the rights to the knowledge are shared among the collaborating partners. In such collaborations benevolence may be observed in the collaborative exchanges and it is also maintained over long periods of time.

Our observations and searches for such pure collaborating knowledge-creating economic organizations suggest that these extreme forms are empirically rare because of problems of *value capture*, which is related to the scarcity of resources and the constraints imposed by markets. Therefore, most cases of interorganizational relations in knowledge-intensive industries represent various hybrid forms of competition and collaboration.[7] Hybrid forms, in which we can observe a duality of competition and collaboration, may be characterized by permeable boundaries shaped by the two relational forces. The permeability can be illustrated by three central elements:[8]

- the level of analysis at which the networks are analyzed
- timing and the organizational product life-cycle
- the institutional environment resulting from the conditioning effects of political, economic, or normative systems in which the networks are embedded.

In the following section, these three elements are elaborated and interwoven with examples from relevant research in the biotechnology industry.

Levels of analysis and differences in collaboration and competition.

It has been argued that in order to get a full picture of interorganizational networks in the biotechnology industry it is important to study

---

[7] Two important streams of study focus on the coexistence of competition and collaboration within networks. One stream is the literature on "coopetition" (Brandenburger & Nalebuff 1996; Bengtsson & Kock, 2000) that uses this concept to show the synergy of these two forces in business networks. Another stream concerns industrial districts (e.g. Saxenian 1985; Hendry, Brown & Defillipi 2000). Since this chapter focusses on knowledge creation in knowledge-intensive industries, it does not directly touch on these streams.

[8] Other elements, such as organizational technology, type of alliances, and product or market characteristics, are also significant elements that have been discussed in the literature.

at least three levels of networking (Oliver & Liebeskind 1998). The *individual* level networks have to be studied at both the *intra-organizational* and the *interorganizational* levels. In addition, it is important to capture interorganizational relations on the organizational level, thus combining micro- and macro-network levels of analysis. Since only an integrative model that incorporates organizational data with individual-level data can capture the complex dynamics in inter-organizational collaborations, we need to show how these levels interact. Capturing the multiple levels of networks in the analysis also reflects what Ring and Van de Ven (1994, p. 103) propose as the interaction between formal and informal processes of negotiation, commitment, and execution, or the suggestion by Nee (1998, p. 85) that "Informal constraints embedded in norms and networks, operating in the shadows of formal organizational rules, can both limit and facilitate economic action." Both Nee (1998) and Ring and Van de Ven (1994) argue that informal norms and networks can facilitate the growth of new industries since they are based on trust and collective action.

Historical and developmental studies of the biotechnology industry may illustrate how norms of informal collaboration have contributed to the scientific growth of organizations. One such study, by Liebeskind *et al.* (1996), focussed on a case study of two major biotechnology firms in the USA. They found that informal individual-level collaborations between firm scientists and university scientists on scientific publications were frequent and very diverse. These collaborations involved scientists from 250 different universities and research centers (within the USA and international universities) over a period of 10 years. These findings show that informal norms of scientific collaboration with academic institutions were one of the main sources of learning for these two firms, whereas formal agreements between the two firms and the universities of the collaborating scientists were numbered and rare. In addition, qualitative findings based on interviews revealed that informal networks for learning were widespread in this industry, although their presence at the organizational level in the shape of formal contracts was limited to a very few instances only (Liebeskind & Oliver 1998).

The dominance of informal exchanges monitored by norms of informal reciprocity was evident in a study of the biotechnology industry in another culture – in Israel (*see* Chapter 6). Interviews with scientists in biotechnology firms and in universities conducted between 1994 and 1997 revealed the fact that, within the scientific community, everyone knows what kind of research is being done in all the other firms despite the high level of organizational secrecy imposed by the managers. This free flow of information was explained by the scientists who were interviewed to result from a few contextual factors. First, the fact that most scientists graduated from three main research universities that are also geographically proximate. Second, owing to the dense scientific and mentoring networks overlapping at conferences and seminars, and finally, because informal relations are highly normative in Israel, a significant free flow of information may be seen between scientists in that country, even though the scientists belong to competing organizations which formally refrain from collaborating with one another. In addition, the exchange of resources, instruments, and materials between competing firms is also common, owing to the scarcity of resources and the high costs of equipment. These scientific instrumental support exchanges are not always known at managerial level, but are one of the strategies used by firms' scientists to acquire necessary information, to exchange ideas, or to share equipment. Nee (1998, p. 88) argues that, "Opposition norms encourage individuals to directly resist formal rules ... when the organizational leadership and formal norms are perceived to be at odds with the interests and preferences of actors and subgroups, informal norms opposing formal rules will emerge to 'bend the bars of the iron cage' of the formal organizational rules." In this respect, the decoupling of the organization's formal rules and the scientists' informal norms illustrate the duality of competition (at the interorganizational–organizational level), and collaboration (at the interorganizational–individual scientist level). Based on the above, we thus propose the following hypothesis (H1) regarding competition and collaboration:

H1: In knowledge-intensive industries, where scientists are embedded in scientific networks and where firm-level competition is apparent we may find a decoupling between the tendency of individual scientists to cooperate and of organizations to compete.

Time and product life-cycle dimension effects on collaboration and competition

Competition between rival firms may turn into collaboration if and when various conditions change. We may find that these dual factors coexist in any interorganizational interaction if we consider the *distributive* versus the *integrative* elements in knowledge-appropriation processes. Distributive properties refer to the share of the joint outcome assigned to the individual firm, whereas integrative properties refer to the total joint outcome to the two collaborating firms. Larsson *et al.* (1998) argue that "Collaboration and competition are highly assertive learning strategies that aim to absorb as much new knowledge as possible" and that both the integrative and the distributive dimensions exist *simultaneously* in all organizational interactions. Inability to account for this coexistence leads to research fallacies:

While the collaborative learning fallacy is to neglect the distributive dimension of knowledge appropriation among the individual partner organizations, the competitive learning fallacy is to neglect the integrative dimension of joint knowledge development." (Larsson *et al.* 1998, p. 290)

Various examples of collaborating competitors appear in the literature. For example, Sakakibara (1993) describes R&D cooperation among competing Japanese semiconductor firms. In the same vein, Hagedoorn, Cyrayannis and Alexander (2001) document an emerging collaboration between IBM and Apple, which resulted in an increasing number of alliances between the two for joint technological development. In their qualitative exploratory case study, these authors show that IBM and Apple did not begin to collaborate until the early 1990s, once the DOS-based paradigm had become dominant. Their collaboration concerned opportunities for future interfaces and concentrated on R&D, while little attention was paid to collaboration in manufacturing or marketing. Hagedoorn, Cyrayannis and Alexander (2001, p. 848) also conclude that the alliances could turn back into competition again: "We can expect that technology alliances between proponents of competing basic designs will break down as the cooperation begins to focus on the design of one company to the detriment of the other." Using the terminology of Larsson *et al.* (1998), we could say that the collaboration between two rival firms will prevail while the integrative dimension becomes more dominant than the distributive dimension.

These observations, in the context of collaboration and competition, yield the two following hypotheses.

H2 (a): Competition may turn into collaborations when the integrative dimension is perceived to be more advantageous than the distributive dimension.

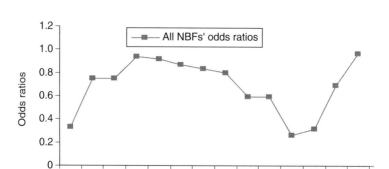

Figure 8.2 New biotechnology firms (NBFs) odds ratios for entering new learning alliances, by NBF age (the best-fitted model including firm and industry control variables).
Source: Oliver 2001

H2 (b): This collaboration may turn into a new phase of competition when interests of the firms begin to overlap so that the distributive dimension is perceived to be more advantageous than the integrative dimension.

The importance of alliances for firm learning is not an obvious one. Hoang and Rothaermel (2006) confront two contrasting theoretical perspectives on alliance-based advantage to examine project-level performance in the biotechnology industry:

The first theoretical perspective underscores alliances as vehicles for learning from the partner: alliances provide a platform to interact with and acquire the partner's capabilities (Lane & Lubatkin 1998). The second theoretical perspective highlights the role of alliances as a means to access the partner's capabilities (Grant & Baden-Fuller, 2004). Hoang & Rothaermel (2006, p. 1).

Thus, in view of a collaborative theoretical framework, alliances are the means for learning and building capabilities for both sides. Yet, through a competitive perspective, alliances are means for appropriating knowledge and capabilities.

In the context of the above presented duality, Oliver (2001)[9] has studied the formation of strategic alliances of biotechnology firms

---

[9] The study was based on 554 biotechnology firms (founded since 1975) over a period of 16 years (1975–1990), and 2034 strategic alliances in which the biotechnology firms were involved.

over their life-cycles. By focussing on longitudinal aspects of the "life-cycle" transition of biotechnology firms and the formation of alliances, she provided evidence that highlighted the interchangeability between stages of competition and stages of collaboration. It is well documented that biotechnology firms tend to form learning alliances (Powell, Koput & Smith-Doerr 1996; Powell *et al.* 2005), thus it may be expected that biotechnology forms will establish more new learning alliances every year of their life-cycles as a means of enhancing their learning capabilities. Yet Oliver (2001) found that there is no increasing linear pattern in the odds of forming new alliances by firm age (the steady increase in alliance formation is in the first four years).[10] Figure 8.2 shows the patterns of forming new alliances for each age-year of the firm. The detailed statistical evidence showed that once the firms reached five years of age the odds for forming new alliances each age-year declined toward age 11 years, followed by an inconclusive (in the form of statistical significance) further increase toward age 14 years. These findings were statistically robust even when additional variables were controlled for. The control variables were, at the firm level – size, number of technologies used by the firm, financial status of the firm, main biotechnology focus of the firm, and number of the firm's different foci, and on the industry level – industry cohort-year effect. Additional findings are of interest here. For example, the finding that the odds ratios for forming new alliances were strongest for firms in the therapeutic area, and the lowest for firms in agriculture biotechnology. This finding emphasizes the differentiated need to rely on alliances within different specializations for firms in the biotechnology industry. In addition, the findings showed that the absence of alliances formed by a firm and other biotechnology firms was associated with firm death. This finding supported the findings of previous studies and corroborated the idea that interorganizational alliances are vital to organizational survival in the biotechnology industry (Lane & Lubatkin 1998; Powell, Koput & Smith-Doerr 1996).

The interpretation for these findings is based on a learning-cycle argument of exploration and exploitation (March 1991; Nooteboom 1999b). This argument characterizes the learning processes in firms as

---

[10] This finding clearly supports the arguments in Powell, Koput and Smith-Doerr (1996, p. 122) that "a firm grew by becoming a player – it did not become a player by growing."

being built on cycles of exploration and exploitation, and these have an impact on the learning networks they establish. The exploration phase that occurs at the early stages of the R&D life-cycle is embedded in learning through collaborations with other firms and universities. This stage supports the "learning-through-networks" argument suggested by Powell and Brantley (1992), Powell, Koput and Smith-Doerr (1996), and Koput and Powell (2002). The wealth of knowledge in the interinstitutional network may help firms to economize on research costs and to explore options for alternative research directions and acquire knowledge on needed technologies. However, the exploration stage is relatively short and it has to be followed by an appropriation of the knowledge acquired, thus the knowledge value has to be captured. The evidence from the study by Oliver (2001) indicates that this stage lasts about five years in biotechnology firms. Now, once the product life-cycle has explored the options of learning from the environment through collaborative strategic alliances, the exploitation stage has been reached. During the exploitation stage, in which all the previously accumulated knowledge needs to be captured within the firm, organizational boundaries are redefined. At this stage, the product is being developed internally, whereby competition concentrates on product specificity or applications, and the "first-to-market" race is on. It is obvious that at this stage a "zero-sum" calculation of interests defines a phase of competition embedded within the collaborative networks.[11,12]

Based on the above argument the next hypothesis is suggested.

H3: Within network-based knowledge relations, collaboration tends to occur during the exploration stage, while competition intensifies during the exploitation stage, as firms aim to capture value from knowledge, thus tending to avoid establishing or re-initiating collaboration.

---

[11] Similarly, in a case study of three industries, Bengtsson and Kock (2000) found that competitors cooperate with activities far from the customer and compete in activities close to the customer.

[12] Additional institutional pressures can account for this life-cycle alliances dynamics, including the need to comply with other types of collaborative arrangement that are necessary for establishing other norms and forms of conduct imposed by venture capital firms or regulatory institutions such as the Food and Drug Administration (FDA) (e.g. the accounts in Martineau (2001) on regulatory pressures, and in Robbins-Roths (2000), on the pressures of venture capital firms to form alliances while going public).

Intensified competition within networks of collaborations may also be associated with vertical integration between firms, which can substitute for continuous alliances. Indeed, Danzon, Epstein and Nicholson (2004) argue that "the pharmaceutical–biotechnology industry has become increasingly concentrated over the past 15 years; in 1985 the 10 largest firms accounted for about 20 percent of worldwide sales, whereas in 2002 the 10 largest firms accounted for 48 per cent of sales. Much of this consolidation is the result of mergers." On the other hand, they argue, "despite rising R&D spending the productivity of the pharmaceutical industry, as measured by the number of compounds approved by the Food and Drug Administration (FDA) has deteriorated since 1996. Furthermore, the number of new drugs entering clinical trials has declined since 1998, which calls into question the effectiveness of mergers and the economies of scale hypothesis more generally. Moreover, several of the largest pharmaceutical firms have been trading at significantly lower price-to-earning ratios than many of their smaller rivals, indicating investors believe the larger firms will experience lower growth rates."[13]

For instance, in December 2001, Amgen, a biotechnology company founded in 1980, announced the acquisition of another biotechnology firm, Immunex.[14] Although there had been three big biotechnology mergers prior to this merger, Amgen is regarded as the first biotechnology company to achieve the stature of a major pharmaceutical company, and this transaction is seen as by far the largest merger in the biotechnology industry. Through this merger Amgen acquired the rights to Immunex's rheumatoid arthritis drug, Enbrel (etanercept), which is expected to reach sales of more than $1 billion next year and which Immunex projects could eventually sell for $4 billion a year. The deal thus allows Amgen to expand its product offering and gain access to a large cash flow to invest in its in-house R&D. Interestingly, the first thing Amgen did after this agreement was signed, was to stop its major collaborative arrangements with other firms – clearly a sign of consolidation and an intention to move from network collaboration toward the internal exploration of knowledge assets.

---

[13] Danzon, Epstein & Nicholson (2004, p. 2).
[14] The acquisition was finalized in July 2002.

An interesting comment made by the two chief executive officers (CEOs) was that they had been contemplating some sort of alliance between their firms for two years, but the merger discussions first became serious when the Immunex stock fell low enough to make the deal attractive for Amgen. The integration between the two firms substituted for, and was preferred to, network-based learning alliances between them.

As to the overall effect of this merger on the biotechnology industry, some analysts expected that many biotechnology R&D-based alliances are likely to turn into mergers between biotechnology firms, for a number of reasons:[15]

- Investors who were burned by the collapse of internet companies were looking for companies which could come up with products that sell quickly, so biotechnology firms with long-term research programs but no market products may be heavily penalized in the stock market.
- A single product on the market is not enough. Biotechnology firms are finding that they need more products to sustain their growth and stock prices, which puts pressure on them to buy other companies or to be acquired.
- It is inefficient for biotechnology firms to sustain their own overheads and sale forces for only a few products.
- There is a shortage of venture capital and initial public offering (IPO) funds, which leads firms to seek other sources of cash to fund their R&D programs.

Thus, because of the intensified competition for funding the pipeline products, and the need to economize on production and sales overheads, it has been observed that the institutionalized arrangement of alliances in biotechnology will generate a relatively consolidated industry, characterized by largely internalized R&D (Danzon, Epstein & Nicholson 2004).

Following the arguments in Child and Faulkner (1998) and Clarke-Hill, Li and Davies (2003) it may be suggested that when competition between two organizations is low and the cooperation high, a merger is anticipated. However, it is also expected that scarcity of

---

[15] *New York Times*, 23 June 2003.

environmental resources will be associated with the promotion of such mergers. This leads to the next suggested hypothesis.

H4: Consolidation within networks of knowledge-intensive organizations is associated with intensified industry-level competition for resources. The consolidation may be caused by increased competition, and may in turn lead to intensified competition for capturing value from knowledge assets.

Finally, in some instances, what appears to be a trust-based collaboration may, in fact, be considered as competition once the undisclosed interests of the collaborating parties becomes apparent. The following illustration may be rather a remote example, but it may be just the tip of an iceberg. One of the largest US biotechnology firms had a long-lasting and satisfactory R&D alliance with a foreign biotechnology firm.[16] In many interviews with scientists and managers in the firm, this collaboration was mentioned as an example of a highly successful alliance. However, one executive told us[17] in confidence that one night, while he was staying late at work, he heard some strange noises from the main R&D office. Peeking out from his office, he was amazed to see that two executives of the allied firm were opening cabinets and taking photos of confidential materials with small "spy" cameras. This action was in direct contravention of the trust-based collaborative relations between the two biotechnology firms. When this executive told his superiors the next day what he had seen, their decision was not to terminate the alliance, nor to disclose their awareness of the betrayal and espionage. Rather, they decided to adapt to the apparently competitive interests of their "collaborators," to establish a subsidiary within the territories of the foreign biotechnology firm, and to spy on their research in return. This story illustrates how firms which are investing in the "learning race" seek to absorb as much knowledge as possible relying on mixed forms of collaboration and competition (Larsson *et al.* 1998; Clarke-Hill, Li & Davies 2003).

Effects of the institutional environment on collaboration and competition

Changes in the institutional environment which reflect political, economic, or social changes may shift the balance between competition

---

[16] Names of firms involved are not disclosed due to agreed confidentiality.

[17] Based on interviews made by Oliver and Liebeskind during 1993.

and collaboration in knowledge-intensive firms. For instance, during a return visit to one of the biotechnology companies where interviews had been conducted four years earlier, Liebeskind and Oliver (1998) noted the increased dominance of formal contractual arrangements in the industry. In contrast to the numerous informal collaborations in the past between the firm's scientists and scientists from the universities or other biotechnology firms, now even the shortest exchange with any external scientist required a formal confidentiality agreement. This emphasis on confidentiality had appeared in the mid-1990s, and Liebeskind and Oliver (1998) argued that the growing emphasis on securing intellectual property rights in the biotechnology industry had had a significant impact on the nature of the interrelationships among academic scientists in molecular biology, because their interests had changed. Monetary-based contracted scientific exchanges became the norm even for many university scientists. In addition, this all resulted in intensified competition over intellectual property rights in the industry, and any overlapping research collaborations between biotechnology firms and academic scientists disappeared to avoid risking the loss of intellectual property rights in the biotechnology firms. Instead, academic scientists now seem to be "captured" by individual biotechnology firms through long-term contractual arrangements that prevent them from collaborating with other firms or even with other academic scientists (without signed contracts, and often they need permission from the firm with whom they have a formal collaboration). This suggests the following hypothesis.

H5: As a result of the intensified use of formal contractual arrangements and the protection of intellectual property rights, increased competition over the right to appropriate knowledge will lead to changes in the scope and width of the collaboration in network-based knowledge relations.

Positive and negative externalities in interorganizational collaboration and competition

The concept of "externalities," originally developed by the economists Pigou (1932) and Coase (1960), refers to the relationship between economic activities and social costs. However, the concept has also recently been introduced into the sociological literature. Callon (1998b) raises the issue of externalities in the sociology of networks and organizations. In economics, externalities are linked to market failures – that is, they are expressed in terms of efficiency. Specifically, an externality occurs when private and social costs (or benefits) are not the same. Therefore, the presence of an externality (positive or negative) in economics portrays the market as inefficient on account of gaps between private marginal income and marginal social costs. If a whole neighborhood can enjoy the wonderful scent of flowers cultivated in a private garden, this is an example of a positive externality. Conversely, if loud music is being played at a party in a private house but can be heard by all the neighbors, we have an example of a negative externality. Thus, negative externalities occur when private decision-makers do not take social costs into account, while positive externalities often discourage private efforts by reducing the ability of private parties to fully capture the fruits of their labors (Callon 1998b, p. 248).

A pure collaborative approach to interorganizational networks would assume that competition had exclusively negative externalities, whereas collaboration had only positive ones. For example, it has been claimed that competition externalities may induce rival firms to introduce new incompatible technologies at an early stage, which would further increase their R&D costs by reducing convergence toward a winning design. On the other hand, firms may collaborate in delaying the introduction of incompatible technologies (Kristiansen 1998), or increase their divergent external learning (Ring 1999) and thereby reduce their costs. In another case, it has been argued that in networks based on horizontal alliances collaboration between firms in similar domains generates positive externalities for both of them (Nault & Tyagi 2001).

In seeking a more balanced and holistic view of networks, and building on the above ideas on the duality of collaboration and competition in network-based knowledge relations, the next section offers some possible examples of the reverse logic, suggesting that competition may yield positive externalities while collaboration may generate negative externalities both for organizations and for the social system as a whole.

Examples of positive externalities of competition in networks

Third-party winners
When knowledge-intensive firms refrain from collaboration because of severe competition, they are still dependent on external learning.

Hence, they may search for other collaborative arrangements for learning with partners who are not active within their own competitive arena. In the biotechnology industry the main winners from the competition between firms are the research universities. Academic scientists conducting basic and applied biotechnology-related research benefit greatly in terms of research funding and collaboration opportunities among other things owing to the competition among the biotechnology firms.[18]

Availability of information to competitors through formal intellectual-property-rights protection

The following example is offered by Callon (1998b, p. 245). A pharmaceutical company is conducting intensive R&D and clinical tests on various active substances that it identifies. In order to protect its findings and possible future profits, the company monopolizes the discoveries by filing patent applications, and discloses some of the information it has produced. This information is valuable to competitors, which are now inspired to rethink the direction of their own research. Competitors can now enjoy, free of charge, the efforts and investments of a company that alone bears all the associated costs and risk.

Stochastic exploration leading to diversity in R&D

Heavy competition may direct biotechnology firms to explore internally unique domains of research, or to apply different and original techniques and methods, rather than exploiting knowledge available from other firms which reflects more routine procedures and accepted practices. When network forms of collaboration are institutionalized and become the norm, alternative intra-organizational paths to innovation may be disregarded. Following the argument of Stark (2001, pp. 72–73), efficient organizational models are based on a mix of Cartesian exploitation and stochastic exploration. If these two processes are conducted within the firm, rather than in networks, they can lead to the emergence of a wide diversity of methods, approaches, and products that will allow for larger-scale innovations, which in turn may lead to positive externalities and the possible production of

---

[18] These academic–industry collaborations also yield some negative externalities for the universities, and these have been discussed elsewhere (e.g. Liebeskind & Oliver 1998), but are beyond the scope of the present chapter.

significant social benefits for society in the form of the products and knowledge generated.

Examples of negative externalities of collaboration

Establishing converging joint cognition, group-think, or learning isomorphism

In dominant interfirm collaborative systems it is possible to observe a process of cognitive "oversocializing" whereby the collaborating firms tend to generate isomorphic learning processes. These similarities may mean that the collaborations generate redundancy in knowledge and mimetic adaptations of R&D practices. This in turn means that research directions all too soon meet in a single track, while limiting forces are imposed on the search for alternative directions and their exploration. Ring (1999, p. 250) suggests that membership in a networked organization might be described as "group-think." As commitment escalates, the actual learning may be diminished while its costs increase. Learning can become even more difficult in embedded networked organizations, as the organizational members are exposed to limited sources of knowledge or of divergent information.

Overly rapid learning

As has been pointed out in recent literature, rapid organizational learning, where limitations at the exploration stage promote speedy exploitation with underperformance, results in reduced organizational efficiency (March 1991; Stark 2001). This argument is based on March's (1991) argument that fast learners tend to move quickly on to the exploitation stage rather than continuing to explore. This then increases the danger of positive feedback and tight coupling (Stark 2001, p. 73) and, owing to the overly rapid learning in collaboration networks, also to the sub-optimization of organizational performance.

Free-riding and opportunism

Long-term collaborations in networks are based on the assumptions of trustworthiness and benevolence on the part of the collaborating parties. Specifically, this assumption is based on the expectation that each side will contribute its best efforts, intentions, and abilities to the common goal of the collaboration, without having to monitor the others' investments. Yet network collaborations can lead to free-riding (Williamson 1991) or hold-up problems (Das, Sen & Beal 1998). Building on the assumptions of the cybernetic model, it has been proposed in a theoretical cybernetic approach to trust (Oliver & Montgomery 2001) that systems which are based on trust and which therefore fail to apply enough negative correcting feedback loops, based upon information and sufficient monitoring, will ultimately witness their own dissolution. Because of the complexity of the inter-organizational learning process and the ambiguity in the measuring of inputs in learning collaborations, early signs of possible dissolution (such as various forms of free-riding and opportunistic behavior) are not adequately noted by other parties in the collaborative learning process. Consequently, the costs of delays or suboptimal product quality, or both, may add to the social costs of the collaboration.

Reduction in learning efficiency as the number of collaborations grows

If all the organizational learning is embedded in interorganizational networks, knowledge-intensive organizations may find themselves involved in multiple and divergent learning collaborations without being able to integrate and exploit the acquired knowledge and learned practices in an efficient way. The literature has shown that knowledge-transfer within firms is a highly complex matter (e.g. Tsai 1991; Schulz 2001). We may therefore expect that a firm's involvement in multiple external learning processes will serve to reduce its organizational efficiency and to cause problems of internalizing and integrating knowledge. There can be many reasons for this, for example multiple redundant learning cycles, non-optimal levels of a unit's "absorptive capacity" (Cohen & Levinthal 1990; Tsai 1991; Osborn & Hagedoorn 1997), problems in collecting, codifying, or combining new knowledge (Shulz 2001), or limited information flows. Further, when R&D units in one organization collaborate with other organizations, we may expect to see a compartmentalized structure between the R&D units in the various firms. As a result, the locus of learning lies in the dyadic interorganizational collaborating R&D units, and learning is not integrated into the different R&D teams in each individual firm. Hence, an "overcollaborating" type of organizational learning may not be adequately integrated, which in turn makes it difficult for the firm to exploit, in-house, the knowledge it has acquired.

Conclusions

Alliances are regarded as a crucial but volatile element in the attempt to gain competitive advantage (Hamel, Doz & Prahalad 1989; Ring & Van de Ven 1994; Larsson *et al.* 1998). However, they also entail complexities, dilemmas, and paradoxes in a variety of forms (Kogut 1998; Larsson *et al.* 1998; Clarke-Hill, Li & Davies 2003). Nor do they always fulfill the functions for which they are designed and may result in failure (Arino & de la Torre 1998; Podolny & Page 1998).

Acknowledging this complexity in the alliance phenomenon, Gnyawali and Madhavan (2001) draw attention to the simultaneous processes of cooperation and competition, and to the vital need for research to examine how network structure and competitive relations co-evolve, and to develop more integrative models of competitive organizational behavior. Following a similar logic, Larsson *et al.* (1998) point out that the emphasis on a "good-partner" behavior model that maximizes the gains from joint interpartner learning, disregards the extent to which individual organizations in fact appropriate this joint learning.

The primary contribution of the duality approach to competition and collaboration proposed in the present chapter lies in its focus on certain parameters that introduce complexity into the study of network-based knowledge relations. Further, the chapter argues that adoption of the prism metaphor allows researchers to seek coexisting instances of interplay between collaborative and cooperative behaviors among firms in networks such as the biotechnology industry. The methodological assumption encapsulated in the prism metaphor encourages researchers to assume that the relations observed may be composed of many subrelations, and that these may sometimes contradict one another. Yet, a prism-less model of observation may miss these dualities, and thus miss the complex analytical implications that recognition of the complexities in networks may bring.

The general argument is that duality is generated by the ongoing reciprocal relationship between exploration and exploitation, and between network-based exploration and privatization, all stemming from the tension surrounding the appropriation of knowledge – a tension in which the learning processes are embedded.

The collaboration–competition duality in networks is also evident in the analysis of possible network externalities. An attempt to "break" the common perception of positive externalities from collaboration and negative externalities from competition, has yielded a few examples of the opposite effects, and it has been suggested that network forms of organization also entail some "social costs" and risks for the participants and for the wider social systems. The competition or collaboration between any two actors may affect other actors in an industry.

9 | *Further directions for understanding interorganizational collaborations and learning*

The aim of this book is to offer a complex mapping of actors, forms, levels, processes, and domain issues associated with issues of learning and knowledge creation in alliances and collaborations within the biotechnology industry. The mapping is not exhaustive or conclusive as it leads to further research directions, new analytical concepts, foci directions, and interrelations that need to be examined. In many respects, the book offers a taste of the many important "flavors" associated with studies on learning, collaborations, and networks in the biotechnology industry. In this final chapter, the general findings and arguments presented in the book are summarized, and a few important directions that future research might explore further are suggested.

The first chapter introduced the concepts of "collaboration" and "learning" in the context of the biotechnology industry. Understanding these concepts is related to issues of levels of analysis, which are needed for understanding of the knowledge creation and learning processes within and between organizations. The aim of the chapter was to establish the analytic elements used in the book and to exemplify the complexity involved in studying exchanges that are embedded in multilevels and multi-units.

The organizational literature on alliances and learning in the biotechnology industry was reviewed in Chapter 2, which introduced the main actors in the industry and highlighted some of the research on them. In addition, the chapter provided some comparison with what is known about other knowledge-intensive industries.

Much research devoted to organizational change uses a macro-level ecological approach which emphasizes the impact of environmental factors on changes in populations of organizations and organizational forms. Chapter 3 tried to widen the focus of new organizational forms to the inheritance of key features from existing parental forms. The elements inherited are associated with internal features and structures, and these are related to learning and collaboration. The chapter started by suggesting that new biotechnology firms (NBFs) constitute a new organizational form and characterized the elements found in this form. Then, it reviewed additional new forms for conducting biotechnology collaborations and learning, including consortia, university spin-offs, and incubators, and their internal features. All these features are based on some sort of synergy between academic basic science and industrial applied science.

Academic-scientific entrepreneurship is a largely growing phenomenon, in general, and in the context of the biotechnology industry, in particular (Rothaermel, Agung & Jiang 2007). On the organizational level, this issue relates to the changing structure and processes within universities toward various modes of entrepreneurial activities. On the individual level, this phenomenon regards scientists who are becoming more involved in the commercialization of their inventions. Chapter 4 is based on a study conducted on such scientific entrepreneurs within Israeli universities and tries to explain the various collaborations they are involved in.

Chapter 5 focussed on issues of knowledge creation, discoveries, and inventions, as well as scientific entrepreneurship. All these issues are embedded in the norms and regulations of the institutional environment and these shape the actions of universities, scientists, and networks of collaboration. In this chapter, the author and Julia Porter Liebeksind explored the effects of institutional context on the conduct and outcomes of scientific research through the lens of property rights arrangements. The chapter investigated the allocation of property rights of two historical breakthrough inventions in biotechnology and asked whether the absence of narrowly defined property rights in these two inventions was a deterrent to the development of subsequent property rights in commercially valuable new inventions that employed them. This chapter brings in the context of the institutional environment and intellectual property rights policies, and their relations to the conduct of inventions in open versus closed science.

Under the new structure of university–industry collaborative science, university scientists and biotechnology scientists and firms are constantly searching for learning collaborations. An investigation of the search processes shows that they are based on a variety of forms, basic assumptions, processes, expected outcomes, and additional characteristics. Yet, analyses of interviews with key players in these exchanges led to the suggested analytical metaphoric distinction between the linear and the chaotic processes for learning-based collaborations, and these were described in Chapter 6.

Chapter 7 brought in an important element in understanding the complex structure of collaborations and learning, namely "trust." Learning may be fully understood only if we take into account the construction of trustworthy relations both at the organizational level and at the individual level. Trust is not only an important, even crucial, element in collaborations: Chapter 7 suggested an argument that the changing norms about knowledge and discoveries had an impact on the trust basis of scientific exchanges and collaborations.

Moving back to the organizational level, Chapter 8 brought in the concepts of collaborations in the context of competition in the biotechnology industry. This chapter is based on the argument that the study of interorganizational networks for learning and knowledge creation requires the adoption of a *duality* framework of collaboration *and* competition and the application of a *prism-like methodology*. Three main search lines for observing this duality are offered. The chapter ended by accounting for learning externalities, both positive and negative, of competition and collaboration in networks of learning.

The book as a whole has tried to provide a wide range of observations on the issue of networks of learning in the biotechnology industry. Each chapter has provided a review, suggested analytical concepts, or opened an array of structural and developmental complexities associated with these issues. The topics covered also result in new possible and needed directions of inquiry. At this point a few emerging questions and new directions for further research are highlighted.

First, based on the directions offered in Chapter 8, will the "learning-through-networks" institution decline in the biotechnology industry over time, as firms grow and the industry becomes more mature, or will the "network form" (Powell 1990) remain the dominant mode of governance?

At this stage it is difficult to offer even an educated guess. Pisano (2002), argues that "While many new biotechnology companies had visions of becoming fully integrated pharmaceutical companies, the high costs of drug development forced virtually all new entrants to pursue a strategy of collaboration with larger, more established pharmaceutical companies. Only a handful of new entrants were able to establish themselves as fully integrated pharmaceutical companies." However, as mergers and acquisitions seem to increase, we may be seeing evidence of a system consolidation. This consolidation may lead, in turn, to more exploitation within firms and more competition between them at the price of less interfirm collaboration for learning.

Another question concerns the direction to adopt in exploring the duality of the two relational forms. Although Khanna, Gulati and Nohria's (1998) argument that the unit of analysis for studying alliances should be not the single alliance but, rather, the broader range of activities pursued by firms, it is also important to acknowledge the paradoxical nature of strategic alliances and the dilemmas in which such alliances are embedded (Larsson *et al.* 1998; Clarke-Hill, Li & Davies 2003). The contextual variation of alliances and collaborations should be further explored (Nooteboom 1999b). Only qualitative in-depth case studies are able to capture the wealth of the contextual variations that are promoted by the duality perspective, so that the prism methodology may be applied.

On the front of the methodological effect on what we know on collaborations and learning, issues of trust in various scientific collaborations were raised in Chapter 7, which suggests that understanding the role of trust in collaboration and its association with the intellectual property rights regimens needs to be further explored through qualitative research based on interviews and observations in collaborative research. Whilst the wealth of publicly available quantitative data available on strategic alliances in biotechnology is impressive, it has attracted many researchers to study these collaborations statistically. Yet, there are very few studies that offer detailed qualitative research on the internal mechanisms of these collaborations and the complexities associated with them. These include, for example, the role of trust, credits, tacit, and explicit knowledge, the nature of the technology, the organization of the scientific work conducted, and the institutional affiliation of the participants. Chapter 3 offered an inside observation on what was titled the NBF as a new organizational form; Chapter 6 explored cognitive metaphors for how collaboration partners should be attracted, whilst Chapter 7 was based on some insightful qualitative observations into the changing role of trust in interorganizational biotechnology collaborations. In addition, some of the author's understanding on the duality of collaboration and competition resulted from qualitative interviews conducted in firms. Thus, more qualitative, detailed, and informative research is needed for a better understanding of collaborations and learning in biotechnology.

The methodology has yet another important aspect regarding the approach used in studying networks of collaborations. The point here is that understanding the effectiveness of network structures in any given context may be greatly enhanced if the entire network structure is analyzed. Most studies of strategic alliances in biotechnology take an organizational unit or project-dyadic unit approach to their analyses of alliances.[1] Yet very few studies are able to study full networks of exchanges and collaborations. Such studies, with the most impressive study by Powell *et al.* (2005), are unique as they require detailed and large scale datasets on all actors involved in alliances at each time-period, in a certain region or industry specialization, and may be analyzed only with advanced statistical, mathematical, or graphic methods.

A full network study may provide answers to more complex issues about collaborations. For example, any given research collaboration between an NBF and a university is likely to be more effective if the NBF collaborates with academic partners who are exclusive to the collaboration (i.e. they do not collaborate with other firms). This information, as well as information about structural holes, is vastly important in understanding competition (Burt 2005), but may be found only if full-scale networks are studied. In addition, network measures, such as structural equivalence, overlapping subgroups, or affiliation properties of actors and events, clustering, structural balance, and transitivity (Wasserman & Faust 1994, especially parts III and IV), may also be observed and understood only when an entire network is studied. Such full network studies will enable us, for instance, to examine the structure of competing interorganizational collaborations for a given biotechnology product. Following the classic definition of

---

[1] When the *organization* is the unit of analysis, the study focusses on questions about trends in strategic alliances, relations between firm characteristics and alliance characteristics, and so on. When the *alliance* is the unit of analysis, the study focusses on the dyads associated with the alliance and asks questions about the composition of partners in the alliances as related to success factors, the nature of previous alliances on the success of the current alliance, or the characteristics of the organizations involved in the alliance and the type of alliance formed.

effectiveness by Yuchtman and Seashore (1967) as the ability to gather and make use of the best environmental resources, such a study may illustrate how competition in the biotechnology industry depends on the ability of individual firms to establish network relations with the best available partners and to initiate these relationships at a sufficiently early point to gain an advantage over competitors. The above-mentioned shortage of studies of full network collaborations in biotechnology leads to a request that we see more full network studies on biotechnology collaborations, which will result in a better understanding of cross-sectional differences and of longitudinal effects.

Finally, how far are the claims made here to be generalized to other industries or contexts? This is a very complex question and it is hard to provide a clear answer. The fact that interorganizational and interinstitutional collaborations are considered unique, intensive, and crucial in the biotechnology industry – and its relation to the wide range of actors and forms for learning and collaborations – makes this industry a unique case. However, it is possible to expect that issues such as search modes, trust, scientific commons, and science privatization, entrepreneurial scientists, and the collaborative–competitive duality depicted above may be expected to appear in other knowledge-intensive industry segments. These areas may be characterized by dominant "learning races," where knowledge is distributed among many actors, where firms collaborate with universities and research centers, and where knowledge may be appropriated, captured, and privatized in patents or in products.

On the other hand, forms of knowledge-intensive organizations such as law firms or consultancies of varied form or scope do not appear to incorporate the elements suggested which makes it less likely that the framework implied here would be applicable to their operation.

Additional implications for studying interorganizational networks

The various chapters in the book, and the multilevel model for studying networks of collaborations and learning specified in Chapter 1, also raise important implications for research on social networks themselves. In the next section, a few valuable directions that should be a part of the research on interorganizational networks are suggested.

Trust in learning networking

Trust is a primary factor in fostering and perpetuating social network relations (Gulati 1995; Oliver 1997; Ring & Van de Ven 1992). In the typical model of social-network relations, exchanges take place within the context of socially established trust relationships, such as those which exist among members of a close community, cultural grouping, organization, or profession (Ouchi 1980; Wilkins & Ouchi 1983; Granovetter 1985; Coleman 1990). In these situations, shared norms, common socialization processes, and informal monitoring and sanctioning systems all engender trust, which then serves as a lubricant for economic exchange (Granovetter 1985; Bradach & Eccles 1989; Coleman 1990; Oliver 1997, Oliver & Montgomery 2001). One question that arises here is how firms foster trust in social-network relations between their own employees and non-employees. One way in which firms may achieve this end is by "free-riding" on existing social networks that encompass both their own employees and others; for instance, a firm's employees may be members of an industry group, profession, or closely knit local community. Firms may also rely on social networks within the firm itself to engender norms of trustworthy behavior that also apply to dealings with outsiders. In addition, a firm may engender trust by enforcing norms of acceptable social behavior among its employees through bureaucratic rules or incentives, or both. Finally, a firm may engender trust by adopting some rules of social behavior from an external community that it wishes to maintain social-network relations with. Understanding and adopting trust-engendering mechanisms within and between firms and within scientific communities are crucial for establishing full-range collaboration in learning networks and further research is required in this arena.

Levels of analysis and formal/informal collaborations

The model suggested in Chapter 1, and partially illustrated in Chapter 8, argued that the use of multiple levels of analysis may lead to a deeper understanding of the nature of interorganizational network relationships. In particular, what may appear at first glance to be a high level of cooperation in interorganizational relationships when considered at one level may be revealed as relationships characterized as conflict when examined at another level – explicitly or implicitly (Hardy & Phillips 1995). For example, the study by Liebeskind *et al.* (1996) of collaborative research relationships in biotechnology might lead us to conclude that there are close and uniformly cooperative research relationships between universities and NBFs. However, when multiple levels of analysis are considered, and when these collaborative relationships are analyzed in a longitudinal framework, they can also be understood to be characterized by a high degree of conflicts of interest between actors. The intended outcome of collaborative research between university scientists and NBF scientists is to convert academic research into commercial products. However, the issue of private property rights and ownership of these rights is an issue of potential conflict of interest between universities and scientists.

The social embeddedness of interfirm partnerships may also be conceptualized at several levels. Hagedoorn (2006) refers to embeddedness levels which correspond to different social contexts that surround interfirm partnerships, and distinguishes between *environmental* embeddedness (e.g. country and industry effects), *interorganizational* embeddedness (e.g. historical setting and previous networks) and *dyadic* embeddedness (e.g. one-on-one characteristics of the linkages between firms).

The comparison of formal and informal exchanges and collaborations is also an important element in the model. As suggested in Chapter 7, what used to be informal university–industry collaborations have now transformed and become based on formal contracts between firms and university technology-transfer offices. In order to protect themselves against undue appropriation of academic knowledge and conflicts of interest among their faculties, universities have moved increasingly to regulate the involvement of their faculties in industrial research (Argyres & Liebeskind 1998). Thus, while scientists may collaborate willingly in research, the institutions for which they work may seek to inhibit cooperation because their own missions are in conflict. This research direction, suggested in Chapter 5 and Chapter 7, on issues of private and public knowledge, the changing structure of universities, and the changing nature of scientific collaborations, is being explored in the current literature but will benefit from further research as it introduces a highly dynamic area of change and entails normative interests as well as incentives, and rewards complexities and transitions.

Process issues in collaborations

Another distinction between network types needs to focus on the processes that enable and facilitate or hamper these learning networks. Following the resource base approach to organizational learning of Nonaka and Hirotaka (1995) we perceive interorganizational collaborations over knowledge as a process in which knowledge is externalized and internalized. More specifically, in order to establish the needed learning collaborations, organizations need to externalize their internal knowledge to other organizations, and to internalize knowledge from other organizations. According to Nonaka's (1994) learning theory, the interaction between individuals who share knowledge requires a process in which tacit knowledge is externalized and becomes explicit, whilst explicit knowledge needs to become internalized by the receiving unit. This learning process is complex and demanding within organizational units, where knowledge is gathered for the joint purpose of organizational profit-maximizing. If this is the case in interorganizational collaborations, it is to be expected that the process will be much more complex since in boundary-crossing collaborations between two or more organizations knowledge becomes unbounded and as a result the knowledge-based utility for each organization may be at risk.

Some examples from the literature exemplify the complexity and problematic aspects of interorganizational learning directed toward generating new knowledge. Strategic alliances are defined by Gulati (1998, p. 293) as "voluntary agreements between firms involving exchange, sharing, or co-development of products, technologies, or services. They can occur as a result of a wide range of motives and goals, take a variety of forms, and occur across vertical and horizontal boundaries." The literature provides evidence that strategic alliances are crucial in some markets, and therefore the rate of formation of strategic alliances has increased in recent decades, especially in technology-intensive industries (Hagedoorn 1993; Mowery, Oxley & Silverman 1996). Powell, Koput and Smith-Doerr (1996) found in their study of the biotechnology industry that because of the intensive use of strategic alliances in this industry firms without ties are becoming rare. They conclude that firms are unlikely to retreat from their use of alliances since the locus of innovation is in the network, and firms use alliances as an admission ticket to new innovations.

Despite all listed advantages in strategic alliance, research must also emphasize the questionable aspects of alliances and their possible costs to firms. On this front, Osborn and Hagedoorn (1997, p. 270) highlight a problematic question related to the learning benefits of strategic alliances: "If organizational learning within a corporate hierarchy is problematic, surely such learning is much more complex in the context of a cooperative effort." In addition, they note that because research-intensive cooperation involves the discovery and absorption of tacit knowledge that cannot be easily transferred, non-equity alliances may not advance absorption back to the sponsors as well as do hierarchical forms, thus learning internalization is problematic as well. In this vein, Park and Ungson (2001) argue that alliances fail because of opportunistic hazards as partners try to maximize their own interests and because it is difficult to coordinate two independent units. But even in cooperative transfers we may encounter failures in collaborations and transfer of knowledge. Sorenson, Rivkin and Fleming (2006, p. 997) point to two main reasons for such possible failure in what they title "recipe transfer." One reason is that the recipient rarely grasps the original recipe completely owing to imperfections in the transfer process as such processes need to *perfectly* understand the recipe. The other reason is that the local ingredients and experience of the sender rarely match those of the recipient. Such failures may be understood only with a process-based follow-up and analysis.

High transaction costs related to alliances should be reevaluated. For example, it has been argued that firms entering alliances face hazards, since partners' behavior is unpredictable and opportunistic behavior likely, and partners may free-ride by restricting their contributions (Williamson 1991). In addition, rapid environmental changes may lead to changes in organizational needs and thus may affect the partners in the alliance. Alliances may also reduce firms' interest in developing certain competencies or technologies (Hamel, Doz & Prahalad 1989), and reduce revenues through profit-sharing (Shan 1990). Using transaction costs arguments, Pisano (1990) examines how two sources of transaction costs, small-number bargaining hazards, and appropriability concerns, may affect established firms' choices between in-house and external sources of research and development (R&D). In a study of 92 biotechnology R&D projects that major pharmaceutical companies had sponsored either in-house or through external contractual arrangements. Pisano (1990) found that small-numbers–bargaining problems motivated firms to internalize R&D. Thus, a pharmaceutical company will be more likely to internalize R&D in those biotechnology product areas in which R&D capabilities are concentrated in fewer suppliers.

In addition, the study found that a pharmaceutical firm will be more likely to undertake a biotechnology R&D project in-house when it has accumulated more in-house R&D experience in the relevant area of biotechnology, and a firm with a higher percentage of its business in pharmaceuticals will be more likely to internalize biotechnology–pharmaceutical R&D projects.

Additional organizational risk factors relate to the incompleteness of contracts. These result from the inability of the partners to anticipate all future contingencies at the time when contractual relations evolve, and from the fact that property rights and future income are not well defined. Thus, the parties are exposed to possible opportunistic exploitation by their partners and also to hold-up problems (Hart 1995; Das, Sen & Beal 1998). Thus, alliances also expose organizations to the risk of being exploited through appropriations of knowledge, ideas, or products, as a result of the interdependence that has been built up.

Owing to the risk associated with alliances it is important to explore the answers to the questions of how organizations reduce selection uncertainty, what mechanisms enable firms to do so, and how organizations form alliances. All these issues are process-based and an inside focus may facilitate our understanding of what counts for success or failure of alliances. For example, in a study of 18 for-profit and two non-profit biotechnology firms, Mitsuhashi (2002) found that the alliance-formation processes were based on five phases, which included defining opportunities, identifying sets of prospective partners, making contacts, proceeding with due diligence processes, and establishing alliances. Three types of selection uncertainty were detected, and included:

- *Uncertainty about the technological competence of prospective partners*: utilizing organizational know-how and structuring subunits to scan environments, collect information, and assess prospective partners (the *internal* mechanism).
- *Uncertainty about behavioral aspects of prospective partners*: the relational mechanism operates on the principle that firms form

alliance networks based on preexisting social ties and personal rapport as a way to reduce selection uncertainty (the *relational* mechanism).

- *Uncertainty about potential commercial success of proposing alliances*: relying upon reputations of prospective partners and usage of reputations of prospective partners to reduce selection uncertainty.

The study of the patterns of changing or maintained structures of networks over time is important for understanding learning collaborations between firms. Evolutionary theory of strategic alliances may, for example, question whether and how routine processes at the partnering-firm level influence the performance of cooperative agreements. Such a question is based on the dyadic level effects of one partner on the routines of the other partner to an alliance. In this context, Zollo, Reuer and Singh (2002) found, based on a sample of 145 biotechnology strategic alliances, that the greater the number of previous alliances established by a firm with the same partner, the better the performance of the focal alliance, and that the positive performance effect of partner-specific experience will be greater for non-equity alliances than for equity alliances.

Learning networks as exploration and exploitation

Exploration and exploitation cycles of learning are highly important for understanding patterns of interorganizational collaborations in knowledge-intensive industries such as biotechnology. As maintained by Powell, Koput and Smith-Doerr (1996), internal capabilities and external learning collaborations are not substitutes but are complementary. Through collaborations, firms establish access to new resources which cannot be developed internally, and these resources may be evaluated and further exploited internally (Nelson 1990). The combination of external learning and internal exploitation is associated with a dynamic view of learning introduced by March (1991) and Nooteboom (1999a). March (1991) distinguished between the two central concepts of exploitation and exploration, whereas Nooteboom (1999a) unfolded the process that connects the stages. Based on the latter's argument, "exploration" starts with radical innovation which is the stage at which a novel practice or idea is introduced. Then there is a stage of consolidation, in which, through trial and error, a dominant design emerges. The exploitation stage which follows starts with generalization associated with consolidation and increase of scale. The model proposed by Nooteboom (1999a) is insightful since it refers to a shift between consolidation and interfirm strategic alliances. To put it in Nooteboom's (1999a, p. 109) words, "disintegration is dynamically efficient to generate 'exploration' while integration into tighter intrafirm networks is needed to achieve productive efficiency in 'exploitation'." These assumptions were the theoretical basis of a longitudinal study of strategic alliances in the biotechnology industry. In this study, Oliver (2001)[2] found that biotechnology firms tend to have a clear life-cycle pattern of alliance-formation over time – the first years of biotechnology firms are associated with increased odds of forming new alliances, whereas after a peak age these odds are decreasing, followed by a further increase again. This finding was interpreted as depicting the exploration–exploitation cycles of learning of biotechnology firms (based on Nooteboom 1999a, 1999b). At the exploration stage, acquiring new knowledge and establishing interorganizational learning alliances are vital for the firm's product development. Thus, we should expect an increasing pattern of alliance formation at this initial stage. Consequently, at the following exploitation stage, the study found that firms tended to reduce the formation of new alliances and exploit the knowledge acquired internally. This pattern was interpreted as an internalization of learning whilst trying to capture and commodify the knowledge acquired during the exploration stage.

The awareness of the dialectic nature of strategic alliances in the organizational literature has increased only in recent years. In this context, de Rond and Bouchikhi (2004) argued that, based on their literature review of strategic alliances, process studies informed by a dialectical theory appear to be markedly absent. They explored the characteristics and contributions of a dialectical approach in understanding interorganizational collaborations and focussed on a longitudinal case study of a biotechnology-based alliance. The case illustrates the co-evolutionary interchange of design and emergence, cooperation and competition, trust and vigilance, expansion and contraction, and control and autonomy. In their view it is important to treat alliances as heterogeneous phenomena and as subject to social

---

[2] This study was also reviewed in Chapter 8.

construction in which unintended consequences are the main change agent. Chapter 8 suggested some specifications of these complexities.

Structure of networks: brokerage and closure in collaborative structures

Issues of the network structure of collaborations matter to a great degree. Many studies have looked at issues of structure and collaboration, but there are additional options in this research domain. In general (Burt 2005), two main structural positions may be termed by the use of network-based structures. Such positions may be important for firms which collaborate for learning, yet they may be associated with different returns. These structural position terms may be titled as two distinct modes:

- *amplified* centrality mode of learning
- *brokerage* centrality mode of learning.

Both terms refer to the centrality position of firms within their networks of collaborations and learning. Yet, centrality may be based on different structures and be associated with different means. The first mode of wide-range access is based on multiple collaborations with many potential partners, in which learning is generated from the processes established with multiple partners. The efficiency of using multiple resources is amplified when the collaborative partners are information sources that are highly central in the network of collaborations. In network terms, this will be evident in a centrality measure that increases as the number of collaborations increase, and as their centrality is high. Thus, the higher the centrality of an actor and the centrality of the actors with whom he collaborates, the higher the access he has to information through collaborators. As a result, the actor may have access to amplified learning opportunities.

The second mode of access is based on the structural position of "structural holes." Structural holes may be characterized as being positioned between other actors who do not communicate directly. The absence of direct communication between any two actors gives the third actor – namely the "broker" – a position of power over the other two actors, and places him in a position to have information access advantages. Burt (2005, p. 59) argues that brokerage across "structural holes" permits many other advantages, including a vision advantage. This advantage results from the opportunity to "learn about things they didn't know they didn't know." The leading hypothesis offered by Burt is that actors who stand near the "holes" in social structures are at higher risk of good ideas. In the organizational context, such brokerage positions will provide access to information that is solely available to the organization due to its structural position. As a result, the organization will have the advantage of integrating various learning opportunities and establishing a unique synergy that will enhance future creative and original scientific products. Thus, the information and learning of the firm will be highly proprietary and unavailable to other members of the networks. Therefore we should expect that higher levels of brokerage centrality will be associated with higher access to proprietary and valuable learning opportunities, and will not be available to other members of the network who are not positioned as brokers.

These two structural modes are offered here as an example of how organizational positions within the structure of networks may be associated with their learning outcomes. However, the advantage of brokerage positioning is only a hypothesis in this context and, of course, even if found to be corroborated in empirical research on biotechnology firms it would depend on many additional features of the organization. Thus, future studies in this context may offer insightful understanding of questions such as "whether one of these positions is of greater benefit for the organization or whether both positions are needed for an efficient learning and collaborating structure?" or "what kinds of collaborative structures are of advantage in what kinds of learning processes?"

Another important network structure measure is density. Schilling and Phelps (2007) argue that the structure of networks influences their potential for knowledge creation. Specifically, dense local clustering provides information transmission capacity in the network by fostering communication and cooperation. These scholars studied the patent performance, longitudinally, of 1106 firms in 11 industry alliances networks. Their empirically supported hypothesis is that firms which are embedded in alliance networks that are highly clustered and offer high reach (a short path average to a wide range of firms) will be more innovative than firms that do not occupy such positions.

In this suggested research vein, when the context is of network structure and firm performance in biotechnology, Maurer and Ebers (2006) conducted a comparative case analysis of six NBFs in Germany and explored how configuration of the evolution of their social capital affected their performance. The importance of this study is also associated with its process-based focus mentioned earlier in this chapter, but, at this point, the contribution of their findings in the context of the structure of networks and its changing features is highlighted.

In their study on social capital of firms, Maurer and Ebers (2006) followed the three dimensions of social capital offered by Nahapiet and Goshal (1998), namely, structural, relational, and cognitive dimensions. Based on qualitative interviews, they identified the inertial forces of social capital that are associated with relational "lock-ins" (based on obligations and norms of reciprocity which lead to inertia in social capital) and cognitive "lock-ins" (that result from cognitive schemes similarity of collaborators and frequency of interactions and lead to inertia in social capital). They argue that firms can overcome the relational and cognitive inertia in their social capital by three major mechanisms: breaking strong and cohesive old relations; establishing new collaborations; and learning new cognitive schemes. From this study about the relations between network structure and organizational outcomes we understand that the internal management of firms' relationships with external partners, and the changes in these collaborations, permit firms to use their social capital in an advantageous way. Thus, not only does the structure of a firm's networks count, but also the degree to which their composition changes and adapts over time to the firm's needs.

This book comes to an end with a recommendation for future research on learning, collaborations, and networks in biotechnology. We will benefit from additional studies that look at the processes in which trust is established and secured in learning collaborations; which take advantage of our ability to look into multiple levels and units of analyses; which focus on untangling process issues in learning collaborations, such as differentiating between exploration and exploitation in learning processes; and which establish meaningful linkages between the structure of collaborative networks and the processes of collaborations and learning, and their outcomes at individual, tie, and firm levels. Obviously, comparative studies with other emerging and existing knowledge-intensive industries are of great importance and value.

References

Abernethy, W. J. and Clark, K. B. (1985) Innovation: mapping the winds of creative destruction. *Research Policy* 14, 3–22.

Agrawal, A. and Henderson, R. (2002) Putting patents in context: exploring knowledge transfer from MIT. *Management Science* 8, 44–60.

Aldrich, H. E. and Pfeffer, J. (1976) Environments of organizations. *Annual Review of Sociology* 2, 79–105.

Aldrich, H. E. and Zimmer, C. (1986) Entrepreneurship through science networks. In Sexton, D. L. and Smilor, R. W. (eds.), *The Art and Science of Entrepreneurship*. Ballinger Publishing.

Anderson, P. (1999) Complexity theory and organization science. *Organization Science* 10, 216–232.

Anderson, P., Mayer, A., Eisenhardt, K., Carley, K. and Pettigrew, A. (1999) Introduction to the special issue: applications of complexity theory to organization science. *Organization Science* 10, 233–236.

Antonelli, C. (1999) The evolution of the industrial organization of the production of knowledge. *Cambridge Journal of Economics* 23, 243–260.

Argyres, S. N. and Liebeskind, J. P. (1998) Privatizing the intellectual commons: universities and the commercialization of biotechnology research. *Journal of Economic Behavior and Organization* 35, 427–454.

(2002) Governance inseparability and the evolution of US biotechnology industry. *Journal of Economic Behavior and Organization* 47, 197–219.

Ariño, A. and de la Torre, J. (1998) Learning from failure: towards an evolutionary model of collaborative ventures. *Organization Science* 9(3), Special issue: Managing partnerships and strategic alliances, 306–325.

Arora, A. and Gambardella, A. (1990) Complementary and external packages linkages: the strategy of the firms in biotechnology. *Journal of Industrial Economics* 38, 361–379.

(1994) The changing technology of technological change: general and abstract knowledge and the division of innovative labour. *Research Policy* 23(5) (September), 523–532.

Arundel, A. (2001) The relative effectiveness of patents and secrecy for appropriation. *Research Policy* 30, 611–624.

Arrow, K. (1962) Economic welfare and the allocation of resources for invention. In Nelson, R. R. (ed.), *The Rate and Direction of Inventive Activity: Economic and Social Factors*. National Bureau of Economic Research.

Bains, W. (1998) Genes to proteins in context. *Trends in Biotechnology* 16, 2–4.

Barley, S. R., Freeman, J. and Hybels, R. C. (1992) Strategic alliances in commercial biotechnology. In Nohria, N. and Eccles, R. (eds.), *Networks and Organizations*. Harvard Business School.

Barrett, F. J. and Cooperrider, D. L. (1980) Generative metaphor intervention: a new behavioral approach for working with systems divided by conflicts and caught in defensive perception. *Journal of Applied Behavioral Science* 26, 219–239.

Baum, J. A. C. and Singh, J. V. (1994) Organizational niches and the dynamics of organizational mortality. *American Journal of Sociology* 100, 346–380.

Beckman, C. and Haunschild, P. R. (2002) Network learning: the effects of partners' heterogeneity of experience on corporate acquisitions. *Administrative Science Quarterly* 47, 92–124.

Ben David, J. (1971) *The Scientist's Role in Society: A Comparative Study*. Prentice-Hall, Inc.

Bengtsson, M. and Kock, S. (2000) "Coopetition" in business networks – to cooperate and compete simultaneously. *Industrial Marketing Management* 29, 411–426.

Berg, P. (1997) Interview conducted by Sally Smith Hughes, Regional Oral History Office, Bancroft Library, University of California, Berkeley.

Bergmann Lichtenstein, B. (2000) Self organized transitions: a pattern amid the chaos of transformative change. *Academy of Management Executive* 14, 128–141.

Bok, D. (1981) President's report: business and the academy. *Harvard Magazine* May–June, 23–35.

Boyer, P. (1997) Interview by Sally Smith Hughes, Regional Oral History Office, Bancroft Library, University of California, Berkeley.

Brandenburger, A. M. and Nalebuff, B. J. (1996) *Co-opetition*. Doubleday.

Bozeman, B., Laredo, P. and Mangematin, V. (2007) Introduction: understanding the emergence and deployment of "nano" S&T. *Research Policy* 36, 807–812.

Bourdieu, P. and Wacquant, L. (1992) *Invitation to Reflexive Sociology*. University of Chicago Press.

Bradach, J. and Eccles, R. (1989) Price, authority, and trust: from ideal types to plural forms. *Annual Review of Sociology* 15, 97–118.

Broekstra, G. (1996) The triune-brain metaphor: the evolution of the living linear. In Grant, D. and Oswick, C. (eds.), *Metaphors and Organizations*. Sage.

Burrill, S. G. and Lee, K. B. (1989) *Biotech 89: Commercialization*. Ernst & Young.

Burt, R. S. (2005) *Brokerage and Closure: An Introduction to Social Capital*. Oxford University Press.

Callon, M. (1998a) Introduction: the embeddedness of economic markets in economics. In Callon, M. (ed.), *The Laws of the Markets*. Blackwell Publishers/*Sociological Review*.

(1998b) An essay on framing and overflowing: economic externalities revisited by sociology. In Callon, M. (ed.), *The Laws of the Markets*. Blackwell Publishers/*Sociological Review*.

Cambrosio, A. and Keating P. (1995) *Exquisite Specificity: The Monoclonal Antibody Revolution*. Oxford University Press.

Cardinal, L. B., Alessandri, T. M. and Turner, S. F. (2001) Knowledge codifiability, resource, and science-based innovation. *Journal of Knowledge Management* 5, 195–204.

Carroll, G. (1984) Organizational ecology. In Turner, R. H. and Short, J. F. (eds.), *Annual Review of Sociology*. Annual Review, Inc.

Casper, S. and Kettler, H. (2001) National institutional frameworks and the hybridization of entrepreneurial business models: the German and UK biotechnology sectors. *Industry and Innovation* 8, 5–30.

Casper, S. and Whitley, R. (2004) Managing competences in entrepreneurial technology firms: a comparative institutional analysis of Germany, Sweden and the UK. *Research Policy* 33, 89–106.

Casper, S., Lehrer, M. and Soskice, D. (1999) Can high-technology industries prosper in Germany? Institutional frameworks and the evolution of the German software and biotechnology industries. *Industry and Innovation* 6, 5–24.

Chandler A. (1962) *Strategy and Culture*. MIT Press.

Child, J. and Faulkner, D. (1998) *Strategies of Co-operation: Managing Alliances, Networks, and Joint Ventures*. Oxford University Press.

Clarke-Hill, C., Li, H. and Davies, B. (2003) The paradox of co-operation and competition in strategic alliances: towards a multi-paradigm approach. *Management Research News* 26, 1–20.

Clegg, S. R. and Gray, J. T. (1996) Metaphors in organizational research: of embedded embryos, paradigms and powerful people. In Grant, D. and Oswick, C. (eds.), *Metaphors and Organizations*. Sage.

Coase, R. (1960) The problem of social cost. *Journal of Law and Economics* 3, 1–44.

Cohen, S. N., Chang, A. C. Y., Boyer, H. W. and Helling, R. B. (1973) Construction of biologically functional bacterial plasmids in vitro. *Proceedings of the National Academy of Science* 70, 3240–3244.

Cohen, W. M. and Levinthal, D. A. (1990) Absorptive capacity: a new perspective on learning and innovation. *Administrative Science Quarterly* 35, 128–153.

Cohen W. M., Nelson R. R. and Walsh J. P. (2000) Protecting their intellectual assets: appropriability conditions and why US manufacturing firms patent (or not). National Bureau of Economic Research, working chapter #7552.

(2002) Links and impacts: the influence of public research on industrial R&D. *Management Science* 48, 1–23.

Coleman, J. S. (1988) Social capital in the creation of human capital. *American Journal of Sociology* 94, S95–S121.

(1990) *Foundations of Social Theory*. Belknap Press of Harvard.

Colyvas, J., Crow, M., Gelijns, A., Mazzoleni, R., Nelson, R. R., Rosenberg, N. and Sampat, B. M. (2002) How do university inventions get into practice? *Management Science* 48, 61–72.

Cooke, P., Kaufmann, D., Levin, C. and Wilson, R. (2006) The biosciences knowledge value chain and comparative incubation models. *Journal of Technology Transfer* 31, 115–129.

Coriat, B. and Orsi, F. (2002) Establishing a new intellectual property rights regime in the United States: origins, content and problems. *Research Policy* 31, 1491–1507.

Corolleur, C. D. F., Carrere, M. and Mangematin, V. (2004) Turning scientific and technological human capital into economic capital: the experience of biotech start-ups in France. *Research Policy* 33, 631–642.

Crane, D. (1968) Social structure in a group of scientists: a test of the "invisible college" hypothesis. *American Sociological Review* 34, 335–352.

(1972) *Invisible Colleges – Diffusion of Knowledge in Scientific Communities*. University of Chicago Press.

Danzon, P. M., Epstein, A. and Nicholson, S. (2004) Mergers and acquisitions in the pharmaceutical and biotech industries. *NBER Working Paper Series, Working Paper* 10536, National Bureau of Economic Research, Cambridge, MA. (Available at: www.nber.org/papers/w10536).

Darby, M. R. and Zucker, L. G. (2002) Going public when you can in biotechnology. *NBER Working Paper Series, Working Paper* W8954.

Das, P. S., Sen, P. and Beal, D. B. (1998) Impact of strategic alliances on firm valuation. *Academy of Management Journal* 41, 27–41.

Das, T. K. and Teng, B. S. (2000) Instabilities of strategic alliances: an internal tensions perspective. *Organization Science* 11, 77–101.

Dasgupta, P. (1988) Trust as a commodity. In Gambetta, D. (ed.), *Trust: Making and Breaking Cooperative Relations*. Basil Blackwell.

Dasgupta, P. and David, P. A. (1987) Information disclosure and the economics of science and technology. In Feiwel, G. (ed.), *Arrow and the Ascent of Modern Economic Theory*. MacMillan Press.

David, P. A. (1992) Path-dependence in economic processes: implications for policy analysis in dynamical systems contexts. Discussion paper, Center for Economic Policy Research, Stanford University.

David, P. A., Mowery, D. and Steinmueller, W. E. (1992) Analysing the economic payoffs from basic research. *Economics of Innovation and New Technology* 2, 73–90.

DeCenzo and Robbins (1996) *Human Resource Management*. John Wiley & Sons.

Deutschman, A. (1994) The managing wisdom of hightech superstars. *Fortune*, October 17, 197–205.

Djerassi, C. (1993) Policy forum – basic research: the gray zone. *Science* 261, 972–973.

Dodgson, M. (1993) Organizational learning: a review of some literatures. *Organization Studies* 14, 375–394.

Doving, E. (1996) In the image of man: organizational action, competence and learning. In Grant, D. and Oswick, C. (eds.), *Metaphors and Organizations*. Sage.

Eisenberg, R. (1987) Proprietary rights and the norms of science in biotechnology research. *Yale Law Journal* 97, 177–231.

(1996) Public research and private development: patents and technology transfer in government-sponsored research. *Virginia Law* 82, 1663–1727.

Eisenberg, R. and Nelson, R. R. (2002) Public vs. proprietary science: a fruitful tension? *Daedalus* 131, 89–102.

Eisenhardt, K. M. (1989) Building theories from case study research. *Academy of Management Review* 14, 532–550.

Eisenhardt, K. M. and Shoonhoven, C. B. (1996) Resource based view of strategic alliance formation: strategic and social effects in entrepreneurial firms. *Organization Science* 10, 136–150.

Etzkowitz, H. (1998) The norms of entrepreneurial science: cognitive effects of the new university–industry linkages. *Research Policy* 27, 823–833.

(1999) Bridging the gap: the evolution of industry–university links in the United States. In Branscomb, L. and Kodama F. (eds.), *Industrialized Knowledge: University–Industry Linkages in Japan and in the United States*. MIT Press.

(2002) *MIT and the Rise of Entrepreneurial Science*. Routledge.

(2003) *Triple Helix: A Manifesto to Innovation, Incubation and Growth.* SNS Press.

Etzkowitz, H. and Leydesdorff, L. (2000) The dynamic of innovation: from national systems and "Mode 2" to a triple helix of university–industry–government relations. *Research Policy* 29, 109–123.

Etzkowitz, H. and Webster, A. (1998) Entrepreneurial science: the second academic revolution. In Etzkowitz, H., Webster, A. and Healey, P. (eds.). *Capitalizing Knowledge: New Intersections of Industry and Academia.* SUNY Series, Frontiers in Education.

Etzkowitz, H., Webster, A. and Healey, P. (eds.) (1998) *Capitalizing Knowledge: New Intersections of Industry and Academia.* SUNY Series, Frontiers in Education.

Etzkowitz, H. A., Webster, C., Gebhardt, B. and Terra, R. C. (2000) The future of the university and the university of the future: evolution of ivory tower to entrepreneurial paradigm. *Research Policy* 29, 313–330.

Feldman, M. (2003) The locational dynamics of the US biotech industry: knowledge externalities and the anchor hypothesis. *Industry and Innovation* 10, 311–328.

Feldman, M. P. and Francis, J. K. (2004) Homegrown solutions: fostering cluster formation. *Economic Development Quarterly* 18, 127–137.

Fligstein, N. (1985) The spread of the multidivisional form among large firms, 1919–1979. *American Sociological Review* 50, 377–391.

Foschi, M. (1991) Gender and double standards for competence. In Ridgeway, C. (ed.), *Gender, Interaction and Inequality.* Springer-Verlag.

Friedkin, N. E. (1978) University social structure and social networks among scientists. *American Journal of Sociology* 83, 1444–1465.

Friedman, J. and Silberman, J. (2003) University technology transfer: do incentives, management, and location matter? *Journal of Technology Transfer* 28, 81–85.

Fukuyama, F. (1995) *Trust.* Free Press.

Galambos, L. and Sturchio, J. L. (1998) Pharmaceutical firms and the transition to biotechnology: a study in strategic innovation. *Business History Review* 72, 250–278.

Gambetta, D. (1988) *Trust: Making and Breaking Cooperative Relations.* Basil Blackwell.

Gilseng, V. and Nooteboom, B. (2005) Density and strength of ties in innovation networks: an analysis of multimedia and biotechnology. *European Management Review* 3, 179–197.

Gittelman, M. and Kogut, B. (2003) Does good science lead to valuable knowledge? Biotechnology firms and the evolutionary logic of citation patterns. *Management Science* 49, 366.

Gnyawali, D. R. and Madhavan, R. (2001) Cooperative networks and competitive dynamics: a structural embeddedness perspective. *Academy of Management Review* 26, 431–445.

Granovetter, M. (1985) Economic action and social structure: the problem of embeddedness. *American Journal of Sociology* 91, 481–510.

Grant, D. and Oswick, C. (1996) Introduction: Getting the Measure of Metaphors. In Grant, D. and Oswick, C. (eds.), *Metaphors and Organizations*. Sage.

Grant, M. (1996) Toward a knowledge-based theory of the firm. *Strategic Management Journal* 17, special issue "Knowledge and the Firm."

Grant, R. M. and Baden-Fuller, C. (2004) A knowledge accessing theory of strategic alliances. *Journal of Management Studies* 41, 61–84.

Gulati, R. (1995) Does familiarity breed trust? The implications of repeated ties for contractual choice in alliances. *Academy of Management Journal* 38, 85–112.

(1998) Alliances and networks. *Strategic Management Journal* 19, 293–317.

Gulati, R. and Higgins, M. C. (2003) Which ties matter when? The contingent effects of interorganizational partnerships on IPO success. *Strategic Management Journal* 24, 127–144.

Gulati, R., Khanna, T. and Nohria, N. (1994) Unilateral commitments and the importance of process in alliances. *Sloan Management Review* 35, 61–70.

Gulbrandsen, M. and Smeby, J.-C. (2005) Industry funding and university professors' research performance. *Research Policy* 34, 932–950.

Hackett, E. J. (1990) Science as a vocation in 1990: the changing organizational culture of academic science. *Journal of Higher Education* 61, 241–279.

Hagedoorn, J. (1993) Understanding the rationale of strategic technology partnering: interorganizational modes of cooperation and sectoral differences. In Grabher, G. (ed.), *The Embedded Firm: On the Socioeconomics of Industrial Networks*. Routledge.

(2002) Inter-firm R&D partnerships: an overview of major trends and patterns since 1960. *Research Policy* 31, 477–492.

(2006) Understanding the cross-level embeddedness of interfirm partnership formation. *Academy of Management Review* 31, 670–680.

Hagedoorn, J. and Duysters, G. (2003) Learning in dynamic inter-firm networks: the efficacy of multiple contacts. *Organization Studies* 23, 525–548.

Hagedoorn, J., Crayannis, E. and Alexander, J. (2001) Strange bedfellows in the personal computer industry: technology alliances between IBM and Apple. *Research Policy* 30, 837–849.

Hamel, G. (1991) Competition for competence and inter-partner learning within international strategic alliances. *Strategic Management Journal* 12, 83–103.

Hamel, G., Doz, Y. L. and Prahalad, C. K. (1989) Collaborate with your competitors and win. *Harvard Business Review* 67, 133–139.

Hannan, M. T. and Carroll, G. R. (1992) *Dynamics of Organizational Populations Density, Legitimation, and Competition.* Oxford University Press.

Hannan, M. T. and Freeman, J. (1977) The population ecology of organizations. *American Journal of Sociology* 82, 929–964.

 (1984) Structural inertia and organizational change. *American Sociological Review* 49, 149–164.

 (1989) *Organizational Ecology.* Harvard University Press.

Hardy, C. and Phillips, N. (1999) No joking matter: discursive struggle in the Canadian refugee system. *Organization Studies* 20, 1–24.

Hardy, C., Phillips, N. and Lawrence, T. B. (2003) Resources, knowledge and influence: the organizational effects of interorganizational collaboration. *Journal of Management Studies* 40, 321–343.

Harmon, B., Ardichvili, A. and Cardozo, R. N. (1997) Mapping the university technology transfer process. *Journal of Business Venturing* 12, 423–434.

Hart, O. (1995). *Firms, Contracts, and Financial Structures.* Oxford University Press.

Heller, A. M. and Eisenberg, R. (1998) Can patents deter innovation? The anticommons in biomedical research. *Science* 280/5364, 698–702.

Henderson, R. and Mitchell, W. (1997) The interaction of organizational and competitive influences on strategy and performance. *Strategic Management Journal* 18 (Summer special issue), 5–14.

Henderson, R., Jaffe, A. and Trajtenberg, M. (1994) Numbers up, quality down? trends in university patenting 1965–2002. Unpublished manuscript, Harvard University.

Henderson, R., Jaffe, A. and Trajtenberg, M. (1998) Universities as a source of commercial technology: a detailed analysis of university patenting 1965–1988. *Review of Economics and Statistics* 80, 119–127.

Hendry C., Brown, J. and Defillippi, R. (2000) Regional clustering of high technology-based firms: opto-electronics in three countries. *Regional Studies* 34, 129–145.

Hicks, D. and Katz, J. S. (1997) *The Changing Shape of the British Industrial Research System.* Steep Special Report 6, University of Sussex.

Hoang, H. and Rothaermel, F. T. (2006) Internal and external capabilities transfer: time to market in new product development. Academy of Management Best Conference Paper, BPS: R1.

Höyssä, M., Bruun, H. and Hukkinen, J. (2004) The co-evolution of social and physical infrastructure for biotechnology innovation in Turku, Finland. *Research Policy* 33, 769–785.

Hughes, S. S. (2001) Making dollars out of DNA. *Isis* 92, 541–575.

Huxham, C. (1996) *Creating Collaborative Advantage*. Sage Publications.

Huygens, C., Baden-Fuller, F., Van Den Bosch A. J. and Volberda, H. W. (2001) Co-evolution of firm capabilities and industry competition: investigating the music industry, 1877–1997. *Organization Studies* 22, 971–1011.

Hybels, R. C. and Popielarz, P. A. (1989) The iron law revisited: the formation of an interorganizational oligarchy through joint ventures. Paper presented at the Academy of Management Annual Meeting, Cincinnati, August 1996.

Inkpen, A. and Tsang, E. (2005) Social capital, networks, and knowledge transfer. *Academy of Management Review* 30, 146–165.

Jackson, S. E. and Schuler, R. S. (1995) Understanding human resource management in the context of organizations and their environments. *Annual Review of Psychology* 46, 237–264.

Kaghan, W. (1997) Contracts and the structuring of deals in university/industry technology transfer. Manuscript, University of Washington School of Business Administration.

Kaplan, S., Murray, F. and Henderson, R. (2003) Discontinuities and senior management: assessing the role of recognition in pharmaceutical firm response to biotechnology. *Industrial and Corporate Change* 12, 203–233.

Kenney, M. (1986) *Biotechnology: The University–Industrial Complex*. Yale University Press.

Khanna, T., Gulati, R. and Nohria, N. (1998) The dynamics of learning alliances: competition, cooperation and scope. *Strategic Management Journal* 19, 193–210.

Khodyakov, D. (2007) Trust as a process: a three-dimensional approach. *Sociology* 41, 115–132.

Kirby, D. A. (2006) Creating entrepreneurial universities in the UK: applying entrepreneurship theory to practice. *Journal of Technology Transfer* 31, 599–603.

Kleinman, D. L. (1998) Untangling context: understanding a university laboratory in the commercial world. *Science Technology and Human Values* 23(3), 285–314.

Kogut, B. (1998) Joint ventures: theoretical and empirical perspectives. *Strategic Management Journal* 9, 319–332.

 (2000) The network as knowledge: generative rules and the emergence of structure. *Strategic Management Journal* 21, 405–425.

Kogut, B., Shan, W. and Walker, G. (1992) The make-or-cooperate decision in the context of an industry network. In Nohria, N. and Eccles, R. (eds.), *Networks and Organizations*. Harvard Business School Press.

Kohler, G. and Milstein, C. (1975) Continuous cultures of fused cells secreting antibody of defined specificity. *Nature (Lond.)* 256, 495–497.

Koput, K. W. (1997) A chaotic model of innovative search: some answers, many questions. *Organization Science* 8, 528–542.

Koput, K. W. and Powell, W. W. (2002) Science and strategy: organizational evolution in a knowledge-intensive field. Working paper, University of Arizona.

Kornberg, A. (1995) *The Golden Helix*, University Science Books.

Kramer, R. M., Brewer, M. B. and Hanna, B. (1996) Collective trust and collective action in organizations: the decision to trust as a social decision. In Kramer, R. M. and Tyler, T. R. (eds.), *Trust in Organizations*. Sage.

Kreiner, K. and Schultz, M. (1993) Informal collaborations in R&D: the formation of networks across organizations. *Organization Studies* 14, 189–209.

Kristiansen, E. G. (1998) R&D in the presence of network externalities: timing and compatibility. *RAND Journal of Economics* 29, 531–547.

Lakoff, G. and Johnson, M. (1980) *Metaphors We Live By*. University of Chicago Press.

Lampel, J. and Shapira, Z. (2001) Judgmental errors, interactive norms, and the difficulty of detecting strategic surprises. *Organization Science* 2, 599–611.

Lane, J. P. and Lubatkin, M. (1998) Relative absorptive capacity and interorganizational learning. *Strategic Management Journal* 19, 461–477.

Larsson, R., Bengtsson, L., Henriksson, K. and Sparks, J. (1998) The interorganizational learning dilemma: collective knowledge development in strategic alliances. *Organization Science* 9, 285–305.

Latour, B. and Woolgar, S. (1979) *Laboratory Life*. Sage.

(1986) *Laboratory Life – The Construction of Scientific Facts*. Princeton University Press.

Ledford, G. E. and Lawler, E. E. (1994) Research on employee participation: beating a dead horse? *Academy of Management Review* 19, 633–636.

Lee, Y. S. (1996) Technology transfer and the research university: a search for boundaries of university–industry collaborations. *Research Policy* 25, 843–863.

(1998) University–industry collaboration on technology transfer: views from the ivory tower. *Policy Studies Journal* 26, 69–84.

Lee, Jr., K. B. and Burrill, G. S. (1995) *Biotech 95: Reform, Restructure, Renewal*. Ernst & Young.

Lehrer, M. and Asakawa, K. (2004) Rethinking the public sector: idio-syncrasies of biotechnology commercialization as motors of national R&D reform in Germany and Japan. *Research Policy* 33, 921–938.

Lewin, A. Y. (1999) Application of complexity theory to organization science. *Organization Science* 10, 215.

Lewin, A. Y., Long, C. P. and Carroll, T. N. (1999) The coevolution of new organizational forms. *Organization Science* 10, 535–550.

Lewis, W. M. (2000) Exploring paradox: toward a more comprehensive guide. *Academy of Management Review* 25, 760–776.

Liebeskind, J. D. (2000) Ownership, governance and incentives in new biotechnology firms. In Blair, M. and Kochan, T. (eds.), *The New Relationship: Human Capital in The American Corporation*, MIT Press.

Liebeskind, J. P. (2000) Internal capital markets: benefits, costs, and organizational arrangements. *Organization Science* 11, 58–76.

(2001) Risky business: university and intellectual property. *Academe* 87, 49–54.

Liebeskind, J. P. and Oliver, A. L. (1998) From handshake to contract: trust, intellectual property and the social structure of academic research. In Lane, C. and Bachmann, R. (eds.), *Trust Within and Between Organizations*. Oxford University Press.

Liebeskind, J. A., Oliver, A. L., Zucker, L. and Brewer, M. (1996) Social networks, learning, and flexibility: sourcing scientific knowledge in new biotechnology firms. *Organization Science* 7, 428–443.

Luhman, N. (1988) Familiarity, confidence, and trust. In Gambetta, D. (ed.), *Trust: Making and Breaking Cooperative Relations*. Basil Blackwell.

McKelvey, B. and Aldrich, H. (1983) Populations, natural selection, and applied organizational science. *Administrative Science Quarterly* 28, 101–128.

McKelvey, M., Alm, H. and Riccaboni, M. (2003) Does co-location matter for formal knowledge collaboration in the Swedish biotechnology–pharmaceutical sector? *Research Policy* 32, 483–501.

McKelvey, W. (1982) *Organizational Systematics: Taxonomy, Evolution, Classification*. University of California Press.

(1997) Quasi-natural organization science. *Organization Science* 8, 352–380.

Malerba, F. and Orsenigo, L. (2002) Innovation and market structure in the dynamics of the pharmaceutical industry and biotechnology: towards a history-friendly model. *Industrial and Corporate Change* 11, 667–703.

March, J. (1991) Exploration and exploitation in organizational learning. *Organization Science* 2, 71–87.

March G. J. and Simon, H. H. (1958) *Organizations*. New York.

Martineau, B. (2001) *First Fruit: The Creation of the Flvr Savr Tomato and the Birth of Genetically Engineered Food.* McGraw-Hill.

Maurer, I. and Ebers, M. (2006) Dynamics of social capital and their performance implications: lessons from biotechnology startups. *Administrative Science Quarterly* 51, 262–292.

Mayer, R. C., Davis, J. H. and Schoorman, F. D. (1995) An integrative model of organizational trust. *Academy of Management Review* 20, 709–734.

Mazzolini R. and Nelson R. R. (1998a) Economic theories about the benefits and costs of patents. *Journal of Economic Issues* 32, 1031–1052.

(1998b) The benefits and costs of strong patent protection: a contribution to the current debate. *Research Policy* 27, 273–284.

Merges, R. P., Menell, P. S., Lemley, M. A. and Jorde, T. M. (1997) *Intellectual Property in the New Technological Age.* Aspen Publishers Inc.

Merton, R. K. (1968) The Matthew effect in science. *Science* 159, 56–63.

(1973) The normative structure of science. In Merton, R. K. (ed.), *The Sociology of Science.* University of Chicago Press.

(1977) The sociology of science: an episodic memoir. In Merton, R. K. and Jerry, G. J. (eds.), *The Sociology of Science in Europe.* Southern Illinois University Press.

Meyer, D. A., Tsui, A. S. and Hinings, R. C. (1993) Configurational approach to organizational analysis. *Academy of Management Journal* 36, 1175–1195.

Meyer, J. and Scott, W. R. (1983) *Organisational Environments: Ritual and Rationality.* Sage.

Meyer, W. J. and Rowan, B. (1977) Institutionalized organizations: formal structure as myth and ceremony. *American Journal of Sociology* 83, 340–362.

Meyer-Krahmer, F. and Schmoch, U. (1998) Science-based technologies: university–industry interactions in four fields. *Research Policy* 27, 835–851.

Mian, S. A. (1996) Assessing value-added contribution of university technology business incubators to tenant firms. *Research Policy* 25, 325–335.

Miles, G. R., Miles, R. E., Perrone, V. and Edvinsson, L. (1998) Some conceptual and research barriers to the utilization of knowledge. *California Management Review* 40, 281–288.

Milstein, C. (2000) With the benefit of hindsight. *Immunology Today* 21, 359–364.

Miner, A. S. (1994) Seeking adaptive advantage: evolutionary theory and managerial action. In Baum, J. A. C. and Singh, J. V. (eds.), *Evolutional Dynamics of Organizations.* Oxford University Press.

Mitsuhashi, H. (2002) Uncertainty in selecting alliance partners: the three reduction mechanisms and alliance formation processes. *International Journal of Organizational Analysis* 10, 109–133.

Morgan, G. (1980) Paradigms, metaphors and puzzle solving in organizational theory. *Administrative Science Quarterly* 25 605–622.

(1983) More on metaphor: why we cannot control tropes in administrative science. *Administrative Science Quarterly* 28, 601–607.

(1986) *Images of Organization.* Sage Publications.

Morrow, J. F., Cohen, S. N., Chang, A. C. Y., Boyer, H. W., Goodman, H. M. and Helling, R. B. (1974) Replication and transcription of eukaryotic DNA in esherichia coli. *PNAS* 71, 1743–1747.

Mowery, D. C., Oxley, J. E. and Silverman, B. S. (1996) Strategic alliances and interfirm knowledge transfer. *Strategic Management Journal* 17 (Winter special issue), 77–91.

Mowery, D. C., Sampat, B. N. and Ziedonis, A. A. (2002) Learning to patent: institutional experience, learning, and the characteristics of US university patents after the Bayh–Dole Act, 1981–1992. *Management Science* 48, 73–89.

Mowery, D. C., Nelson, R. R., Sampat, B. N. and Ziedonis, A. A. (2001) The growth of patenting and licensing by US universities: an assessment of the effects of the Bayh–Dole act of 1980. *Research Policy* 30, 99–119.

Nahapiet, J. and Goshal, S. (1998) Social capital, intellectual capital, and the organizational advantage. *Academy of Management Review* 23, 242–266.

Nault, B. R. and Tyagi, R. K. (2001) Implementable mechanisms to coordinate horizontal alliances. *Management Science* 47, 787–799.

Nee, V. (1998) Norms and networks in economic and organizational performance. *American Economic Association Papers and Proceedings* May, 85–89.

Nelkin, D. (1984) *Science as Intellectual Property: Who Controls Scientific Research?* Macmillan.

Nelkin, D., Nelson, R. R. and Kiernan, C. (1987) University–industry alliances – commentary. *Science, Technology & Human Values* 12, 65–74.

Nelson, L. (1998) The rise of intellectual property protection in the American university. *Science* 279(5356), 1460.

Nelson, R. R. (1990) Capitalism as an engine of progress. *Research Policy* 19, 193–214.

(2002) The market economy of the republic of science. Working paper, Columbia University.

(2004) The market economy and the scientific commons. *Research Policy* 33, 455–472.

Nesta, L. and Mangematin, V. (2002) Industry life cycle, knowledge generation and technological networks. In De la Mothe, J. and

Link, A. E. (eds.), *Networks, Alliances and Partnerships in the Innovation Process*. Kluwer Academic.

Nicolaou, N. and Birley, S. (2003) Academic networks in a trichotomous categorization of university spinouts. *Journal of Business Venturing* 18, 333–359.

Niosi, J. (2003) Alliances are not enough explaining rapid growth in biotechnology firms. *Research Policy* 32, 737–750.

Niosi, J. and Bas, T. G. (2001) The competencies of regions – Canada's clusters in biotechnology. *Small Business Economics* 17, 31.

Nonaka, I. (1994) A dynamic theory of organizational knowledge creation. *Organization Science* 5, 14–37.

Nonaka, I. and Hirotaka, H. (1995) *The Knowledge-Creating Company: How Japanese Companies Create the Dynamics of Innovation*. Oxford University Press.

Nonaka, I. and Konno, N. (1998) The concept of "Ba:" building a foundation for knowledge creation. *California Management Review* 40, 40–54.

Nooteboom, B. (1999a) The dynamic efficiency of networks. In Grandori, A. (ed.), *Interfirm Networks: Organization and Industrial Competitiveness*. Routledge.

(1999b). *Inter-Firm Alliances: Analysis and Design*. Routledge.

(2002) *Trust: Forms, Foundations, Functions, Failures and Figures*. Edward Elgar.

Oliver, A. L. (1993) New biotechnology firms: a multilevel analysis of interorganizational relations in an emerging industry. Bringing process into structure. Unpublished dissertation, UCLA.

(1997) On the nexus of organizations and professions: networking through trust. *Sociological Inquiry* 67, 227–245.

(2001) Strategic alliances and the learning life-cycle of biotechnology firms. *Organization Studies* 22, 467–489.

(2004) Biotechnology entrepreneurial scientists and their collaborations. *Research Policy* 33, 583–597.

(2007). University–industry collaborations in the Israeli biotechnology industry. Work in progress, Department of Sociology and Anthropology, The Hebrew University of Jerusalem.

Oliver, A. L. and Liebeskind, J. P. (1998) Three levels of networking for sourcing intellectual capital in biotechnology: implications for studying interorganizational networks. *International Studies of Management & Organization* 27, 76–104.

Oliver, A. L. and Liebeskind, J. P. (2003) Public research and intellectual property rights: a tale of two inventions. Working paper, The Hebrew University of Jerusalem.

Oliver, A. L. and Montgomery, K. (2000) Creating a hybrid organizational form from parental blueprints: the emergence and evolution of knowledge firms. *Human Relations* 53, 33–57.

Oliver, A. L. and Montgomery, K. (2001) Cybernetics and the theory of trust development. *Human Relations* 54, 1045–1065.

Oliver, A. L. and Ramati, A. (2003) Historical accounts of scientific entrepreneurship. Unpublished working paper, The Hebrew University of Jerusalem.

Orsenigo, L. (1989) *The Emergence of Biotechnology: Institutions and Markes in Industrial Innovation*. Pinter Publishers.

(2001) The (failed) development of a biotechnology cluster: the case of Lombardy. *Small Business Economics* 17, 77–92.

Osborn, R. and Hagedoorn, J. (1997) The institutionalization and evolutionary dynamics of interorganizational alliances and networks. *Academy of Management Journal* 40, 261–278.

Ouchi, G. W. (1980) Markets, bureaucracies and clans. *Administrative Science Quarterly* 28, 129–141.

Ouchi, W. and Jaeger, A. (1978) Type Z organization: stability in the midst of mobility. *Academy of Management Review* 3, 305–314.

Oviatt, B. M. and McDougall, P. P. (1995) Global start-ups: entrepreneurs on a worldwide stage. *Academy of Management Executive* 9, 30–44.

Owen-Smith, J. (2003) From separate systems to a hybrid order: accumulative advantage across public and private science at research one universities. *Research Policy* 32, 1081–1104.

Owen-Smith, J. and Powell, W. W. (2001a) To patent or not: faculty decisions and institutional success at technology transfer. *Journal of Technology Transfer* 26, 99–114.

(2001b) Careers and contradictions: faculty responses to the transformation of knowledge and its uses in the life sciences. *Research in Sociology or Work* 10, 109–140.

(2003) The expanding role of university patenting in the life sciences: assessing the importance of experience and connectivity. *Research Policy* 32, 1695–1711.

(2005) Accounting for emergence and novelty in Boston and Bay area biotechnology. In Braunerhjelm, P. and Feldman, M. (eds.), *Cluster Genesis: The Emergence of Technology Cluster and their Implication for Government Policies*. Cambridge University Press.

Owen-Smith, J., Riccaboni, M., Pammolli, F. and Powell, W. W. (2002) A comparison of US and European university–industry relations in the life sciences. *Management Science* 48, 24–44.

Pace, G. (2001) The role of development agencies for the entrepreneurial promotion: Israeli case studies. (Available at: http://econwpa.wustl. edu:8089/eps/urb/papers/0311/03111003.pdf).

Packer, K. and Webster, A. (1996) Patenting culture in science: reinventing the scientific wheel of credibility, science technology. *Science, Technology, and Human Values* 21, 427–453.

Park, S. O. and Ungson, G. R. (2001) Interfirm rivalry and managerial complexity: a conceptual framework of alliance failure. *Organization Science* 12, 37–53.

Petersa, L., Groenewegenb, P. and Fiebelkornb, N. (1998) A comparison of networks between industry and public sector research in materials technology and biotechnology. *Research Policy* 27, 255–271.

Pigliucci, I. (2000) Skeptic. *Altadena* 8, 62–71.

Pigou, A. C. (1932) *The Economics of Welfare*, 4th ed. Macmillan.

Pirnay, F., Surlemont, N. and Nlemvo, F. (2003) Toward a typology of university spin-offs. *Small Business Economics* 21, 355–369.

Pisano, G. P. (1990) The R&D boundaries of the firm: an empirical analysis. *Administrative Science Quarterly* 35, 153–176.

   (1991) The governance of innovation: vertical integration and collaborative arrangements in the biotechnology industry. *Research Policy* 20, 237–249.

   (1994) Knowledge, integration, and the locus of learning: an empirical analysis of process development. *Strategic Management Journal* 15, 85–100.

   (1996) Learning-before-doing in the development of new process technology. *Research Policy* 25, 1097–1111.

   (2002) The economics and technology of pharmaceutical R&D in the age of molecular biology. Working paper, Harvard Business School.

Podolny, J. M. and Page, K. L. (1998) Network forms of organization. *Annual Review of Sociology* 24, 57–76.

Porter, K., Whittington, B. and Powell, W. W. (2005) The institutional embeddedness of high-tech regions: relational foundations of the Boston biotechnology community. In Breschi, S. and Malerba, F. (eds.), *Clusters, Networks, and Innovation*. Oxford University Press.

Powell, W. W. (1990) Neither market nor hierarchy: network form of organization. *Research in Organization Behavior* 12, 295–336.

   (1998) Learning from collaboration. *California Management Review* 40, 228–240.

Powell, W. W. and Brantley, P. (1992) Competitive cooperation in biotechnology – learning through networks? In Nohria, N. and Eccles, R. (eds.), *Networks and Organizations: Structure, Form and Action*. Harvard Business School.

Powell, W.W. and Owen-Smith, J. (1998) Universities and the market for intellectual property in the life sciences. *Journal of Policy Analysis and Management* 17, special issue "The Commercialism Dilemma of the Nonprofit Sector."

Powell, W.W., Koput, K.W. and Smith-Doerr, L. (1996) Interoganizational collaboration and the locus of innovation: networks of learning in biotechnology. *Administrative Science Quarterly* 41, 116–45.

Powell, W.W., Koput, K.W., Smith-Doerr, L. and Owen-Smith, J. (1999) Network position and firm performance: organizational returns to collaboration in the biotechnology industry. In Andrew, S. and Knock, D. (eds.), *Research in the Sociology of Organizations*. JAI Press.

Powell, W.W., White, D.R., Koput, K.W. and Owen-Smith, J. (2005) Network dynamics and field evolution: the growth of interorganizational collaboration in the life sciences. *American Journal of Sociology* 110, 1132–1205.

Prigogine, I. and Stengers, I. (1984) *Order Out of Chaos*. Bantam Books.

Quinn, J.B. (1986) Innovation and corporate strategy: managed chaos. In Horwitch, M. (ed.), *Technology in the Modern Corporation: A Strategic Perspective*. Pergamon Press.

Rabinow, P. (1996) *Making PCR*. University of Chicago Press.

Ramer, S., Hwee Ang, S. and Baden-Fuller, C. (2001) Dealing with uncertainties in the biotechnology industry: the use of real options reasoning. *Journal of Commercial Biotechnology* 8, 95–105.

Reimers, N. (1997) Stanford's office of technology licensing and the Cohen/Boyer cloning patents. Oral History, by Sally Smith Hughes, Regional Oral History Office, Bancroft Library, University of California, Berkeley.

Rhoades, G. and Slaughter, S. (1991) Professors, administrators, and patents: the negotiation of technology transfer. *Sociology of Education* 64, 65–77.

Ring, P.S. (1997) Processes facilitating reliance on trust in interorganizational networks. In Ebers, M. (ed.), *The Formation of Inter-Organizational Networks*. Oxford University Press.

(1999) The Costs of Networked Organization. In Grandori, A. (ed.), *Interfirm Networks: Organizational and Industrial Competitiveness*. Routledge.

Ring, P. and Van de Ven, A. (1992) Structuring cooperative relations between organizations. *Strategic Management Journal* 13, 483–498.

Ring, P.S. and Van de Ven, A.H. (1994) Developmental processes of cooperative interorganizational relations. *Academy of Management Review* 19, 90–118.

Robbins-Roth, C. (2000) *From Alchemy to IPO: The Business of Biotechnology*. Perseus Publishing.

de Rond, M. and Bouchikhi, H. (2004) On the dialectics of strategic alliances. *Organization Science* 15, 56–69.

Romanelli, E. (1991) The evolution of new organizational forms. *Annual Review of Sociology* 17, 79–103.

Rothaermel, F. T. (2001) Complementary assets, strategic alliances, and the incumbent's advantage: an empirical study of industry and firm effects in the biopharmaceutical industry. *Research Policy* 30, 1235–1251.

Rothaermel, F. T. and Thursby, M. (2007) The nanotech versus the biotech revolution: sources of productivity in incumbent firm research. *Research Policy* 36, 832–349.

Rothaermel, F. T., Agung, S. and Jiang, L. (2007) University entrepreneurship: a taxonomy of the literature. *Industrial and Corporate Change* 16, 691–791.

Sakakibara, K. (1993) R&D cooperation among competitors: a case study of the VLSI semiconductor research project in Japan. *Journal of Engineering and Technology Management* 10, 393–407.

Saxenian, A. (1985) Silicon Valley and Route 128: regional prototypes or historic exceptions? In Castells, M. (ed.), *High Technology, Space, and Society*. Sage.

   (1994) *Regional Advantage: Culture and Competition in Silicon Valley and Route 128*. Harvard University Press.

Schilling, M. A. and Phelps, C. C. (2007) Inter-firm collaboration networks: the impact of large-scale network structure on firm innovation. *Management Science* 53, 1113–1126.

Schulz, M. (2001) The uncertain relevance of newness: organizational learning and knowledge flows. *Academy of Management Journal* 44, 661–682.

Schumpeter, J. A. (1934/1975) *The Theory of Economic Development*, trans. Opie, R. Harvard University Press.

Scott, W. R. (1995) *Institutions and Organizations: Theory and Research*. Sage Publications.

Seitzer, D. (1999) Technology transfer – a flexible link between research, university and industry. *European Journal of Engineering Education* 24, 139–150.

Selznick, P. (1957) *Leadership in Administration: A Sociological Interpretation*. University of California Press.

Senker, J. and Faulkner, W. (1992) Industrial use of public sector research in advanced technologies: a comparison of biotechnology and ceramics. *R&D Management* 22, 157–175.

Shan, W. (1990) An empirical analysis of organizational strategies by entrepreneurial high technology firms. *Strategic Management Journal* 11, 129–140.

Shane, S. and Stuart, T.E. (2002) Organizational endowments and the performance of university start-ups. *Management Science* 48, 154–171.

Silverman D. (1970) *The Theory of Organisations: A Sociological Framework*. Heinemann.

Simon, A.H. (1976) *Administrative Behavior: A Study of Decision Making Behavior in Administrative Organizations*. Free Press.

Sorensen, J.B. and Stuart, T.E. (2000) Ageing, obsolescence, and organizational innovation. *Administrative Science Quarterly* 45, 81–112.

Sorensen, O., Rivkin, W. and Fleming, L. (2006) Complexity, networks and knowledge flow. *Research Policy* 25, 994–1017.

Stark, D. (2001) Ambiguous assets for uncertain environments: heterarchy in postsocialist firms. In DiMaggio, P. (ed.). *The Twenty-First-Century Firm: Changing Economic Organization in International Perspective*. Princeton University Press.

Stinchcombe, A.L. (1965) Social structure and organizations. In March, J.G. (ed.), *Handbook of Organizations*. Rand McNally.

Stuart, T.E. (1998) Network positions and propensities to collaborate: an investigation of strategic alliance formation in a high-technology industry. *Administrative Science Quarterly* 43, 668–698.

Stuart, T.E. and Podolny, J.M. (1996) Local search and the evolution of technological capabilities. *Strategic Management Journal* 17 (Summer special issue), 21–38.

Subramaniam, M. and Youndt, M.A. (2005) The influence of intellectual capital on the types of innovative capabilities. *Academy of Management Journal* 48, 450–463.

Sydow, J. (1997) Understanding the constitution of interorganizational trust. In Lane, C. and Bachmann, R. (eds.), *Trust Within and Between Organizations*. Oxford University Press.

Tansey, E.M. and Catterall, P.P. (eds.) (1995) Technology transfer in Britain: the case of monoclonal antibodies. Wellcome witnesses to twentieth century medicine. *Contemporary Record* 9, 409–444.

Teece, D.J. (1986) Profiting from technological innovation. *Research Policy* 15, 285–305.

(1992) Strategies for capturing the financial benefits from technological innovation. In Rosenberg, N., Landau, R. and Mowery, D.C. (eds.), *Technology and the Wealth of Nations*. Stanford University Press.

(1998) Capturing value from knowledge assets: the new economy, markets for know-how, and intangible assets. *California Management Review* 40, 55–79.

Teece, D.J. and Pisano, G. (1994) The dynamic capabilities of firms: an introduction. *Industrial and Corporate Change* 3, 537–556.

Todeva, E. and Knoke, D. (2005) Strategic alliances and models of collaboration. *Management Decision* 43, 123–148.

Torero, M., Darby, M. R. and Zucker, L. G. (2001) The importance of intellectual human capital in the birth of the semiconductor industry. Working paper, University of California.

Tsai, W. (1991) Knowledge transfer in intraorganizational networks: effects of network position and absorptive capacity on business unit innovation and performance. *Academy of Management Journal* 44, 996–1004.

Tushman, M. L. and Anderson, P. (1986) Technological discontinuities and organizational environments. *Administrative Science Quarterly* 31, 439–465.

Uzzi, B. (1996) The sources and consequences of embeddedness for the economic performance of organizations: the network effect. *American Sociological Review* 61, 674–698.

(1997) Social structure and competition in interfirm networks: the paradox of embeddedness. *Administrative Science Quarterly* 42, 35–67.

(1999) Embeddedness in the making of financial capital: how social relations and networks benefit firms seeking financing. *American Sociological Review* 64, 481–505.

Van de Ven, A. H., Venkatraman, S., Polley, D. and Garud, R. (1989) Processes of new business creation in different organizational settings. In Van de Ven, A. H., Angle, H. and Poole, M. S. (eds.), *Research on the Management of Innovation*. Ballinger Press.

Vohora, A., Wright, M. and Lockett, A. (2004) Critical junctures in the development of university high-tech spinout companies. *Research Policy* 33, 147–175.

von Hippel, E. (1998) Economics of product development by users: the impact of "sticky" local information. *Management Science* 44, 629–644.

Walker, G., Kogut, B. and Shan, W. (1997) Social capital, structural holes and the formation of an industry network. *Organization Science* 8, 109–125.

Wasserman, S. and Faust, K. (1994) *Social Network Analysis: Methods and Applications*. Cambridge University Press.

Watzman, H. and Avitzour S. P. (2001) Israel's great expectations. *Nature Biotechnology* 19, 518–20.

Weick, K. E. (1976) *The Social Physiology of Organizing* (2nd edition). Addison-Wesley.

Werth, B. (1995) *The Billion Dollar Molecule*. Simon Schuster/Touchstone.

Wiggins J. and Gibson, D. V. (2003) Overview of US incubators and the case of the Austin technology incubator. *International Journal of Entrepreneurship and Innovation Management* 3, 56–66.

Wilkins, A. L. and Ouchi, W. G. (1983) Efficient cultures. Exploring the relationships between culture and organizational performance. *Administrative Science Quarterly* 28, 468–481.

Williamson, O. (1981) The economics of organization: the transaction cost approach. *American Journal of Sociology* 87, 548–577.

Williamson, O. E. (1975) *Markets and Hierarchies: Analysis and Antitrust Implications*. Free Press.

(1985) *The Economic Institutions of Capitalism*. Free Press.

(1991) Comparative economic organization: the analysis of discrete structural alternatives. *Administrative Science Quarterly* 36, 269–296.

Woolley, J. L. (2006) The origins of organizational communities: nanotechnology in the United States. Working paper, The Paul Merage School of Business, University of California, Irvine.

Woolley Eisenhardt, K. M. (1989) Building theories from case study research. *Academy of Management Review* 14, 532–550.

Wright, M., Birley, S. and Mosey, S. (2004) Entrepreneurship and university technology transfer. *Journal of Technology Transfer* 29, 235–246.

Yin, R. (1984) *Case Study Research*. Sage Publications.

Youndt, M., Snell, S., Dean, J. and Lepak, D. (1996) Human resource management, manufacturing strategy, and firm performance. *Academy of Management Journal* 39, 836–866.

Yuchtman, E. and Seashore, S. E. (1967) A system resource approach to organizational effectiveness. *American Sociological Review*, 891–903.

Zollo, M. J., Reuer, J. and Singh, H. (2002) Interorganizational routines and performance in strategic alliances. *Organization Science* 13, 701–713.

Zollo, M. and Winter, S. G. (2002) Deliberate learning and the evolution of dynamic capabilities. *Organization Science* 13, 339–351.

Zucker, L. G. (1986) Production of trust: institutional sources of economic structure 1840 to 1920. *Research in Organizational Behavior* 8, 53–111.

Zucker, L. G. and Darby, M. R. (1996) Star scientists and institutional transformation: patterns of invention and innovation in the formation of the biotechnology industry. *Proceedings of the National Academy of Science* 93(12), 709–12, 916.

(1997) Individual action and the demand for institution. *American Behavioral Scientist* 4, 502–513.

(1997) Present at the biotechnological revolution: transformation of technological identity for a large incumbent pharmaceutical firm. *Research Policy* 26, 429–446.

Zucker, L. G. and Darby, M. (2001) Capturing technical opportunity via Japan's star scientists: evidence from Japanese firms' biotech patents and products. *Journal of Technology Transfer* 26, 37–58.

Zucker, L. G. and Darby, M. R. (2003) Grilichesian breakthroughs: inventions of methods of inventing and firm entry in nanotechnology. NBER Working paper, No. 9825.

Zucker, L. G., Darby, M. R. and Armstrong, J. (1998) Geographically localized knowledge: spillover or markets, *Economic Inquiry* 36(1), 65–86.

(2002) Commercializing knowledge: university science, knowledge capture, and firm performance in biotechnology. *Management Science* 48, 138–153.

Zucker, L. G., Darby, M. R. and Brewer, M. B. (1998) Intellectual human capital and the birth of US biotechnology enterprises. *American Economic Review* 88, 290–306.

Zucker, L. G., Darby, M. R. and Torero, M. (2002) Labor mobility from academe to commerce. *Journal of Labor Economics* 20, 629–660.

Zucker, L. G., Brewer, M. B., Oliver, L. G. and Liebeskind, J. (1993) Basic science as intellectual capital in firms: information dilemmas in rDNA biotechnology research. Working paper, Institute for Social Science Research, Los Angeles.

Zucker, L. G., Brewer, M., Darby, M. and Peng, Y. (1996) Collaboration structure and information dilemmas in biotechnology: organizational boundaries as trust production. In Kramer, R. and Tyler, T. (eds.), *Trust in Organizations*. Sage Publications.

Zucker, L. G., Darby, M. R., Furner, J., Liu, R. C. and Ma, H. (2007) Minerva unbound: knowledge stocks, knowledge flows, and new knowledge production. *Research Policy* 36, 850–864.

Index